# POSTHUMOUS WORKS

## A Selection of Allan Kardec's Writings

Allan Kardec

# POSTHUMOUS WORKS

## A Selection of Allan Kardec's Writings

Allan Kardec

*CONSELHO ESPÍRITA INTERNACIONAL – CEI (International Spiritist Council – ISC)*
*SGAN Quadra 909 – Conjunto F*
*70790-090 – Brasília (DF) - Brasil*

*First Edition – 2026*

*ISBN: 978-1-948109-51-2*
*LCCN: 2026939420*

*Original title in French:*
*ŒUVRES POSTHUMES*
*(Paris, 1890)*



*UNITED STATES SPIRITIST COUNCIL – USSC*
*United States Spiritist Council*
*10900 Research Blvd 160c-1157*
*Austin, TX 78759*
*www.spiritist.us*

*Library of Congress – In Publication Data*

*Kardec, Allan, 1804-1869.*
*ŒUVRES POSTHUMES / by Allan Kardec; translated by Darrel W. Kimble and Marcia M. Saiz. Ilse Reis – New York (NY), USA: USSC 2026. Reviewed by the United States Spiritist Council.*

*ISBN: 978-1-948109-51-2*
*1. Mediums. 2. Spiritism.*

# Contents

# BIOGRAPHY OF ALLAN KARDEC

It is under the blow of profound grief caused by the early departure of the venerable founder of Spiritism that we approach a task that may have been simple and easy for his wise and experienced hands, but whose weight and gravity would crush us if we could not count on the effective help of good spirits and the indulgence of our readers.

Who among us, without being branded as presumptuous, could ever boast of possessing the spirit of method and organization with which all of the master's works shine? Only his powerful mind could have focused on such diverse materials, mill them and transform them to spread them afterwards like beneficent dew upon souls desirous of understanding and love.

Incisive, concise and profound, he knew how to please and to make himself understood in a language that was both simple and elevated, as removed from the familiar style as from the obscurities of metaphysics.

Incessantly spreading himself all around, he had been able to handle everything until now. However, the daily increase of his relationships and the ongoing growth of Spiritism made him sense the need to appoint a few intelligent aides. At that time, he was also preparing the new organization of Spiritism and its endeavors, when he left us to go to a better world to reap the blessing of a mission accomplished and to gather elements for a new work of devotion and sacrifice.

He was in a class by himself!... We shall call ourselves *legion,* and as weak and inexperienced as we may be, we hold the inner conviction that we will remain worthy of the situation, if, starting from established principles and incontestable facts, we set our minds on carrying out, as well as possible and according to the needs of the moment, the future plans that Mr. Kardec himself intended to complete.

As long as we follow in his footsteps and as long as all those of goodwill join in a common effort for the intellectual and moral progress of humankind, the spirit of the great philosopher will be with us and will aid us with his powerful influence. May he make up for our insufficiency and may we render ourselves worthy of his concourse by dedicating ourselves to the work with much devotion and sincerity, albeit lacking his knowledge and intelligence!

On his banner he inscribed these words: *Labor, Solidarity, Tolerance.* Like him, let us be untiring; according to his wishes, let us be tolerant and unified; and let us not be afraid to follow his example, returning over and over again to the principles that are still being discussed. We call upon the assistance of all, of all minds. We shall try to progress with sureness rather than with haste, and our efforts will not be unfruitful if, as we are persuaded – and we will be the first to set this example – each of us endeavors to fulfill his or her duty, putting aside all personal issues in order to contribute to the overall good.

We could not enter under more favorable auspices the new phase that is opening up for Spiritism than to provide our readers with a brief sketch of this man, who was righteous and honorable throughout his entire life, this intelligent and profound scholar whose memory will be carried over to future centuries surrounded by the radiance of the benefactors of humankind.

Born in Lyon on October 3, 1804, to an old family that had distinguished itself in magistracy and law, Allan Kardec (*Léon-Hippolyte-Denizard Rivail*) did not pursue the same career. Early in his youth, he felt drawn to the study of the sciences and philosophy.

Educated at Pestalozzi's School in Yverdun, Switzerland, he became one of the famous professor's most eminent disciples and a zealous propagator of his educational system, which had such a great influence on the reformation of schooling in France and Germany.

Endowed with a remarkable intelligence and attracted to teaching by his character and special aptitudes, when he was only fourteen years old he would teach what he knew to his fellow students who had learned less than he had. It was at this school that the ideas developed that would later place him in the class of progressive individuals and free thinkers.

Born into Catholicism but educated in a protestant country, the acts of intolerance that he had to endure because of it soon led him to conceive of the idea of a religious reform, toward which he worked silently for several years with the idea of achieving the unification of all beliefs. However, he lacked the indispensable element for the solution to this gigantic problem.

Spiritism would appear later on to furnish it and to imprint his labors with a special direction.

Having concluded his studies, he returned to France. Fluent in German, he translated various educational and moral works into that language, especially those of Fenelon, who had most particularly impressed him.

He was a member of several learned societies, among them the Royal Academy of Arras, which in a competition in 1831 awarded him for a remarkable dissertation on the issue: "*What study system is the most harmonious with the needs of the time?*"

From 1835 to 1840 in his home on Sèvres Street, he taught free courses in chemistry, physics, comparative anatomy, astronomy, etc., an enterprise worthy of praise at any time, but especially when only a very small number of minds dared to take such a road.

Always concerned with making educational systems attractive and interesting, he invented, simultaneously, an ingenious method for learning to count and a mnemonic table of the history of France. The objective was to fix in the memory the dates of noteworthy events and discoveries that illustrated each kingship.

Among his numerous educational works we would cite the following: *Plan proposé pour l'amélioration de l'instruction publique* (1828) [*Proposed Plan for Improving Public Education*]; *Cours pratique et théorique d'arithmétique, d'après la méthode de Pestalozzi, à l'usage des instituteurs et des mères de famille* (1829) [*Practical and Theoretic Course on Arithmetic, according to the Pestalozzi Method, for use by Teachers and Family Mothers*]; *Grammaire française classique* (1831) [*Classic French Grammar*]; *Manuel des examens pour les brevets de capacité* ; *Solutions raisonnées des questions et problèmes d'arithmétique et de géométrie* (1846) [*Manual of Examinations for Certificates of Capacity*; *Rational Solutions to Questions and Problems in Arithmetic and Geometry*]; *Catéchisme grammatical de la langue française* (1848) [*Grammatical Primer of the French Language*]; *Programme des cours usuels de chimie, physique, astronomie, physiologie* [*Standard Course Syllabus for Chemistry, Physics, Astronomy, Physiology*], which he taught at the Lycée Polymathique; *Dictées normales des examens de l'Hôtel de ville et de la Sorbonne* [*Normal Dictations for Examinations of City Hall and the Sorbonne*] accompanied by *Dictées spéciales sur les difficultés orthographiques* (1849) [*Special Dictations on Orthographic Difficulties*], a work very much appreciated at the time of its appearance and still published in new editions until recently.

As one can see, before Spiritism popularized the pseudonym Allan Kardec, he had already made himself well-known through works of quite a different nature, but they all had the objective of enlightening the masses and connecting them more to their family and country.

Around 1855[1], upon inquiring into the issue of spirit manifestations, Kardec devoted himself to persevering

1 It was actually 1854. See Part 2 of this book, the section entitled: *My*

observation of these phenomena, focusing primarily on deducing their philosophical consequences. From the very beginning, he foresaw in them the principle of new natural laws—laws governing the relations between the visible and invisible worlds. He recognized in the activities of the invisible world one of the powers of nature and understood that grasping its workings would shed light on a multitude of problems long regarded as unsolvable. He also perceived its significance from a religious perspective.

His principle works on the subject were: *The Spirits' Book*, for the philosophical aspect, and whose first edition appeared on April 18, 1857; *The Mediums' Book*, for the experimental and scientific aspect (January 1861); *The Gospel according to Spiritism*, for the moral aspect (April 1864); *Heaven and Hell*, or God's Justice according to Spiritism (August 1865); *Genesis, Miracles and Predictions* (January 1868); *Revue Spirite: Journal of Psychological Studies,* a monthly collection that began publication on January 1, 1858. On April 1, 1858, he founded the first regularly-constituted Spiritist Society in Paris under the title *Parisian Society for Spiritist Studies*, whose sole purpose was the study of everything that might contribute to the progress of the new science. Kardec flatly denied having written anything under the influence of preconceived or theoretical ideas. A man of an unruffled and calm character, he observed the phenomena, and from his observations, he deduced the laws that governed them. He was the first to present a theory and to form a methodical and normal body of doctrine from them.

By demonstrating that phenomena erroneously regarded as supernatural are actually subject to laws, he treated them as phenomena of nature, thus destroying the last refuge of the extraordinary and one of the elements of superstition.

During the early years of spirit phenomena, their manifestations were more of an object of curiosity than a

---

*Initiation into Spiritism.* – Tr.

subject of serious study. *The Spirits' Book* brought the matter under a new light. The turning tables were abandoned, for they had been only a prelude, and attention started to be focused on a body of doctrine that encompassed all the issues of interest for humankind.

The appearance of *The Spirits' Book* marked the true founding of Spiritism, which until then possessed only scattered, uncoordinated elements, and whose impact no one would ever have guessed. From that moment on, Spiritism grabbed the attention of serious individuals and began to develop rapidly. In only a few years, its ideas found numerous adherents in all social classes and in several countries. Such unprecedented success was undoubtedly connected with the affinity such ideas encountered, but was also largely due to the book's clarity, which is one of the distinctive characteristics of Kardec's writings.

By avoiding abstract metaphysical formulations, the author knew how to make his writings easy to read, an essential condition for popularizing an idea. His argumentation on every controversial point was tightly logical and offered little opportunity for refutation, predisposing instead to conviction. The material proofs provided by Spiritism on the existence of the soul and the future life tend to destroy materialistic and pantheistic ideas. One of the most fertile principles of Spiritism and which derives from the preceding, is that of the *plurality of existences*, which was already foreseen by a multitude of ancient and modern philosophers, most recently by *Jean Reynaud, Charles Fourier, Eugène Sue* and others. However, it remained in a hypothetical and theoretical state, whereas Spiritism demonstrated its reality and proved that it is one of the essential attributes of humankind. From this principle derives the solution of all the apparent anomalies of human life, of all intellectual, moral and social inequalities; thus, humans know where they have come from, where they are going, what their purpose on earth is and why they suffer on it.

Innate ideas are explained by knowledge acquired in previous lifetimes; the progress of peoples and humankind, by the action of individuals of times past who reincarnate after having progressed; sympathies and antipathies, by the nature of previous relationships. These relationships, which connect the great human family throughout all time, are the basis for the very laws of nature, and the great principles of fraternity, equality, liberty and universal solidarity are no longer mere theory.

Instead of the principle, "*Without the Church there is no salvation*," which feeds the separation and animosity among the different sects, and which has led to the shedding of so much blood, Spiritism has as its maxim, "*Without charity there is no salvation*"; that is, equality of men and women before God, tolerance, freedom of conscience and mutual benevolence.

Instead of *blind faith*, which annuls freedom of thought, Spiritism says: *"Unshakable faith is only that which can meet reason face to face in every human epoch". A foundation is needed for faith and this foundation is perfect intelligence concerning the object to be believed in. In order to believe, it is not enough to merely see; above all, one must comprehend. Blind faith is no longer apropos for this century. It is precisely the dogma of blind faith that has given rise today to such a large number of disbelievers, because it wants to impose itself and requires the abolition of two of the most precious of the human faculties: reason and free will."* (The Gospel according to Spiritism)

A tireless worker, always the first to take on an endeavor and the last to leave it, Allan Kardec passed away on March 31, 1869, while preparing for a change of location, required by the considerable expansion of his multiple occupations. Several works that he was about to finish, or for which he had awaited the right time to bring to light, would one day demonstrate even more the extent and power of his convictions.

He died as he had lived: working. For many years he had suffered from a heart condition that could only be controlled by intellectual repose and a certain amount of physical activity. But completely dedicated to his work as he was, he refused anything that might have absorbed one moment at the expense of his favorite occupations. The same happened to him that happens to all strongly tempered souls: the blade wore out the sheath.

His body slowed down and refused him its services, but his spirit, more alive, more energetic and more fertile, continued widening the circle of its activity.

In this unequal struggle, matter could not endure for long. One day it finally gave up; the aneurism broke and Allan Kardec was struck down. A man departed the earth, but a great name took its place among the illustrious of this century; a great spirit left to re-temper itself in the Infinite, where all those whom he had consoled and enlightened had been waiting impatiently for his arrival!

"Death," he said just recently, "strikes with redoubled blows against illustrious ranks!... To whom will it now turn to set free?"

Like so many others, he left to be re-tempered in the spirit world, to seek new elements to restore his organism, spent on a life of incessant labor. He left with those who will be the beacons of a new generation, to return with them soon to continue and complete the work left behind in devoted hands.

The man is no longer here; his soul, however, will remain among us. It will be a sure guardian, one more light, a tireless worker that has been added to the phalanxes of the spirit world. As on earth, without harming anyone, he will enable all to listen to his opportune counsels; he will temper the premature zeal of the extreme, support the sincere and the selfless, and stimulate the apathetic. He now sees and knows everything he had foreseen just a little while ago! He is no longer subject to uncertainty or impairments, and he will enable us to share in his conviction by enabling us to touch the goal, pointing the way to us in that clear, precise language that has made him noteworthy in literary annals.

The man is no more – we repeat; but Allan Kardec is immortal and his memory, his endeavors, his spirit will always be with those who firmly raise the banner that he always knew how to make respected.

A mighty individual comprised the work. He was the guide and beacon for all. On earth, the work will replace the individual. We will no longer rally around Allan Kardec; we will rally around Spiritism such as he has structured it, and with his counsels and under his influence, we will advance with sure steps toward the blissful phases promised to regenerated humankind.

*Revue Spirite*, May 1869

# EULOGY
# AT THE TOMB OF ALLAN KARDEC

## by
## CAMILLE FLAMMARION

Ladies and gentlemen:

In accepting with deference the kind invitation from the friends of the industrious thinker whose earthly body now lies at our feet, I remember a dreary day in December of 1865. At that time, I pronounced the final farewell at the tomb of the founder of the *Librairie Académique*, the honorable publisher Didier, who was Allan Kardec's convinced collaborator in the publication of the fundamental works of a doctrine that was dear to him, and who passed away all of a sudden as well, as if heaven wanted to spare these two righteous spirits the philosophical embarrassment of leaving this life differently than the usual way. The same consideration applies to the death of Mr. Jobard, our late colleague from Brussels.

Today, however, my task is even greater because I would like to be able to present to the minds of those who are listening to me and those of the millions of people who, throughout Europe and in the New World, have been concerned with the problem of the still-mysterious phenomena designated as "Spiritist"; I would like – as I said – to be able to present them with the scientific interest and the philosophical future of the study of these phenomena, in which, as everyone knows, eminent fellows among our contemporaries have participated. I would like to give them a glimpse of the unknown horizons that will open up to the human mind as its positive knowledge of the natural forces acting around us unfolds; to show them that these findings are the most effective antidote for the leprosy of atheism that seems to have stricken our time of transition in particular; and lastly, to testify publicly regarding the eminent service that the author of *The Spirits' Book* rendered to philosophy, *calling for attention to and discussion about* facts that until then belonged to the morbid and fatal realm of religious superstition.

In fact, here before this eloquent tomb, it would be important to establish that, rather than renewing the spirit of superstition and weakening the force of reason, the methodical examination of the phenomena, wrongly labeled "supernatural," instead clears away the errors and illusions of ignorance and *serves progress much better* than the spurious denials of those who do not want to put forth the effort to see.

However, this is not the place to open up an arena for disrespectful argument. Let us only allow our testimonies of affection and sentiments of grief – which lie around him in his tomb like an embalmment of the heart – descend from our minds upon the impassible face of the man lying before us.

And because we know that his eternal soul has survived these mortal remains just as it had also existed before them; because we know that indestructible ties connect our visible world to the invisible one; because that soul exists today just as it did three days ago, and because it is quite possible that it is present before me at this very moment; let us tell him that we do not want to let his corporeal image vanish and to bury him in his grave without unanimously honoring his work and his memory, and without paying a tribute of recognition to his earthly incarnation, which was so usefully and so worthily fulfilled.

I shall first draw a quick sketch of the principal lines of his literary career.

Deceased at age 65, Allan Kardec devoted the first part of his life to writing fundamental classical works designed mostly for use by teachers of young people. When, around 1855, the apparently new manifestations of turning tables, raps without any apparent cause, and the unusual movements of objects and furniture started to catch the public's attention, causing in excitable minds a sort of fever due to the novelty of such experiences, Allan Kardec, who was studying magnetism and its odd effects, followed with the greatest patience and a judicious perspicacity the numerous experiments and attempts taking place in Paris at the time. He collected and organized the results that were obtained during this lengthy observation and with them composed the body of the doctrine published in 1857 in the first edition of *The Spirits' Book*. You all know the success this work had both in France and abroad.

Published today in its 15$^{th}$ edition[2], this body of fundamental doctrine (which is not new in its essence, because the Pythagorean School in Greece, along with the Druids in our poor[3] Gaul, used to teach its principles) began to spread to all classes. However, it constituted a true form of novelty due to its connection with the phenomena.

After that initial work came, successively, *The Mediums' Book, or Experimental Spiritism*; *What is Spiritism?* or a summary in the form of questions and answers; *The Gospel according to Spiritism*; *Heaven and Hell*; and *Genesis*. Then, death took him at the moment in which, in his tireless activity, he was working on a book about how magnetism and Spiritism are related.

Through the *Revue Spirite* and the Parisian Society, of which he was president, he established himself, more or less, as the center where everything converged, the link between

---

2 At the time of the present edition of this volume, *The Spirits Book* has reached its 52nd edition. – Tr.

3 In the May 1869 issue of *The Spiritist Review,* in which this Eulogy was first printed, this word in French is not *pauvre* but *propre,* which would translate into English as *own*. – Tr.

all researchers. A few months ago, sensing the end of his life was at hand, he prepared the conditions of vitality for such studies after his death and formed the central Committee which succeeds him.

He aroused rivalries. He gained followers in a personal way. There is still some division between "Spiritualists" and "Spiritists." Henceforth, ladies and gentlemen, we should all be united in a fraternal solidarity and make a unified effort to address the problem in our general and impersonal desire for the truth and the good (such is, at least, the wish of the friends of truth).

Some have objected that our worthy friend, to whom we are paying our last respects today, was not a *scientist*, that he was not a physicist, a naturalist or an astronomer, and that he tried to establish a body of moral doctrine before having submitted the reality and nature of the phenomena to scientific discussion.

But perhaps it is best that things started like that. We cannot always discount the value of the sentiments. How many hearts have been comforted by this religious belief! How many tears have been dried! How many consciences have been opened to the beams of spiritual beauty! Not everyone is happy down here. Many hearts have been broken! Many souls have been benumbed by skepticism! Thus, isn't it something to have brought to spiritualism so many individuals who used to be floating around in doubt and who loved neither physical nor intellectual life any longer?

Had Allan Kardec been a man of science, there can be no doubt that he would not have been able to offer this all-important service and spread it afar as an invitation to all hearts.

He was what I would simply call "common sense incarnate." With an upright and judicious mind, he thoughtfully applied the innermost indications of common sense to his ongoing work. This was no small quality in the order of things that concern us. It was – one could say – the main one and the most valuable of all, without which the work could neither have become popular nor have set down its vast roots throughout the world. Most of those who have engaged in these studies can remember having personally witnessed unexplainable manifestations in their youth or under certain special circumstances. There are few families who have not observed evidence of this kind in their history. The starting point was to apply the firm reasoning of simple common sense to them and to study them according to the principles of the positive method.

As the organizer of this slow and difficult study foresaw, this complex study must now enter its scientific phase. The physical phenomena – which we did not insist on in the beginning – must now become the object of experimental criticism, to which we owe the magnificence of modern progress and the wonders of electricity and steam. This method has to understand, examine, measure and define the phenomena of the still-mysterious order that we continue to witness.

For, ladies and gentlemen, Spiritism is not a religion but a science, a science about which we barely know the *ABC's*. The time of dogma is over. Nature enfolds the universe, and God himself, who formerly was made in the image of man, can only be seen as a *Spirit in Nature* by modern metaphysics. The supernatural does not exist. The manifestations obtained through mediums, such as those of magnetism and somnambulism, *are of a natural order* and must be strictly submitted to the control of experimentation. There are no longer any miracles. We are witnessing the dawn of an unknown science. Who can foresee the consequences of the positive study of this new psychology for the world of thought?

Henceforth, science will govern the world, and, ladies and gentlemen, it would not be out-of-line for this eulogy to comment on its current work and the new inductions it is revealing precisely with regard to our studies.

Never before in history has science opened up such grand horizons before humankind's wondering eye. We now know that *the earth is a heavenly body* and that *our current life will be completed in the heavens.* By analyzing their light, we know which elements burn in the sun and in the stars millions and trillions of leagues from our terrestrial observatory. We can use calculus to determine the history of the heavens and earth, in their distant past as well as in their future – neither of which exists for the immutable laws. Through observation, we have weighed the celestial lands that gravitate in space. The globe on which we stand has become a stellar atom flying through space in the middle of the infinite depths, and our own existence on this globe has become an infinitesimal fraction of our eternal life. But what rightly strikes us even more deeply than all these is the surprising result of the physical works that have been pursued over the past few years: *the fact that we live in the midst of an invisible world* that is constantly active all around us. Yes, ladies and gentlemen, this is a tremendous revelation. For instance, contemplate the light radiating in the atmosphere right now from the shining sun; contemplate that soft azure of the heavenly canopy; notice the emanations of warm air caressing our faces; look at these monuments and this soil. Well, even though our eyes are wide open, we cannot actually see what is happening! Out of a hundred beams of light emanating from the sun, only one-third are discernible to our sight, whether directly or whether reflected by all these objects. The other two-thirds exist and act around us, but in an invisible, albeit real, way. They are warm but are not luminous to us; even so, they are much more active than those we can sense, for they are the ones which attract flowers towards the sun, and which produce all the chemical actions.[4] And they are also the ones that

4 Our retina is insensitive to these rays, but other substances can *see* them; for example, iodine and silver salts. The solar chemical spectrum, which our eye cannot perceive, has been photographed. No visible image ever ap-

invisibly carry water vapor up into the atmosphere to form clouds – thereby constantly occultly and silently exerting all around us a colossal force that is mechanically equivalent to the work of several billions horses!

If the calorific rays and chemical rays that constantly act in nature are invisible to us, it is because the former do not strike our retina fast enough, and because the latter strike it too fast. Our eye only sees things between two limits, below and above which it does not see anything. Our earthly organism can be compared to a harp with two strings, which are the optic and auditory nerves. Certain types of movement make the former vibrate and other types of movement cause the latter to vibrate. Therein resides *all human sensation*, which is more restricted than that of other living beings, such as insects, for example, whose very same "strings" of sight and hearing are more sensitive. However, in nature there are actually not two but ten, a hundred, a thousand kinds of movements. Therefore, physics teaches us that we live in the midst of a world that is invisible to us, and that it is not impossible that beings (also invisible to us) live on this earth too, in an order of sensations completely different than ours. We cannot perceive their presence unless they manifest themselves to us by means of phenomena that fall within the order of our senses.

In light of such truths – which have just started to become known – how absurd and worthless an *a priori* denial is! When we compare how little we know and our limited sphere of perception with the sum of all that exits, we cannot help concluding that we know nothing and that all is left to know. What, then, gives us the right to use the word "impossible" when faced with phenomena that we witness, without being able to determine their unique cause?

---

pears on the photographic plate when leaving the darkroom, even though it has been imprinted, since a chemical operation will reveal it. – Original note in the French.

Science has unfolded perspectives that are as credible as previous ones regarding the phenomena of life and death and regarding the force that animates us. We just need to observe the circulation of existences.

Everything is nothing but metamorphosis. Caught up in their eternal course, the atoms that make up matter pass incessantly from one body to another, from the animal to the plant, from the plant to the atmosphere, from the atmosphere to the human being; and throughout our entire life, our own body continuously changes its constitutive substances, just like the flame that only burns thanks to elements that are continuously renewed. And when the soul has taken flight, this same body, already transformed so many times during its lifetime, finally returns all of its molecules to nature, never to receive them back again. The unacceptable dogma of the resurrection of the flesh has been replaced by the lofty doctrine of the reincarnation of the soul.

Here is the April sun shining in the sky, flooding us with its first warm morning dew. The meadows are awakening; the first blossoms are opening up; springtime is blooming; the blue sky is smiling, and resurrection is in progress. Nonetheless, this new life comes only from death and covers only ruins! Where does the sap of these trees, which are turning green once again in this field of the dead, come from? Where does this moisture that nourishes their roots come from? Where do all the elements that give birth to the little silent flowers and the singing birds under the caresses of May come from? From death!... ladies and gentlemen... from all these corpses buried in the sinister night of the tomb!... A supreme law of nature, the body is merely a temporary assemblage of particles which do not belong to it, and which the soul has brought together according to its own type in order to create organs connecting it to our physical world.

And as our body is thus renewed bit by bit by means of the continuous exchange of matter; as one day it drops dead as an inert mass never to rise again, our spirit, the personal being, has constantly kept its indestructible *identity*, has ruled as sovereign over the matter it has clothed itself with, thereby establishing, by this constant and universal fact, its independent personality, its spiritual essence – which is not subject to the realm of space and time – its individual grandeur, its *immortality*.

What does the mystery of life consist of? By what links is the soul connected to the organism? How does it free itself in the end? In what form and under what conditions does it exist after death? Which memories, which affections does it keep? My friends, these are problems that are far from being resolved and together they will form the psychological science of the future. Some may deny the existence of the soul, as well as the existence of God; they may state that moral truth does not exist, that there are no intelligent laws in nature, and that we, spiritualists, are being duped by a great illusion. On the other hand, others may state that, due to a special privilege, they understand the essence of the human soul, the shape of the Supreme Being, the state of the future life, and they regard us as atheists because our minds refuse their faith. My friends, neither of the two will keep us from facing the greatest problems, from being interested in these things (which are not at all unfamiliar), and from having the right to apply the experimental method of contemporary science in the search for truth.

It is by means of the positive study of the effects that we may appraise the causes. In the order of the studies that are grouped together under the generic label of "Spiritism," *the phenomena do exist,* although no one knows how they are produced. They exist as surely as electrical, light and heat phenomena exist, but we know neither biology nor physiology. What is the human body? What is the brain? What is the absolute action of the soul? We do not know. Nor do we know the essence of electricity or the essence of light. Thus, it is wise to observe all these phenomena impartially and to try to determine their causes, which are perhaps of different kinds and are more numerous than we have ever assumed until now.

Let those whose sight is limited because of pride or prejudice not understand the eagerness of our knowledge-hungry minds; let them cast their sarcasm or anathemas over this type of study; we lift our thoughts much higher!... You were the first, O my master and friend! You were the first, who, from the beginning of my career in astronomy, displayed a profound affinity for my deductions regarding the existence of celestial humanities. Taking into your hands the book *The Plurality of Inhabited Worlds*, you placed it at once at the base of the doctrinal edifice that you dreamed about. So often, you and I discussed this highly mysterious celestial life; now, O soul, you know by direct sight what the spirit life to which we all return and which we forget during our existence consists of!

You have returned to that world whence we came, and you are reaping the fruits of your earthly studies. Your envelope of flesh rests at our feet; your brain has shut down; your eyes have closed to open no more; and your words shall no longer be heard... We know that we will all arrive at the same final sleep, the same lifelessness, the same dust. But we do not place our glory and hope in this envelope. The body fails but the soul remains and returns to the spirit world. We will meet again in that better world; and in the immense heavens, where our most powerful faculties will be applied, we will continue our studies, which on earth had a theater that was too confining to contain them.

We prefer to know this truth rather than to believe that your whole being rests in this corpse and that your soul has been destroyed because an organ stopped working. Immortality is the light of life, just as this glowing sun is the light of nature.

Farewell, my dear Allan Kardec, farewell.

# TO SUBSCRIBERS OF REVUE SPIRITE

Until now, *Revue Spirite* has been essentially the work and creation of Allan Kardec, like all the other doctrinal works that he published.

When death took him, the multiplicity of his endeavors and the new phase that Spiritism had entered made him desirous of appointing a number of convinced collaborators to carry out, under his direction, projects that he could not carry out by himself.

We have resolved not to depart from the path he traced out for us; nevertheless, we believed it to be our duty to devote to the Master's labors, under the title *Posthumous Works*, a certain number of pages that would doubtless have been preserved had he remained among us in the corporeal state. The abundance of documents contained in his study will enable us, for several years to come, to publish in each issue—besides such instructions as he may see fit to communicate to us as a Spirit—one of those valuable articles which he possessed the rare gift of rendering intelligible to all.

We thus mean to satisfy the desires of all those whom the Spiritist philosophy has brought into our ranks, and who knew how to appreciate in the author of *The Spirits' Book,* the man of the good, the untiring and devoted worker, the convinced mind, who applied and practiced in his private life the principles he taught in his works.

Revue Spirite, Year 12, June, 1869

# POSTHUMOUS WORKS OF ALLAN KARDEC

## PART ONE

# THE PROFESSION OF THE SPIRITIST FAITH RATIONALIZED

God
The Soul
Creation

## I – GOD

1. *There is one God, the supreme intelligence, the first cause of all things.*

The proof of God's existence is expressed in the axiom: *There is no effect without a cause.* We constantly observe a countless multitude of effects, whose cause does not lie in humanity, because humanity is powerless to produce them or even to explain them; hence, their cause is above humanity. We call this cause *God, Yahweh, Allah, Brahma, Fo Hi, The Great Spirit*, etc., according to languages, times and places.

Such effects are not produced by accident, fortuitously and without order. From the organization of the tiniest insect and the smallest seed up to the law that governs the worlds moving in space, everything attests to a thought, a design, a foresight, a solicitude that surpasses all human conceptions. This cause, therefore, is supremely intelligent.

2. *God is eternal, immutable, immaterial, one, omnipotent, and supremely just and good.*

God is *eternal.* If God had a beginning, then something must have existed before God; otherwise, God would have come from nothingness or would have been created by a prior being. This is how, little by little, we work backwards to the infinite in eternity.

God is *immutable.* If God were subject to change, the laws that govern the universe would have no stability.

God is *immaterial,* which means that God's nature differs from everything that we call matter; otherwise, God would be subject to the fluctuations and transformations of matter, and would not be *immutable.*

God is *one.* If there were many gods, there would be many wills, and then there would be neither unity of purpose, nor unity of power in the governance of the universe.

God is *omnipotent* because God is *one.* If God did not possess supreme power, something would be more powerful. God would not have made all things and those that God did not make would be the work of another God.

God is *supremely just and good.* The providential wisdom of the divine laws is revealed in the tiniest things as well as in the greatest, and this wisdom does not allow doubt either about God's justice or God's goodness.

**3.** *God is infinite in all God's perfections.*

If just one of God's attributes were imagined to be imperfect; if the least particle of God's *eternality*, *immutability*, *immateriality*, *oneness*, *omnipotence*, *justice* or *goodness* were removed, then another being that possessed what God lacked could be imagined, and that being, more perfect than God, would actually be God.

## II – THE SOUL

**4.** *Within human beings there is an intelligent principle known as the SOUL or SPIRIT, which is independent of matter and which gives them their moral sense and their faculty of thought.*

If thought were a property of matter, one would see basic matter thinking. However, since inert matter has never been endowed with intellectual faculties, and since the body, once dead, no longer thinks, one must conclude that the soul is independent of matter and that the organs are nothing more than instruments that assist humans in manifesting their thought.

**5.** *Materialist doctrines are incompatible with morality and subversive to the social order.*

If, according to materialists, thought were secreted by the brain – as bile is secreted by the liver – it would follow that, at the death of the body, humans' intelligence and all their moral qualities would reenter nothingness; that family, friends and all those who had been esteemed would be irretrievably lost; that individuals of genius would be without merit, since they would owe their transcendent faculties only to the happenstance of their physical organization; that between the imbecile and the scholar the only difference would be that of the quantity of cerebral matter.

The consequences of this doctrine would be that humankind, with nothing to hope for beyond this life, would have no interest in practicing the good; that it would be very natural for people to seek the greatest amount of pleasure possible, even at the expense of others; that it would be foolish to deprive oneself for the sake of others; that selfishness would be the most rational sentiment; that those who were consistently unfortunate on the earth would have nothing better to do than to kill themselves because, having to dissolve back into nothingness, it would be neither worse nor better for them and it would at least shorten their suffering.

The materialist doctrine is thus the sanction of selfishness, the source of all vice, the negation of charity – the source of all virtues and foundation of the social order – and the justification of suicide.

**6.** *The independence of the soul is proven by Spiritism.*

The existence of the soul is proven by humans' intelligent acts, which must have an intelligent cause and not an inert one. The soul's independence from matter is patently demonstrated by spirit phenomena, which show that the soul is acting by itself, and especially through the experience of its autonomy *during life,* which allows it to manifest itself, to think and to act without a body.

One could say that, if chemistry has separated the elements of water, if it has thereby disclosed those elements' properties, and if it can make and unmake a composite body at will, then Spiritism can just as easily isolate the two constitutive elements of the human being: *spirit and matter, soul and body*, and can separate and reunite them at will, which can leave no doubt about their independence.

**7.** *The human soul survives the body and retains its individuality after death.*

If the soul did not survive the body, humans would be faced only with the perspective of nothingness – just as if the faculty of thought were simply the product of matter. If the soul did not retain its individuality, that is, if it were lost in the common reservoir called the *Great Whole,* like drops of water in the ocean, it would represent for humans the nothingness of thought, and the consequences would be exactly the same as if they had no soul at all.

The soul's survival after the death of the body has been irrefutably proven, and in a way made tangible through spirit communications, where the soul's individuality is demonstrated by the character and qualities peculiar to each individual. These qualities, which distinguish souls from one another, constitute their personality. If souls were mixed into a common whole, their qualities would all be uniform.

Besides these intelligent proofs, there is also the physical proof of visual manifestations or apparitions, which are so common and authentic that they cannot be questioned.

**8.** *The human soul is happy or unhappy after death, according to the good or evil it practiced during life.*

If one believes in a supremely good and just God, one cannot believe that all souls have the same fate. If the future position of a criminal and of a virtuous individual were the same, it would exclude all usefulness of trying to practice the good. Thus, supposing that God sees no difference between the one who practices the good and the one who commits evil would be to deny God's justice. Since during earthly life evil is not always punished, nor is good always rewarded, one must conclude that justice will be served afterwards; otherwise, God would not be just.

Moreover, future punishments and rewards are materially proven by the communications humans can establish with the souls of those who have lived and who come to describe their happy or unhappy conditions, the nature of their happiness or sufferings, and what caused it.

**9.** *God, the soul, the survival and individuality of the soul after the death of the body, and future sorrows and rewards are the fundamental principles of all religions.*

Spiritism has come to add to the moral proofs of such principles the material proofs of the facts and experimentation, putting an end to the sophisms of materialism. In the presence of these facts, disbelief has no more reason to be; it is thus that Spiritism has come to restore the faith of those who have lost it and to dispel the doubts of the unsure.

## III – CREATION

**10.** *God is the creator of all things.*

This proposition is the consequence of the proof of God's existence.

**11.** *The beginning of all things remains one of God's secrets.*

Everything says that God is the author of all things, but how and when did God create them? Like God, has matter existed from all eternity? We do not know. Regarding anything that God has not deemed appropriate to reveal to us, we can only construct theories that are more probable or less so. From the effects we can go back to certain causes. However, there is a boundary that is impossible for us to cross. We would be wasting our time and exposing ourselves to getting lost if we tried to go beyond it.

**12.** *In their investigation of the unknown, humans have the attributes of God as a guide.*

In the investigation of the mysteries that we are allowed to probe through reason there is one sure criterion, one infallible guide: the attributes of God.

Since we believe that God must be *eternal*, *immutable, immaterial, one, omnipotent* and *supremely just and good,* and that God is infinite in God's perfections, then all scientific or religious doctrine or theory that tended to take away a fraction of just one of God's attributes would necessarily be erroneous, because it would tend to negate God's very divinity.

**13.** *Physical worlds had a beginning and will have an end.*

Whether matter has existed throughout all eternity like God, or whether it was created at some particular time, it is obvious from what happens every day before our eyes that the transformations of matter are temporary, and that such transformations result in the various bodies that are incessantly born and destroyed.

Because the various worlds are the products of the agglomeration and transformation of matter, then like all material bodies they must have a beginning and an end according to laws unknown to us. Up to a certain point, science can establish the laws of their formation and go back to their primitive state. Any philosophical theory that contradicts the facts demonstrated by science is necessarily erroneous, unless it can prove that it is science that is in error.

**14.** Besides the physical worlds, God also created the intelligent beings that we call *spirits*.

**15.** The origin of spirits and the way they are created are unknown to us. We only know that they are created simple and ignorant; that is, without the knowledge and understanding of good and evil, but perfectible and with an equal aptitude to acquire and know everything there is to know over time. At their beginning, they are in a sort of infancy, lacking their own will and full awareness of their existence.

**16.** As the spirit progresses from its point of departure, ideas develop in it – like in a child – and with such ideas, free will; that is, the freedom to do or not to do, and to follow this or that pathway for its advancement, which is one of the essential attributes of the spirit.

**17.** The final objective of all spirits is to reach the perfection of which the individual is susceptible. The result of this perfection is the enjoyment of supreme bliss that is its consequence, to which spirits arrive more quickly or less so, according to the use they have made of their free will.

**18.** Spirits are the agents of the divine power. They constitute the intelligent force of nature and partake in the execution of the objectives of the Creator for maintaining the overall harmony of the universe and the immutable laws of creation.

**19.** In order to contribute as agents of the divine power in the work of the material worlds, spirits temporarily clothe themselves in a material body.

Incarnate spirits make up humankind. A human soul is an incarnate spirit.

20. The spirit life is the spirit's normal life: it is eternal; the corporeal life is transitory and temporary: it is no more than an instant in eternity.
21. The incarnation of spirits lies in the laws of nature; it is necessary for their advancement and for the execution of God's works. Through the labor their corporeal life requires of them, they perfect their intelligence, and by observing God's law, they acquire the merit that leads them to eternal bliss.

Thus, while contributing to the overall work of creation, spirits toil for their own advancement.

22. The perfecting of the spirit is the fruit of its own labor. It advances based on its greater or lesser activity, or its good will in acquiring the qualities it lacks.
23. Since the spirit cannot acquire in only one lifetime all the moral and intellectual qualities that will lead it to its goal, it gets there through a string of existences, taking a few steps forward in each one on the pathway of progress and cleansing itself of a few imperfections.
24. To each new existence the spirit brings what it acquired in intelligence and morality during its preceding existences, as well as the seeds of the imperfections it has not yet rid itself of.
25. When a lifetime has been badly used by the spirit, that is, if it made no progress on the pathway of the good, such existence is of no profit to it and it will have to begin once more under conditions that are more painful or less so because of its negligence or ill will.
26. Since with each corporeal existence the spirit should acquire something good and rid itself of something bad, it follows that, after a certain number of incarnations, it is purified and reaches the state of pure spirit.

**27.** The number of corporeal existences is indeterminate; it depends on the spirit's will to lessen the number by actively working on its moral progress.

**28.** In the interval between corporeal existences, the spirit is *errant*[5] and lives the spirit life. The errant state is not of a set duration.

**29.** When, on one world, spirits have acquired the sum of the progress that the state of that world allows, they leave it behind to incarnate on another, more advanced world, where they acquire new knowledge. This process continues successively until incarnation in a corporeal body is no longer necessary; from then on they begin to live the spirit life exclusively, during which they also progress in a different sense and by other means. Upon reaching the culminating point of progress, they enjoy supreme bliss. Admitted into the Councils of the Omnipotent, they identify with its thought and become its messengers, its direct ministers in the governance of worlds, having under their orders spirits at different levels of advancement.

---

5 In the spirit world. – Tr.

# SPIRIT MANIFESTATIONS

## The Character and Religious Consequences of Spirit Manifestations

The Perispirit as the Principle of Manifestations
Visual Manifestations
Transfiguration. Invisibility
The Emancipation of the Soul
Apparitions of Living Persons. Bi-corporeality
Mediums
Obsession and Possession

1. The souls or spirits of those who have lived make up the invisible world that populates space and the environment in which we live. The result is that since there are human beings, there are spirits, and if the latter have the ability to manifest themselves, they must have had this ability in every epoch of history. This is shown to be the case in the history and religions of all cultures. Nevertheless, in these latter times, spirit manifestations have undergone a large development and have acquired a more authentic character, for it was in the objectives of Providence to put an end to the plague of disbelief and materialism by means of obvious proofs, allowing those who have left the earth behind to return to attest to their existence and to reveal to us their happy or unhappy situations.
2. Since the visible world lives in the midst of the invisible world – with which it is in constant

contact – it follows that these two incessantly interact with each other. This interaction is the source of a huge number of phenomena that used to be regarded as supernatural because the cause behind them was unknown.

The action of the invisible world upon the visible world, and vice-versa, is one of the laws, one of the forces of nature that is as necessary for universal harmony as the law of attraction. If this action were to cease, harmony would be disrupted, like a machine from which a part has been removed. Since this action is founded on a law of nature, the result is that there is nothing supernatural about any of the phenomena it produces. They only used to seem so because their cause was unknown. The same was true of other phenomena such as electricity, light, etc.

**3.** The basis for all religions is the existence of God and their objective is the future of the individual after death. This future, which is of crucial interest to the individual, is necessarily connected to the existence of the invisible world. In every epoch of history, finding out about that world has been the object of human investigation and preoccupation. Humankind's attention has, of course, been focused on the phenomena that tend to prove the existence of that world, and there have never been phenomena as conclusive as spirit manifestations, through which the actual inhabitants of that world reveal their existence. That is why such phenomena have been the basis for the majority of the dogmas of all religions.

**4.** Since humans instinctively possess the intuition about a higher power, in every epoch they have been led to attribute to the *direct* action of that power the phenomena whose cause was unknown to them and which to their eyes amounted to miracles and supernatural effects. This tendency has been considered by certain

> disbelievers to be a consequence of people's love for the extraordinary; however, they have not looked for the source of this love. Quite simply, it resides in the hard-to-define intuition of a natural order of things extra-corporeal. With the progress of science and the knowledge about the laws of nature, these phenomena have slowly passed from the realm of the extraordinary to the realm of natural effects, in such a way that what used to seem supernatural is no longer viewed as such today, and that what is still seen as supernatural nowadays will no longer be viewed as such tomorrow.

Since by their very nature the phenomena depend on spirit manifestations, they have furnished a large contingent of facts reputed to be extraordinary. But a time had to come when the law that governs them would be known, and they would re-enter the order of natural events. That time has come indeed, and in making that law known, Spiritism has provided the key to most of the incomprehensible sacred Scripture passages that allude to it, and to events regarded as miraculous.

> **5.** The characteristic of a miraculous event is that it has to be unusual and exceptional; it is a derogation from the laws of nature; hence, if a particular phenomenon is reproduced under identical conditions, it is because it is subject to a law and is not miraculous. The law itself might be unknown, but its existence is no less real. Time is in charge of making it known.

The movement of the sun – or rather, the earth – stopped by Joshua would be a true miracle because it would be a manifest derogation from the law that governs the movement of the heavenly bodies. However, if such an event could be reproduced under certain conditions, it would be subject to some law, and consequently, would cease to be miraculous.

> **6.** The Church is wrongly afraid at seeing the circle of miraculous events narrowing, because God proves God's grandeur and power even better through the wonderful ensemble of God's laws than through a few infractions of these same laws. The Church is even more mistaken when it attributes to the Devil the ability to work wonders, which would imply that if the Devil is able to interrupt the course of the divine laws, he would be as powerful as God. To dare to say that the Spirit of Evil can suspend the action of God's laws is blasphemy and a sacrilege.

Far from religion losing its authority by relegating reputedly miraculous events to the order of natural events, it can only gain by doing so; first, because if an incident is wrongly reputed to be miraculous, it means there has been an error, and religion can only lose by supporting an error, especially if it persists in regarding as a miracle something that is not; second, because many people, by not accepting the possibility of miracles, deny reputedly miraculous events and consequently religion itself, which rests upon such events. On the other hand, if the possibility of those same events were demonstrated to be the effects of natural laws, there would no longer be any grounds for rejecting them than there would be for religion to proclaim them.

> **7.** Events proven peremptorily by science cannot be denied by any contrary religious belief. Religion can only increase its authority by following the progress of scientific knowledge, and it can only lose authority by lagging behind or by protesting against such knowledge in the name of its dogmas, for no dogma will ever prevail against or annul the laws of nature. A dogma founded

on the negation of a law of nature can never be an expression of the truth.

Founded upon the knowledge of laws that had been incomprehensible until now, Spiritism has not come to destroy religious phenomena, but rather to sanction them by providing a rational explanation for them. It has come only to destroy the erroneous consequences that have been deduced from them due to ignorance of those laws, or to their wrong interpretation.

**8.** Ignorance of the laws of nature, which leads people to look for fantastic causes behind any phenomenon they do not understand, is the source of superstitious ideas, some of which are due to misunderstood spirit phenomena. An understanding of the laws that govern such phenomena destroys such superstitious ideas, putting things under the light of reality and demonstrating a limit on what is possible and what is not.

## I – THE PERISPIRIT AS THE PRINCIPLE OF THE MANIFESTATIONS

**9.** As stated elsewhere, spirits have a fluidic body called the *perispirit.* Its substance is absorbed from the universal or cosmic fluid, which shapes and nourishes it, just as air shapes and nourishes the physical human body. The perispirit is more ethereal or less so, according to the world the spirit is inhabiting and the degree of the spirit's purification. On less evolved worlds, its nature is denser and closer to brute matter.

**10.** During incarnation, the spirit retains its perispirit: its physical body is only a secondary envelope, denser and more durable, appropriate for the functions it must fulfill, and which it rids itself of at death.

The perispirit is the intermediary between the spirit and the body. It is the organ of transmission of all sensations. Regarding the sensations that come from outside the body, one could say that the body receives the impression, the perispirit transmits it, and the spirit – the sensitive and intelligent being – receives it. When an action is initiated by the spirit, one could say that the spirit wills, the perispirit transmits and the body executes the action.

**11.** The perispirit is by no means enclosed within the limits of the body as in a box. Because of its fluidic nature, it is expandable; it radiates outward, forming around the body a sort of atmosphere that thought and will power can extend to a greater or lesser degree. Thus, it follows that there are individuals who, without being in physical contact with each other, may be in contact through their perispirits and unknowingly exchange impressions, and sometimes, even the intuition of their thoughts.

**12.** Since the perispirit is one of the constitutive elements of human beings, it plays an important role in all psychological phenomena, and to a certain degree in physiological and pathological phenomena as well. When medical science finally takes into account the influence of the spiritual element in the functioning of the individual, it will have taken a large step and completely new horizons will open up to it. Many causes of diseases will then be explained and powerful means of fighting them will be found.

**13.** It is by means of the perispirit that spirits act upon inert matter and produce the various phenomena of manifestations. Its ethereal nature is not a problem, because we know that the most powerful motive forces may be found in the most rarified and imponderable fluids. Thus, it should come as no surprise to see spirits use this lever to produce certain physical effects such as raps and noises of all sorts, or the lifting, carrying or hurling of objects. In order to explain these occurrences, there is no need to resort to the extraordinary or to supernatural effects.

**14.** In acting upon matter, spirits can manifest themselves in many different ways: through physical effects, such as noises and movements of objects; and through the transmission of thought, through sight, hearing, speech, touch, writing, drawing, music, etc. In other words, through any means that may serve to put them in touch with humans.

**15.** Spirit manifestations can either be spontaneous or caused. The former occur unexpectedly and fortuitously. They are often produced by persons who are completely foreign to Spiritist ideas. In some cases, and under the control of certain circumstances, manifestations may be caused by willpower, under the influence of individuals gifted with special faculties to this effect.

Spontaneous manifestations have occurred in all epochs and in all countries. Of course, the means of causing them was also known in ancient times, but it was the privilege of certain castes that only rarely revealed it to initiates under strict conditions, keeping them hidden from the common folk in order to dominate them with the prestige of a secret power. Nevertheless, the means continued among a few individuals down through the ages until our day, but they were nearly always disfigured by superstition or mixed in with the ridiculous practices of magic, which contributed to their discredit. There has been nothing much until now but a few seeds scattered here and there. Providence had reserved for our time the complete knowledge and popularization of such phenomena in order to free them from bad associations and make them useful for the betterment of humankind, which is finally mature enough to understand them and benefit from them.

## II – VISUAL MANIFESTATIONS

**16.** By its very nature, and in its normal state, the perispirit is invisible, a fact in common with a great number of fluids that we know exist but that we have never seen. But like certain fluids, the perispirit can also undergo modifications that make it perceptible to sight, whether by a sort of condensation or by a change in its molecular structure. It can even take on the properties of a solid and tangible body, but can instantly return to its ethereal and invisible state. It is possible to get an idea of this effect by observing steam, which can go from invisibility to the misty state, then the liquid and finally to the solid state, and vice-versa.

These different states of the perispirit are the result of the spirit's will and not some outside physical cause, as is the case with gases. When a spirit appears, it is because it has put its perispirit in the proper state to render it visible. The spirit's will, however, is not always sufficient: in order for this modification of the perispirit to occur, the cooperation of certain outside circumstances is necessary. Furthermore, the spirit must have permission to make itself visible to this or that person, and such permission is not always granted, or is granted only in certain circumstances for reasons unknown to us.[6]

Another property of the perispirit connected with its ethereal nature is *penetrability*. Matter is no obstacle; it can pass through anything just as light passes through transparent objects. Thus, there is no enclosure that can keep spirits out.

---

6 See *The Mediums' Book*, no. 105. – Auth.

They can visit prisoners in their cell as easily as they can visit someone in the middle of a field.

**17.** The commonest visual manifestations normally occur in dreams during sleep: these are *visions*. *Apparitions* per se occur during the waking state, when one is in full possession of and has complete freedom of one's faculties. Apparitions usually appear in a vaporous and diaphanous form, sometimes vague and fuzzy: frequently, at first sight, an apparition is a whitish glow, whose outline becomes clearer little by little. At other times, the form is clearly accentuated and the smallest details of the face can be discerned to the point of making a very precise description possible. The manners and appearance resemble those of the spirit when it was alive.

**18.** Since the spirit can assume any appearance, it shows itself under the one that will best make it recognizable if that is its desire. Also, even though as a spirit it no longer has a bodily infirmity, it will show itself as being deformed, disabled, wounded or scarred if that is what is needed to prove its identity. The same applies to clothing. The garment of spirits who have retained nothing of their earthly penchants usually consists of flowing robes, together with flowing, graceful hair.

Spirits often appear with the attributes characteristic of their elevation, such as a halo, wings for those one might regard as angels, or a resplendent luminous appearance, while others display characteristics that evoke their earthly occupations. Thus, a warrior might appear in armor, a scholar with books, an assassin with a dagger, etc. High order spirits have a beautiful, noble and serene face; those of the lowest orders appear somewhat ferocious and bestial, and some still bear the vestiges of the crimes they committed or the punishments they endured – for them, this appearance is a reality; that is, they believe they are just as they appear; it is a punishment for them.

> **19.** A spirit who wants to appear, or who actually can, sometimes assumes an even clearer form, having all the appearances of a solid body, to the point of creating a complete illusion and leading one to believe one is seeing a corporeal being.

In some cases and under the control of certain circumstances, tangibility can become real, meaning that one can touch, feel and sense the same resistance and warmth as that of a living body, but this tangibility does not keep it from vanishing like a flash of lightning. Thus, a person can be in the presence of a spirit, with whom he or she can exchange words and ordinary gestures, supposing he or she is dealing with an ordinary mortal without even suspecting that it is a spirit.

> **20.** Whatever the aspect in which a spirit presents itself – even in tangible form – it can, at that moment, be visible only to certain individuals. In a gathering, therefore, it can show itself to one only or to several members. Of two people right next to each other, one might be able to see and touch it, while the other sees and feels nothing at all.

The phenomenon of an apparition appearing only to one person among several can be explained by the fact that an apparition must be produced by a combining of the perispiritual fluid of the spirit with that of the person. For this to occur there must be between these fluids a sort of affinity that enables the combination. If the spirit does not find the necessary organic aptitude, the apparition cannot be produced; if the aptitude exists, the spirit is free to take advantage of it or not. The result is that if two persons who are equally gifted with this aptitude are in the same place, the spirit can perform the fluidic combination only with the one to whom it wants to show itself. If it does not perform the combination with the other, he or she will not see it. The same would occur with two individuals, each one having a blindfold over his or her eyes: if a third person wanted to appear only to one of the two, he or she would remove the blindfold only from that person's eyes. However, if that person were blind, it would do no good to remove the blindfold – he or she would not have the faculty of sight in the first place.

**21.** Tangible apparitions are quite rare, but vaporous ones are quite common. They especially occur at the moment of death. The disengaged spirit seems to be in a hurry to see its family and friends in order to advise them that it has just left the earth, and to tell them that it is still alive. Let anyone search his or her memories and he or she will see how many authentic yet inexplicable incidents of this kind have occurred not only at night but in full daylight and in the fullest waking state.

## III – TRANSFIGURATION. INVISIBILITY

**22.** The perispirit of living persons possesses the same properties as the perispirit of spirits. As was stated earlier, the perispirit is not at all confined within the body, but radiates outward to form a kind of fluidic atmosphere. Thus, in certain cases and depending on the circumstances, it undergoes a transformation similar to what has already been depicted: the real and physical form of the body can disappear under this fluidic layer – if we may so describe it – and momentarily assume an entirely different appearance, even the appearance of another person or that of the spirit who combines its fluid with that of the individual; or it can even make a homely face look beautiful and radiant. Such is the phenomenon called transfiguration, a surprisingly common phenomenon that is produced principally when the circumstances allow for a more abundant expansion of fluid.

The transfiguration phenomenon can manifest with a much different intensity, depending on the perispirit's degree of purity, which always corresponds to the spirit's moral stature. At times it is limited to a simple change in the facial appearance, whereas at other times it gives the perispirit a luminous and splendid appearance.

Hence, the material form can disappear behind the perispiritual fluid, but there is no need for this fluid to assume another aspect. Sometimes, it can simply shield an inert or living body, rendering it invisible to one or several persons as would a layer of vapor.

We refer to this solely as a point of comparison, and not to establish a perfect analogy, which does not exist.

**23.** These phenomena might appear strange only because the properties of the perispiritual fluid are not known. For us it is a new body that must possess new properties, which one cannot study through ordinary scientific procedures, but which are natural properties nonetheless, having nothing extraordinary about them but the novelty.

## IV – THE EMANCIPATION OF THE SOUL

**24.** During sleep, only the body rests; the spirit does not sleep. It takes advantage of the body's rest and moments when its presence is not necessary so that it can act by itself and go wherever it wants; it enjoys its freedom and the full use of its faculties. During incarnation, the spirit is never completely separated from the body; no matter how far it might travel, it is always connected to it by a fluidic cord that serves to call it back when its presence is required. This cord is broken only at death.

"Sleep partially frees the soul from the body. When humans sleep, they momentarily find themselves in the state which they will be in permanently after death. Spirits who quickly free themselves from matter upon death had intelligent dreams during earthly life. Such spirits, while their body is sleeping, rejoin the company of those who are more evolved; they travel with, converse with and learn from them. They even work on projects that they find completed upon dying. From these facts you should once more learn not to fear death, because you die daily – as a saint once stated.

"This applies only to more highly evolved spirits; however, the mass of spirits, who at death must remain in a state of confusion for some time – that uncertainty of which we have already spoken to you – either go to worlds even less evolved than earth, where former affections call to them or where they seek out pleasures that are perhaps even baser than those they indulge in here. They go to take in doctrines even viler, more ignoble and more noxious than those they profess among you. What engenders sympathies on earth is nothing other than the fact that upon awakening, they feel linked to the hearts of those with whom they have just spent eight or nine hours of happiness or pleasure. Moreover, the insuperable antipathies they feel at the bottom of our heart for certain individuals may be explained by the fact that they have a consciousness that is different from their own; they recognize these individual without having ever seen them before. It is furthermore what explains people's indifference when they do not seek to make new friends – they know that those who love and cherish them are elsewhere. In a word, sleep has more influence than you think on your life.

"During sleep, incarnate spirits are always in touch with the spirit world, and that is what leads high order spirits, without too much aversion, to consent to incarnate among you. During their contact with earthly vices, God grants them the freedom to re-strengthen themselves during sleep at the source of the good in order not to fail in their commitment to instruct others. Sleep is the door that God opens to them for contacting their friends in heaven. It is their break after work while they await the great deliverance, the final liberation that must restore them to their true environment.

"A dream is the memory of what your spirit has seen during sleep. However, notice that you do not always dream, because you do not always remember what you have seen, or everything that you have seen. This happens because your soul is still under development, so that frequently you retain nothing more than the confused memory that accompanies your departure and your return, which is mixed in with the memory of what you have done or what concerns you have had while awake. Otherwise, how do you explain those absurd dreams that both the wisest and the simplest individuals endure? Bad spirits also use dreams to torment weak and cowardly souls.

"Furthermore, you will soon see another type of dreaming develop; a type as ancient as the kind you already know about but of which you are ignorant. It is the dream of Joan of Arc, the dream of Jacob, the dream of the Jewish prophets and certain Indian seers: this sort of dream is the remembrance of the soul entirely disengaged from the body, the memory of that other life of which I have just spoken to you.

"Try hard to distinguish between these two types of dreams among those that you remember; unless you do, you will fall into contradictions and errors that could be disastrous for your faith." [7]

**25.** The independence and emancipation of the soul most obviously manifests in the phenomena of natural and magnetic somnambulism, catalepsy and lethargy. Somnambulistic lucidity is nothing

---

7 *The Spirits' Book*, no. 402 et seq. – Auth. (3rd Edition, International Spiritist Council, 2010) – Tr.

more than the faculty the soul possesses to see and feel without the aid of the physical organs. This faculty is one of its attributes; it resides in the soul's entire being; the body's organs are only narrow channels by which certain perceptions reach the body. Sight at distance, which some somnambulists possess, results from a dislocation of the soul, which sees what is occurring in the places to where it travels. In its wanderings, the soul is always clothed by its perispirit, the agent of its sensations, but which is never completely disconnected from the body, as we have already stated. The disengagement of the soul causes inertia in the body, which sometimes appears to be deprived of life.

**26.** This disengagement can also occur to various degrees in the waking state, but then the body never engages in its normal activity completely; there is always a certain disconnection, a degree of detachment from earthly matters. The body is not asleep; it walks and acts, but the eyes look without seeing; one can see that the soul is elsewhere. Just as in somnambulism, the soul sees distant things; it experiences perceptions and sensations unknown to us; sometimes, it has a prescience about certain future events through the connection it makes with present events. Upon entering the invisible world, it sees spirits with whom it may carry on a conversation and whose thoughts it may transmit to us.

Upon its return to the normal state, the soul usually forgets what has happened, but sometimes it retains a more or less vague memory of it, like that of a dream.

**27.** Sometimes, the soul's emancipation deadens the physical senses to the point that it produces true insensitiveness, which, in moments of exaltation, enables the body to endure the most intense pain indifferently. This insensitiveness results from the disengagement of the perispirit, the transmitting agent for bodily sensations. The absent spirit does not feel the injuries to the body.

**28.** In its simplest expression, the emancipating faculty of the soul produces what is known as daydreaming; it also endows some persons with the prescience that constitutes presentiment; in more advanced degrees of development, it produces the phenomenon known as "second sight," "dual sight," or "waking-state somnambulism."

**29.** *Ecstasy* is the highest degree possible of the emancipation of the soul. "In both dreams and somnambulism, the soul wanders through terrestrial worlds, whereas in ecstasy, it enters an unknown world, that of ethereal spirits, with whom it communicates, without, however, overstepping certain limits – if it did, the soul would completely break the ties connecting it to the body. A resplendent and entirely new brilliance surrounds this soul. Harmonies unknown on earth enrapture it, an indefinable well-being permeates it, the spirit enjoys a foretaste of celestial beatitude, and it may be said that it has set one foot on the threshold of eternity. In the state of ecstasy, the nullification of the body is almost complete. It only maintains organic life per se and it feels that the soul is connected to it by only one single thread, which with any further effort would break forever."[8]

**30.** As with all the other degrees of the soul's emancipation, ecstasy is not without its errors; hence, revelations by ecstatics are far from always expressing absolute truth. The reason

8 *The Spirits' Book*, no. 455. – Auth. (ibid) – Tr.

for this rests in the imperfection of the human spirit. Only when it has reached the pinnacle of the spirit hierarchy can it judge matters infallibly. Before then, it is allowed neither to see everything nor to understand everything. If, after death, when the disengagement is complete, it cannot always see things accurately; if there are those who remain imbued with life's prejudices, who do not comprehend the things of the invisible world in which they find themselves, more rightly does the same apply to the spirit still connected to the flesh.

At times, among ecstatics there is more over-excitement than true lucidity, or rather, their over-excitement impairs their lucidity; consequently, their revelations are frequently a mixture of truths and errors, of sublime and ridiculous things. Moreover, low order spirits may take advantage of this over-excitement – which is always a cause of weakness when one does not know how to control it – in order to dominate the ecstatic. To do so these spirits assume *appearances* that hold ecstatics to their ideas or prejudices in such a way that their visions and revelations are often no more than reflections of these spirits' own beliefs. This is a scourge that only high order spirits can escape, a situation that requires observers to be on their guard.

**31.** The perispirit of certain individuals is so identified with their body that the disengagement of the soul occurs only with extreme difficulty, even at the time of death. Usually, it affects those who have lived more materially. Death for them is also more painful, more filled with anguish; their agony lasts longer and is more dolorous. On the other hand, there are others whose soul is held to the body by such fragile ties that separation occurs without trouble, with the greatest ease, and quite often before the actual death of the body. When the end of life approaches, the soul has already foreseen the world into which it will enter and it longs for the moment of its full deliverance.

## IV – APPARITIONS OF LIVING PERSONS. BI-CORPOREALITY

**32.** The emancipating faculty of the soul and its disengagement from the body while alive may give way to phenomena analogous to those produced by discarnate spirits. While the body is asleep, the spirit travels to various places; it can render itself visible and can appear in vaporous form, whether in a dream or in the waking state. It can also appear in tangible form, or at least with an appearance that seems so real that a number of people can attest to the fact of having seen it in two different places at the same time. In fact, this has happened; however, the real body was in one place only – at the other site there was only the spirit. Nevertheless, this phenomenon is very rare and has given rise to the belief in double individuals – a phenomenon known as *bi-corporeality*.

As extraordinary as it may be, this phenomenon, like all others, is to be included in the order of natural phenomena, because it rests upon the properties of the perispirit and natural law.

## V – MEDIUMS

**33.** Mediums are individuals capable of receiving the influence of spirits and transmitting their thoughts.

Every person that senses the influence of spirits is by that simple fact a medium. This faculty is inherent to humans, and consequently, is in no way an exclusive privilege; moreover, there are few people who do not possess at least a rudimentary element of it. One could thus say that everyone is a medium to some degree. However, according to normal usage, the label applies only to those whose mediumistic faculty manifests itself by ostensible effects of a certain intensity.

**34.** The perispiritual fluid is the agent for all spirit phenomena; such phenomena can only occur through the reciprocal action of the perispiritual fluids emitted by both medium and spirit. The development of the mediumistic faculty depends on the degree of the expandable nature of the medium's perispirit and the greater or lesser ease with which it may be assimilated by spirits. It thus depends on the medium's physical make-up and may be developed if the principle exists; but it cannot be acquired if the principle is not there at all. Mediumistic predisposition is independent of sex, age and temperament. There are mediums in all categories of individuals, from the youngest to the oldest.

**35.** Relations between spirits and mediums are established through their perispirits, and the ease of these relations depends on the degree of affinity between their perispiritual fluids. Some combine easily, while others repel each other, from which it follows that it is not enough merely to be a medium to communicate with all spirits indiscriminately; there are mediums who can communicate only with certain spirits or categories of spirits, while there are others who communicate only by the transmission of thought, without any outward manifestation.

**36.** By means of the assimilation of perispiritual fluids, a spirit can identify – so to speak – with the person it wants to influence. Not only does it transmit his or her thoughts, but it can exert a physical influence, making the person act or speak to its liking, making him or her say what it wants. In sum, it uses the person's organs as if they were its own. It can even end up neutralizing the action of the person's spirit and paralyzing his or her free will. Good spirits utilize this influence for the good, bad ones for evil.

**37.** Spirits can manifest themselves in infinitely different ways, but only if they find a person capable of receiving and transmitting this or that type of impression according to that person's aptitude. Since there are none who possess all aptitudes to the same degree, the result is that some obtain effects that are impossible for others. This diversity of aptitudes produces different varieties of mediums.

**38.** The medium's will is not always necessary. A spirit who wants to manifest itself looks for an individual capable of receiving its impression, and often uses the person without him or her even realizing it. On the other hand, there are individuals who are aware of their faculty and can precipitate certain manifestations; hence, there are two categories of mediums: *unconscious mediums* and *facultative mediums*. In the former, the spirit takes the initiative; in the latter, the medium.

**39.** *Facultative mediums* are found only among persons who have a more or less complete understanding of the means of communicating with spirits, and are thereby willing to use their faculties to do so; *unconscious mediums*, on the other hand, are found among those – even among the most disbelieving individuals – who have no idea either about Spiritism or spirits, but who serve as spirits' instruments without wanting to or even being aware of it. Spirit phenomena of all kinds can occur due to their influence, and they have been found in every era and in every culture. Ignorance and gullibility have attributed them with supernatural power, and depending on the time and place, have regarded them as saints, witches, lunatics or visionaries. Spiritism shows us that they were merely exhibiting a simple, spontaneous manifestation of a natural faculty.

**40.** Among the different varieties of mediums, we may distinguish principally *physical effects mediums*; *sensitive or impressionable mediums*; *hearing, speaking, seeing mediums; inspired, somnambulistic and healing mediums, and writing* or *psychographic mediums*. Here we will describe only the most essential.[9]

**41.** *Physical effects mediums*. These are more especially capable of producing physical phenomena such as the movement of inert objects, noises, dislocations, the raising and transporting of objects, etc. Such phenomena may either be spontaneous or artificially caused. In all cases, however, they require the witting or unwitting cooperation of mediums endowed with special faculties. Such effects usually originate from less evolved spirits, since more highly evolved ones only concern themselves with intelligent and instructive communications.

**42.** *Sensitive or impressionable mediums*. This applies to persons susceptible of sensing the presence of spirits through a vague impression, a sort of light tingling in their limbs that cannot be explained. This faculty can acquire such subtlety that those endowed with it can determine by the impression they receive not only the good or evil nature of the spirit at their side, but even who it is – like a blind person instinctively recognizing

9 For complete details, see *The Mediums' Book*. – Auth.

the presence of this or that person. While a good spirit always causes a gentle and agreeable impression, a bad one causes a painful, afflictive and unpleasant feeling: there is sort of an impure smell about it.

**43.** *Hearing mediums.* These hear the voices of spirits. Sometimes it is an inner voice that resounds within them; at other times, it is a clear and distinct voice outside of them, like that of a living person. Hearing mediums may also converse with spirits. When they habitually communicate with certain spirits, they recognize them immediately by the sound of their voice. Those who are not hearing mediums themselves may communicate with a spirit through a hearing medium who transmits the words.

**44.** *Speaking mediums.* Hearing mediums, who do nothing more than transmit what they hear, are not *speaking mediums* per se; the latter generally hear nothing at all. The spirit acts on their organs of speech, in the same way that they act on the hand of writing mediums. Whenever a spirit wants to communicate, it uses the most flexible organ available: in one medium, it might be the hand; in another, the vocal cords; in a third, the ears. Generally, speaking mediums speak without being aware of what they are saying, and they often say things that are completely outside the range of their normal ideas and knowledge, and even beyond the scope of their intelligence. Illiterates and persons of average intelligence are sometimes seen in such instances expressing themselves with true eloquence and skillfully addressing issues they would otherwise be incapable of discussing in their ordinary state.

Although speaking mediums may be fully awake, they rarely remember what they have said; however, such passivity is not always complete. Some have an intuition of what they are saying at the time they are saying it.

Regarding speaking mediums, speech is an instrument spirits use so that third parties can communicate with the spirit in the same way they do through hearing mediums. The difference between speaking mediums and hearing mediums is that the latter wittingly repeat what they hear, whereas the former speak unwittingly.

**45.** *Seeing mediums.* This designation is given to individuals who, in the normal state and while fully awake, have the ability to see spirits. The ability to see them while dreaming is incontestably a type of mediumship, but persons who can do this are not seeing mediums per se. We explain the theory of this phenomenon in the chapter "Visual Manifestations" in *The Mediums' Book*.

Apparitions of spirits that appear to persons they have loved or known are very common. While persons who have had such an experience may be regarded as seeing mediums, the designation is more generally given to those who have a more or less ongoing ability to see almost all spirits. Among them there are those who see only spirits who have been evoked, and whom they can describe with minute precision, including their gestures, facial expressions, the clothes they are wearing and even the sentiments that seem to be animating them. There are others whose faculty is even wider: they can see the entire surrounding spirit population coming and going, and one might say, going about their affairs. These mediums are never alone; they are always surrounded by a society that they may choose as they please according to their tastes, because by an act of their will, they can keep away spirits whom they do not like, or they can attract those for whom they have an affinity.

**46.** *Somnambulistic mediums.* Somnambulism may be considered a variety of the mediumistic faculty, or rather, these are two orders of phenomena that are frequently found together. Somnambulists act under the influence of their own spirit. In moments of emancipation, their own soul is what sees, hears and perceives beyond the limits of their physical senses. What they express they draw from themselves; their ideas are usually more correct than when they are in the normal state, and their knowledge is more expansive because their soul is free. In other words, they live the spirit life in advance. Mediums, on the other hand, are instruments used by an outside intelligence; they are passive and what they say does not come from themselves.

In sum, somnambulists express their own thoughts, whereas mediums express the thoughts of others. However, the spirit who communicates with a medium may also communicate with a somnambulist. Frequently, the emancipated state of the soul during somnambulism can render communication easier. Many somnambulists see spirits and describe them as precisely as seeing mediums can. They can converse with them and transmit their thoughts to us; if what they say is outside the ambit of their personal knowledge, it is because other spirits have suggested it to them.

**47.** *Inspired mediums.* In these mediums the outward signs of mediumship are the least apparent. The action of spirits upon them is entirely intellectual and mental, and is displayed in the smallest circumstances of life as well as in the greatest. It is especially from this perspective that one can state that everyone is a medium, because there is not a single person that does not have protecting and familiar spirits employing all their efforts to suggest wholesome ideas to him or her. It is often difficult for inspired mediums to distinguish their own thoughts from those that are suggested to them; what especially characterizes the latter is spontaneity.

Inspiration is most evident in the great works of intelligence. Individuals of genius of all categories – artists, scholars, orators – are undoubtedly advanced spirits capable of understanding and conceiving great things; thus, it is precisely because they are deemed capable that the spirits who want to accomplish certain works suggest their ideas to that end, and consequently, most often such individuals are *mediums without even realizing it.* Nevertheless, they have a vague intuition of some kind of outside assistance, because those who appeal for inspiration are doing nothing more than making an evocation. If they did not expect to be heard, why would they write so frequently: "My good spirit, come to my aid!"

**48.** *Prescient mediums.* These are persons who under certain circumstances have a vague intuition of ordinary future events. This intuition may come from a type of second sight, which allows glimpsing the consequences of present matters and the sequence of events; but frequently such intuition results from secret communications that render such persons a variety of *inspired medium.*

**49.** *Prophetic mediums.* This is also a variety of inspired medium. With God's permission and with more precision than prescient mediums, they receive revelations of future things of a general interest, which they are charged with making known to humankind for its instruction. Prescience is given to most people in some way for their own personal use; the gift of prophecy, on the other hand, is exceptional and implies the idea of an earthly mission.

If there are true prophets, there are many more false ones, who take the fancies of their imagination as revelations

– if they are not hypocrites who, because of ambition, pass themselves off as prophets.

True prophets are *individuals of the good inspired by God.* They can be recognized by their words and actions. God cannot use the mouth of a liar to teach the truth.[10]

**50.** *Writing or psychographic mediums.* We use this name to designate persons who write under the influence of spirits. Just as spirits can act upon speaking mediums' organs of speech and cause them to speak words, they can also use mediums' hands to cause them to write. Psychographic mediumship displays three quite distinct varieties: *mechanical*, *intuitive* and *semi-mechanical.*

As for *mechanical mediums*, spirits act directly upon the hand, thereby giving it impulse. What characterizes this type of mediumship is complete unawareness of what is being written. The movement of the hand is independent of the will; it proceeds without interruption and in spite of the medium for as long as the spirit has something to say, and it stops when the spirit has finished.

As for *intuitive mediums*, the transmission of the spirit's thought is done through the medium's spirit. The discarnate spirit, in this case, does not act upon the hand to guide it, but upon the soul with which it identifies and on which it impresses its will and ideas. The medium receives the foreign thought and transcribes it. In such a situation, mediums write voluntarily and are aware of what they write, even though it is not their own thought.

It is often quite difficult to distinguish between the mediums' own thoughts and those that are suggested to them, which leads *many mediums of this type to doubt their faculty*. However, they can identify suggested thoughts by the fact that they had never had them before; that they surface while the mediums are writing and that they are frequently

---

10 *The Spirits' Book*, no. 624. – Auth.

the opposite of the idea they had previously formed. These thoughts can even be outside the knowledge and capabilities of the mediums.

There is much similarity between intuitive mediumship and inspiration; the difference consists in that the former is most often limited to current issues and can be applied outside the intellectual abilities of the medium. Through intuition a medium can address a subject that is completely foreign to him or her. Inspiration, on the other hand, extends to a much broader field and usually comes to assist the abilities and concerns of the incarnate spirit. The characteristics of this type of mediumship are generally less evident.

*Semi-mechanical* or *semi-intuitive* mediums share in the other two types. In purely mechanical mediums, the movement of the hand is independent of their will; in intuitive mediums, the movement is voluntary and facultative. Semi-mechanical mediums feel an impulse given to their hand in spite of themselves, but at the same time, they are aware of what they are writing as the words are formed. With the first type, the thought comes after the act of writing; with the second, it precedes it; with the third, it accompanies it.

**51.** Since mediums are nothing more than instruments that receive and transmit a discarnate spirit's thought – instruments that follow the mechanical impulse that the spirit gives them – there is nothing they cannot do outside their scope of knowledge if they are endowed with the necessary mediumistic flexibility and aptitude. Consequently, there are *drawing*, *painting*, *musical* and *poetic* mediums, even though they are foreign to the arts of drawing, painting, music and poetry; illiterate mediums that write without knowing how to read or write; polygraphic mediums that reproduce different handwritings – sometimes with perfect exactitude the handwriting of a particular spirit when it was alive; polyglot mediums that write or speak in languages unknown to them, etc.

**52.** *Healing mediums.* This type of mediumship consists in the faculty certain persons have of being able to heal with a mere touch, with the laying-on of their hands, with a look, or even with a gesture without the aid of any kind of medication. Such a faculty undeniably has its principle in the magnetic power; it differs from it, however, by the energy and instantaneousness of the action, in that magnetic healings require a methodical treatment for a longer or shorter amount of time. All magnetizers are able to heal to some degree if they know how to proceed properly; they have an acquired knowledge. In healing mediums, however, the faculty is spontaneous and some of them possess it without ever having heard of magnetism.

The ability to heal with the laying-on of hands obviously has its principle in an exceptional power of expansion, but it is increased by several causes, among which purity of sentiments, disinterestedness, benevolence, an ardent desire to provide relief, fervent prayer and trust in God must be placed first: in sum, all the moral qualities. Magnetic power, on the other hand, is purely organic. Like muscular power, it may be given to anyone, even bad individuals; however, only persons of the good use it exclusively for the good without any ulterior personal motives and without satisfying their pride or vanity. Their purified fluids possess beneficent and restorative properties that the fluids of bad or self-serving individuals cannot have.

As already stated, every mediumistic effect is the result of the combining of the fluids emitted by a spirit and by a medium. Through this union these fluids acquire new properties that they would not possess separately, or at least not to the same degree. Prayer, which is actually a form of evocation, attracts good spirits, always eager to second the efforts of well-intentioned individuals; the beneficent fluids of the former easily combine with those of the latter, whereas the fluids of bad individuals combine with those of the bad spirits that surround them.

Persons of the good who did not possess this fluidic power could do but very little by themselves. Their only alternative would be to call for assistance from good spirits, but their own personal action would be almost nil; however, a large fluidic power allied with the greatest possible number of moral qualities can work true healing wonders.

**53.** Furthermore, the fluidic action is powerfully aided by the trust of the patient, and God often rewards his or her faith with success.

**54.** Only superstition could link any virtue to certain words, and only ignorant or deceiving spirits could feed such ideas by prescribing formulas. Nevertheless, it might happen that for persons who are less enlightened and incapable of comprehending purely spiritual matters, the use of a prayer formula or a certain ritual could contribute to providing them with faith. In that case, however, it is not the formula per se that is effective, but the faith that is increased by the idea attached to the use of the formula.

**55.** *Healing mediums* should not be confused with *medical mediums*; the latter are simply writing mediums whose specialty consists in most easily serving as spirits' interpreters for the purpose of prescribing medications; they do nothing more than transmit the spirit's thought without exerting any of their own influence.

## VI – OBSESSION AND POSSESSION

**56.** Obsession is the control that bad spirits have over certain persons in order to dominate and subject them to their will for the pleasure they experience in doing evil.

When a good or bad spirit wants to act on an individual, it envelops him or her, so to speak, in its perispirit as if it were a robe. The pair's fluids intermingle, their thoughts and wills mix, and the spirit can then use the individual's body as if it were its own, making it act according to its wishes, speaking, writing or drawing as mediums do. If the spirit is good, its action is gentle and beneficent; it impels the individual to do only good things. If it is bad, it forces him or her to do evil. If the spirit is perverse and malevolent, it constrains the person as if in a net, paralyzing his or her will and even his or her judgment, which it smothers under its fluids just as one smothers a fire under a layer of water. It makes the person think, speak and act according to its will, and in spite of whether the person agrees or not, it impels him or her to commit extravagant or ridiculous acts; in other words, it magnetizes and puts the person into a state of moral catalepsy, and he or she becomes a blind instrument of the bad spirit's will. Such is the cause of obsession, fascination and subjugation, which are displayed in highly diverse degrees of intensity. The ultimate subjugation is what is commonly called *possession*. One should note that in this state the individual is often aware that what he or she is doing is ridiculous, but is forced to do it anyway, as if a much stronger individual were making him or her move arms, legs and tongue against his or her will.

**57.** Since spirits have always existed throughout time, they have always performed this same role because it is a part of nature; the proof of this lies in the large number of obsessed, or, if one prefers, possessed persons, way before any mention of spirits was made, or nowadays for those who have never heard of either Spiritism or mediums. Thus, the action of good or bad spirits is spontaneous; the latter cause a huge number of disturbances in the moral and even physical

> resources of persons, which due to ignorance of their true cause used to be attributed to erroneous causes.

Bad spirits are invisible enemies who are all the more dangerous when their actions are not suspected. By unmasking them, Spiritism has disclosed a new cause for certain ills of humankind. With the cause understood, people will no longer try to combat evil by means that are known to be useless; they will look for others that are more effective. And what has led to the discovery of that cause? Mediumship. It is through mediumship that these hidden enemies have betrayed their presence. Mediumship did to them what the microscope did to infinitely small organisms: it revealed a whole other world.

Spiritism did not in any way attract bad spirits; it disclosed them and furnished the means of paralyzing their action, and consequently, of holding them at bay. Thus, Spiritism did not provide this evil, since it has existed throughout all time; on the contrary, it brought the remedy for the evil by pointing out its cause. Once the workings of the invisible world are recognized, we will have the key to a multitude of misunderstood phenomena, and science, enriched with this new law, will see new horizons open up to it. WHEN WILL SCIENCE ARRIVE AT THAT POINT? *When it no longer professes materialism*, because materialism hinders its flight and poses an insurmountable barrier.

**58.** Since there are bad spirits who obsess and good spirits who protect, one might ask if bad spirits are more powerful than good ones.

It is not that the good spirit is the weaker; it is the medium, who is not strong enough to throw off the mantle that has been cast over him or her, who is not strong enough to break free from the clutch of the arms that enlace him or her, and in which, it must be said, the medium sometimes is actually pleased to be held. In such a case, the good spirit cannot prevail, since the bad one is preferred. Now, let us suppose the person has the desire to get rid of this fluidic envelope with which he or she is interpenetrated – like an article of clothing is interpenetrated by moisture. Desire is not enough; even willpower is often not enough.

It involves a struggle against an adversary. When two men fight hand-to-hand, the stronger one will defeat the other, but when a spirit is involved, the struggle is not hand-to-hand, but spirit-to-spirit; and again, it will be the stronger who wins. Here, the strength lies in the *authority* that may be exerted over the obsessor spirit and this authority depends on moral superiority. Moral superiority is like the sun, which scatters the fog with the power of its rays. By strengthening themselves in the good, by becoming better than they already are, by purifying themselves of their imperfections – in sum, by morally elevating themselves as much as possible – this is the means for acquiring the power to control low order spirits to keep them away; otherwise, they will merely ridicule your orders.[11]

Nonetheless, one might say, why do protector spirits not simply order obsessors to withdraw? Undoubtedly, they could and sometimes they actually do; however, in allowing the struggle, they also allow the merit of victory. If they let worthy individuals struggle in certain situations, it is to test their perseverance and enable them to acquire more strength in the good; it is a sort of *moral calisthenics*.

Certain people will obviously prefer an easier recipe for expelling bad spirits: certain words to say, or certain signs to make, for example, which would be easier than having to correct their defects. Unfortunately, we know of no effective means of *overcoming such an enemy except by making oneself stronger than it is*. Whenever we are ill, we must resign ourselves to take our medicine, no matter how bitter; but if we have had the courage to drink it, how good and strong we feel afterwards! Thus, we must persuade ourselves that, in order to achieve satisfactory results, there are no sacramental words, no

---

11 *The Mediums' Book*, nos. 252, 279. – Auth.

formulas, no talismans or any physical signs. Bad spirits only laugh at them and often take delight in prescribing a few of their own, always being careful to say that they are infallible in order to better win the trust of those they want to dupe. Trusting in the power of the process, their victims will hand themselves over without fear.

Before anyone hopes to control a bad spirit, he or she must first have complete self-control. Of all the means of acquiring enough strength to have such control, the most effective is willpower aided by prayer; that is, prayer with the heart and not with words in which the lips play a greater part than thought. We must ask our guardian angel and good spirits to assist us in the struggle, but it is not enough to simply ask them to expel the bad spirit; we must remember the maxim, "Heaven helps those who help themselves," and ask especially for the strength we lack for overcoming our bad inclinations. These tendencies are actually worse for us than bad spirits, because such inclinations are what attract them in the first place, like a rotting carcass attracts vultures. Also, by praying for the obsessor spirit, we repay its evil with good and we show ourselves to be better than it is, and this is already a display of superiority. If we persevere, we will often end up inducing it to better sentiments and our persecutor becomes a grateful friend.

In sum, fervent prayer and serious efforts to improve oneself morally are the sole means of repelling bad spirits. They recognize as their superiors those who practice the good, and while formulas merely make them laugh, anger and impatience incite them. One must wear them down by being more patient than they are.

However, it sometimes happens that subjugation increases to the point of paralyzing the will of the obsessed person, and one cannot expect any serious cooperation on his or her part. This is when the intervention of third parties becomes especially necessary, whether through prayer or through magnetic action. Even then, the power of such intervention depends on the moral ascendancy that the intervener has over the bad spirit; if the former's is no greater than the latter's, whatever he or she does will be fruitless. Magnetic action in this case has the effect of introducing a better fluid into the obsessed person's fluid and removing that of the bad spirit. In this work, the magnetizer must have the double purpose of opposing one moral power with another, of producing upon the patient a sort of chemical reaction – to use a material comparison – getting rid of one fluid by replacing it with another. That way, not only does a salutary disengagement occur, but strength is given to organs that have been weakened by a long and often powerful oppression. Consequently, we understand that the power of fluidic action is due not only to the power of the will, but especially to the quality of the fluid introduced, and according to what we have stated, this quality depends on the education and moral qualities of the magnetizer. Thus, it follows that an ordinary magnetizer who acts mechanically to purely and simply magnetize will produce little or no effect. More than anything else, a *Spiritist* magnetizer is needed, acting with full knowledge of the facts, with the intention of producing not somnambulism or an organic healing, but the effects we have just described. Furthermore, it is obvious that a magnetic action applied in this sense could be very useful in the case of an ordinary obsession, because then, if the magnetizer is seconded by the will of the obsessed person, the bad spirit is being fought by two adversaries instead of just one.

We must also state that discarnate spirits are often blamed for wrongdoing when they are, in fact, innocent. Certain sickly states and certain aberrations attributed to an occult cause are sometimes simply due to the individual's own spirit. The troubles that people ordinarily harbor within them – especially love-related disappointments – make them commit many crazy acts that are wrongly attributed to obsession. People are frequently their own obsessors.

Finally, we will add that certain tenacious obsessions, especially those involving honorable individuals, may be part of the trials to which they are submitted. Sometimes an obsession, when simple, is a task imposed on the one who is obsessed, who must work for the obsessor's improvement like the parent of a naughty child.[12]

Prayer is generally a powerful means for helping to free obsessed individuals; however, a prayer using mere words spoken indifferently and as a banal formula can never be effective in such a case. Ardent prayer is required, which at the same time acts as a sort of mental magnetization. Through thought, a healthful fluidic current can be directed at the patient; the potency of this current is equal to the potency of the intent. Hence, prayer not only has the effect of invoking outside help, but it exerts a fluidic action as well. What one person cannot do alone, several persons united by intent in a collective and reiterated prayer often can do together, the potency of the prayer being increased by the number of persons praying.

**59.** Experience has proven the ineffectiveness of exorcism in cases of possession; in fact, it has been shown that most of the time exorcism increases the problem instead of lessening it. The reason for this is that its influence rests entirely in the moral ascendancy exerted on bad spirits and not an outward action using mere words and gestures. Exorcism consists in rites and formulas that bad spirits laugh at, whereas they yield to the moral authority imposed upon them. They see that one wants to control them through powerless means, that one tries to intimidate them with some meaningless apparatus, and so they tend to show who is the stronger by doubling their efforts. They are like a spooked horse, which bucks off the unskilled rider but obeys when it meets its master. Thus, the true master here is the person with the purest heart,

12 For more details, see *The Mediums' Book*. – Auth.

because he or she is the one most listened to by good spirits.

**60.** What one spirit can do with one individual, many spirits can do with many individuals at the same time, thereby giving obsession an epidemic character. A swarm of bad spirits may invade a locale and manifest themselves in various ways. It was just such an epidemic that struck Judea at the time of Christ. Because of his immense moral superiority, Christ had such authority over demons, or bad spirits, that it was enough for him to order them to withdraw, and they did so without him using any gestures or formulas.

**61.** Spiritism is founded on the observation of phenomena that result from relations between the visible and invisible worlds. These phenomena, being of a natural order, have been produced in all eras and are abundant especially in the sacred books of all religions, having served as the basis for most beliefs. It is because they have not been understood that the Bible and the Gospels present so many obscure passages interpreted in so many different ways. Spiritism is the key that will facilitate their understanding.

# HUMAN DOUBLES. APPARITIONS OF LIVING PERSONS

Nowadays, it is a proven and fully explained fact that when detached from a living body, the spirit can, with the help of its fluidic perispiritual envelope, appear in a different place than where its physical body is. Until now, however, theory, in agreement with experience, seemed to demonstrate that this separation can occur only during sleep, or at least during the inactivity of the corporeal senses. If they are accurate, however, the following incidents would prove that the separation may also occur during the waking state. They are taken from the German work, *The Mystical Phenomena of Nature,* by Maximillian Perty[13], professor at the University of Bern, published in 1861 (Leipzig and Heidelberg).

> **1.** "A plantation owner was seen by his coachman in his stables inspecting his horses at the exact same time in which he was taking Communion in church. The owner later told his priest, who asked him what he had been thinking about at the time of Communion: 'Well, to tell you the truth, I was thinking about my horses.' 'Well, that explains your apparition,' replied the cleric."

The priest was right; since thought is the essential attribute of the spirit, the spirit must be where its thought is. The question involves knowing if in the waking state the spirit's disengagement can be sufficient enough to produce an apparition, which would imply a sort of doubling of the

13 Joseph Anton Maximillian Perty, German Zoologist, 1804-1884. – Tr.

spirit, one part which would animate the fluidic body and the other the physical body. There would be nothing impossible about this, considering that, when the thought is focused on a distant point, the body acts only mechanistically by means of a sort of mechanical impulse; this occurs especially in persons when they are distracted: they are animated only by physical life; their mental life accompanies the spirit. Consequently, it is probable that the man in the above example had experienced a strong distraction at that moment, and that his horses concerned him more than Communion did.

The following incident belongs to the same category, but it displays a more remarkable particularity:

> **2.** "One day, District Judge J… in Fr… sent his assistant to an outlying village. After some time, the judge saw the assistant enter, take a book from the shelf and leaf through it. He sternly asked the assistant why he had not left yet. But as soon as he said this, the assistant vanished. The book dropped to the floor and the judge put it on top of a table and opened it to where it had been before falling. That evening, when the assistant returned, the judge asked him if anything had happened along the way and if he had returned to the room where he was at this moment. 'No,' answered the assistant, 'I made the trip with a friend. As we were going through the forest, we started arguing about a plant that we had found, and I told him that if we were back at the house, it would be easy for me to show him the page from Linnaeus[14] that would prove me right.' It was the exact same book that had remained open to the page indicated."

---

14 Carl Linnaeus, also known as Carl von Linné or Carolus Linnaeus (1707-1778). His system for naming, ranking, and classifying organisms is still in wide use today (with many changes). http://www.ucmp.berkeley.edu. – Tr.

As extraordinary as this incident may seem, it cannot be said to be physically impossible, for we are still far from knowing all the phenomena of the spirit life. Nevertheless, it needs confirmation. In cases such as this, one would have to positively verify the state of the body at the moment of the apparition. Until proven otherwise, we doubt that the incident would be possible, since the body was mentally engaged at the time.

The following incidents are more extraordinary still, and frankly, we must confess that they raise even more questions. We can easily understand that the apparition of a still-living person's spirit can be seen by another person, but not that an individual can see his or her own apparition, especially in the situations described below.

**3.** "A government official from Triptis, in Weimar, went to the chancellery to look for a package of documents he needed very badly and saw himself already there, sitting in his usual chair with the documents in front of him. Startled, he returned home and sent his servant with orders to pick up the documents located in their customary place. The servant went there and also saw her master sitting in his chair."

**4.** "Becker, professor of mathematics in Rostok, was sitting at a table in his house with some friends. A theological argument erupted. Becker went to his library to look for a book that would decide the matter and saw himself sitting at his usual place. Looking over the shoulder of his other self, he saw it pointing to the following passage in an open Bible: 'Put your house in order, for you are going to die.' He went back to his friends, who in vain tried to convince him that he was crazy to attribute the least bit of importance to his vision. *He died the following day.*"

**5.** "Hoppack, author of *Matériaux pour l'étude de la psychologie* (Materials for the Study of Psychology) said that the priest Steinmetz, having visitors in his den at home, saw himself at the same time in his favorite spot in his garden. Pointing to himself and then to his other self, he said, 'This Steinmetz is the mortal; that one is the immortal.'"

6. "F… (who later became a judge), from the town of Z…, while spending some time in the country during his youth, was asked by a young lady of the house to go fetch an umbrella she had left in her room. He went there and saw the girl sitting at her desk, but looking paler than when he had left her. She was staring straight ahead. Despite his fear, F… picked up the umbrella from beside her and took it to her. Noticing his distraught demeanor, she said to him, 'Admit that you saw something, that you saw me. But don't worry; I'm not about to die. I'm a double (in German, *Doppelgaenger*[15], which literally means double goer). In thought, I was next to my work, and many times I have already seen my image right beside me; we don't do anything to each other.'"
7. "Count D… and his watchmen claim to have seen Empress Elizabeth of Russia one night, seated on her throne in her throne room and dressed in her royal robes, while at the same time she was lying asleep. Her handmaid on duty was also sure of this and went to awaken her. The Empress then went to the throne room and saw her image there. She ordered a watchman to make a fire and the image disappeared. The Empress died three months later."

---

15 In German folklore, a wraith or apparition of a living person, as distinguished from a ghost. The concept of the existence of a spirit double, an exact but usually invisible replica of every man, bird, or beast, is an ancient and widespread belief. To meet one's double is a sign that one's death is imminent. www.britannica.com. – Tr.

8. "A student named Elger became very melancholy after having seen himself frequently in the red outfit he normally wore. He never saw his face, but only the contours of a vaporous form that looked like him, and always in late afternoon or in the moonlight. He saw the image at the place where, for a long time, he used to study."
9. "A French school teacher, Emile Sagee, lost her position nineteen times because she would appear everywhere *in double*. The girls from a boarding house in Neuwelke, Livonia[16], would sometimes see her in the lounge or in the garden, while, in reality, she was somewhere else. At other times, they would see two Miss Sagees in front of the blackboard during the lesson, standing beside each other, equally alike, making the same motions, but with the sole difference that the real Sagee would hold the chalk while writing on the board."

Mr. Perty's book contains a large number of incidents of this type. One should note that, in all the examples cited, the intelligent principle is equally active in both individuals, and is even more active in the physical one – when it should be just the opposite. However, what seems radically impossible to us is that there could be contradiction, a divergence of ideas, thoughts and sentiments.

This difference is demonstrated especially in incident no. 4, where one being warns the other about its death, and in no. 7, where the Empress orders fire against her other self.

Accepting the division of the perispirit and a fluidic energy that is strong enough to maintain normal activity in the body, and accepting also the division of the intelligent principle, or a radiation capable of animating both beings and giving them a sort of ubiquity, this principle is one and must be identical; that is, it cannot have a will on one side that

16 Present-day Latvia. – Tr.

it does not have on the other, unless we believe that there are twin spirits, just as there are twin bodies, which would mean that two identical spirits have incarnated in the same body, which is hardly plausible.

If there is something to learn from all these fantastic accounts, there is also much to discard and to take into consideration as legend. Rather than inducing us to accept them blindly, Spiritism helps us separate truth from fiction, the possible from the impossible with the help of the laws it reveals to us regarding the composition and role of the perispirit. However, let us not hurry in rejecting *a priori* everything we do not comprehend, because we are far from understanding all such laws and because nature has not yet told us all her secrets. The invisible world is still a new field of observation, and it would be presumptuous to claim to have probed all its depths when new wonders incessantly appear before our very eyes. Nonetheless, there are incidents that logic and known laws demonstrate to be materially impossible. One such incident was reported in *Revue Spirite* of February 1859[17], p. 41, under the heading *Mon ami Hermann*[18]. It deals with a young, upper-class German who was gentle, benevolent and honorable, and who, every afternoon at sunset, fell into a death-like state. During this time, his spirit would awaken at the antipode[19], in Australia, in the body of a crook who ended up being hanged.

Plain commonsense says that, even if such corporeal duality were possible, the same spirit could not alternate between being an honest man during the day in one body and a crook at night in another body. Those who say that Spiritism believes in such fables prove they know nothing about it, for it furnishes the means of showing how absurd

---

17 Th Spiritist Review 1859, translated to English and published by the United States Spiritist Council.

18 "My friend Hermann." – Tr.

19 A direct or exact opposite (*Random House: Webster's College Dictionary*, 1991) – Tr.

they are. However, at the same time that it demonstrates the error of a belief, it proves that often such belief rests on a true principle that has been disfigured or exaggerated by superstition. One must rid the fruit of the rind surrounding it.

How many ridiculous tales were invented concerning lightning before the law of electricity became known! The same applies to relations with the visible and invisible world. Having explained the law presiding over these relations, Spiritism has reduced them to reality; but this reality is still too much for those who believe neither in souls nor in the invisible world. To them, everything outside the visible, tangible world is superstition. That is why they denigrate Spiritism.

# THE CAUSE AND NATURE OF SOMNAMBULISTIC CLAIRVOYANCE

## Explanation of the Phenomenon of Lucidity

Since the perceptions that occur in the somnambulistic state are of a different nature than those in the waking state, they cannot be transmitted via the same organs. It is obvious that, in this case, sight is not effectuated through the eyes, which, by the way, are usually closed and may even be shielded from light so that any suspicion is impossible. In addition, sight at a distance and through opaque objects rules out the possibility of the use of the ordinary organs of sight. Thus, one has to accept the fact that in the somnambulistic state there is the use of a new sense, the seat of new faculties and perceptions that are unknown to us and which we cannot explain except through analogy and reasoning. There is nothing impossible about this; but what is the seat of this sense, exactly? That cannot be easily determined. Somnambulists themselves cannot give a precise answer in this regard. In order to see better, some place the objects on their abdomen, others on their forehead or on the back of their head. Hence, this particular sense does not seem to be circumscribed to a specific area; it is certain, however, that its main activity resides in the nerve centers. What is obvious is that somnambulists do, in fact, see. But by what means? This is something they themselves cannot define.

Nonetheless, we must add that, in the somnambulistic state, the phenomena of sight and the accompanying sensations are essentially different than what occurs in the normal state. Therefore, we will use the verb "to see" only for comparison, and, of course, because we lack a term for something unknown to us. A nation of people blind from birth would have no word for "light," and would compare the sensations it makes them feel with those they do understand because such sensations would be familiar to them.

Someone tried to explain to a blind person the bright and shiny impression of light upon his eyes: *"I understand,"* the blind person said, *"it is like the sound of a trumpet."* Another, undoubtedly a little more prosaic, to whom someone tried to make understand the emission of rays in beams or luminous cones, replied: *"Ah, yes! It's like cone sugar*[20]*."* We are in the same position regarding somnambulistic lucidity. We are truly blind, and like the blind with regards to light, we compare it to what for us is the most analogous to our faculty of sight. But if we want to establish an absolute analogy between these two faculties and judge one by the other, we will mislead ourselves, just like the two blind persons in the above examples. This is the mistake of almost all those who seek to be convinced by means of experimentation: they want to submit somnambulistic clairvoyance to the same tests as ordinary sight, without realizing that there is no relationship between the two except the name we have given them; and since the results do not always meet their expectations, they find it easier to simply deny it.

If we proceed by analogy, we would say that the magnetic fluid scattered throughout nature, and whose main focus seems to be animate bodies, is the vehicle for mediumistic clairvoyance, just as the luminous fluid is the vehicle for images perceived by our faculty of sight. Thus, just as the luminous fluid renders the bodies through which it freely travels transparent, the magnetic fluid, penetrating all bodies without exception, renders them no longer opaque

---

20 "Cone sugar was the product when sugar was separated from molasses before centrifuges were developed in the late 1800s. The sugar-molasses mix was poured into small vertical cones which had a hole in the bottom. The molasses would drain out of the hole, leaving the sugar in a cone shaped block. http://www.amalgamatedsugar.com – Tr.

to somnambulists. This is the simplest and most natural explanation of lucidity from our point of view. We think it is accurate because the magnetic fluid undoubtedly plays an important role in this phenomenon, but it does not account for all the facts. There is another one that can encompass all of them, but a few preliminary explanations regarding it are indispensable.

In sight at a distance, the somnambulist does not discern a far-off object as we could by using binoculars. *It is not the object that gets closer to the somnambulist through an optical illusion;* rather, IT IS THE SOMNAMBULIST THAT GETS CLOSER TO THE OBJECT. Somnambulists see objects exactly as if they were right beside them – they even see themselves in the location they are observing; in other words, they go there. Somnambulists' bodies at that moment seem non-existent, their speech is more subdued and the sound of their voice has something strange about it. Corporeal life seems nonexistent to them; their spirit life is entirely in the place where their thought has taken them; only their physical body remains where it was. Hence, there is a part of our being that separates from our body to travel instantly through space, conducted by thought and will. This part is obviously immaterial; otherwise, it would produce some of the effects of matter: it is this part of ourselves that we call the *soul.*

Yes, it is the soul that gives somnambulists their marvelous abilities; the soul that, in the given instance, manifests by partially and momentarily freeing itself from its corporeal envelope. For anyone who has closely observed the phenomenon of somnambulism in all its purity, the existence of the soul is a patent fact, and the idea that everything about us ends when our animal life does is sheer nonsense, as amply demonstrated. Thus, one could state with some certainty that magnetism and materialism are incompatible. If there are magnetizers who seem to stray from this rule and who profess materialist doctrines, it is undoubtedly due to the fact that they have done a very superficial study of the physical phenomena of magnetism, and that they have not seriously looked for a solution to the problem of sight at a distance. Whatever the case may be, we have never seen one single *somnambulist* who was not imbued with a profound religious sentiment, *regardless of what his or her opinions might be in the waking state.*

Let us return to the theory of lucidity. Because the soul is the principle of the somnambulistic faculties, it is in the soul that clairvoyance necessarily resides, and not in this or that circumscribed part of the body. That is why somnambulists cannot point to the organ of this faculty, as they would point to the eye for exterior sight; they see through their whole moral being, that is, through their entire soul, because clairvoyance is one of the attributes of every part of the soul, just as light is one of the attributes of all the parts of a lit match. Thus, wherever the soul can enter, there is clairvoyance; hence the cause of somnambulists' being able to see through all bodies, beneath the thickest and at any distance.

One objection to this theory naturally arises, and we must hasten to answer it: If the somnambulistic faculties are the same for the soul freed from its body, why are not such faculties continuous? Why are some subjects more lucid than others? Why does lucidity vary in the same individual? One can conceive of the physical imperfection of an organ, after all, but not of the soul.

The soul is connected to the body through mysterious ties that were impossible to understand before Spiritism pointed out the existence and role of the perispirit. Since this question has been specifically addressed in *Revue Spirite* and the fundamental works of Spiritism, we will not dwell on it here. We will limit ourselves to saying that it is through our material organs that the soul manifests itself to the outside. In our normal state, these manifestations are naturally subordinate to the imperfection of the instrument, just as the best artisan cannot fashion a perfect work with bad tools. As wonderful as the structure of our body may be, whatever the foresight of nature in regards to our organism for the accomplishment of its vital functions, apart from these organs subject to all the disturbances of matter, there is the subtlety of our soul. Therefore, as long as the soul is connected to the body, it endures the body's impediments and vicissitudes.

The magnetic fluid is not the soul; it is a link, an intermediary between the soul and the body. It is through its greater or lesser action upon matter that it renders the soul more, or less, independent; hence the diversity of the somnambulistic faculties. Somnambulists are persons who are unburdened of only part of their garment, but whose movements are still hindered by the part of the garment that remains.

The soul will enjoy the fullness and complete freedom of its faculties only when it has rid itself of its last earthly garment, like the butterfly leaving its chrysalis. If a magnetizer were powerful enough to give the soul complete freedom, the earthly tie would be broken and death would be the immediate consequence. Somnambulism enables us to put one foot in the future life; it lifts a corner of the veil beneath which are hidden the truths that Spiritism enables us to foresee right now; but we will not know this future life in its essence except when we are fully unburdened of the material veil that obscures it here below on the earth.

# SECOND SIGHT[21]

## Knowledge of the Future – Foreknowledge

If, in the somnambulistic state, the manifestations of the soul become somehow ostensible, it would be absurd to think that, in the normal state, the soul would be confined completely to its envelope, like a snail confined to its shell. It is not the magnetic influence that discloses the soul; the magnetic influence only renders the soul evident through the action it exerts on the organs. The somnambulistic state is not always an indispensable condition for this manifestation; the faculties we see produced in this state sometimes develop spontaneously in the normal state in certain individuals. For them, the result is the faculty of being able to see beyond the limits of their senses; they perceive things far away, wherever the soul extends its action; they see – if we may use this expression – by means of ordinary sight, and the images they describe are presented to them like the effect of a mirage, a phenomenon called *second sight.* In somnambulism, clairvoyance is produced by the same cause; the difference is that, in this state, it is isolated, independent of the corporeal life, whereas it is simultaneous in those who possess it in the waking state.

Second sight is almost never lasting. Normally, it is produced spontaneously at certain given moments without being an effect of the will, and it causes a sort of altered state that sometimes perceptibly modifies the physical state: the eyes seem somewhat empty; they seem to look without seeing; the entire face reflects a sort of exaltation.

21 Also known as remote viewing. Editor's Note.

It is worth noting that persons endowed with it are not aware of it; the faculty seems to them as natural as seeing through the eyes. It is an attribute of their being and does not seem exceptional at all. In addition, forgetfulness quite often follows this temporary lucidity, and therefore the remembrance becomes more and more vague, and ends up finally disappearing like the remembrance of a dream.

There are infinite degrees in the power of second sight, from a feeling of confusion to as clear and clean of a perception as occurs in somnambulism. We have no specific word to designate this special state, and especially the individuals who are capable of it; thus, we must use the word *seer*, and although it does not convey the meaning exactly, we shall use it until something better comes along.

If we compare the phenomena of somnambulistic clairvoyance and second sight, we will understand that seers can have the perception of things that are not in their range of physical sight; like somnambulists, they see at a distance; they follow the course of events, determine what direction they are heading, and in some cases, foresee how they might end.

It is this gift of second sight which, in its rudimentary expression, gives certain persons tact, discernment and a kind of sureness in their actions, and which we may define as the ability to evaluate on first contact another person's moral character. Developed further, it reveals events that have already happened or that are in the process of happening. At its peak, it is ecstasy awakened.

The phenomenon of second sight, as we have stated, is almost always natural and spontaneous, but it seems to occur most often under certain circumstances. Times of crisis, calamity, and great emotions – in short, all the causes that overexcite the mind – cause it to manifest. It seems that, in the presence of the most imminent dangers, Providence increases our ability to foresee them.

There have been seers in all times and all cultures, and it seems that certain peoples are more naturally predisposed to it; it is said that the gift of second sight is quite common in Scotland, for example. It is also found frequently among country folk and mountain dwellers.

Seers have been viewed differently according to the times, customs and level of civilization. To the eyes of skeptics, they come across as having deranged hallucinating brains; religious sects have made them into prophets, sibyls and oracles; in times of superstition and ignorance, they were witches deserving of being burned at the stake. For sensible persons who believe in the infinite power of nature and the inexhaustible goodness of the Creator, second sight is a faculty that is inherent to the human species, through which God reveals the existence of our material essence. Who would not recognize such a gift in Joan of Arc and a multitude of other characters whom history qualifies as having been inspired?

We have often heard of fortunetellers who say things that are surprisingly true. Far be it from us to make ourselves apologists for fortunetellers who exploit the credibility of weak minds, and whose ambiguous language lends itself to all combinations of a suggestible imagination. Nonetheless, there is nothing impossible about certain persons in this trade having the gift of second sight, even if unbeknownst to them. The cards in their hands are nothing but a means, a pretext, a basis for conversation; they speak according to what they see and not according to the cards they barely gaze at.

The same applies to other means of divination, such as the reading of palms, coffee grounds, egg whites and other mystic symbols. Palm reading perhaps has more value than other means, not because of the palm reading per se, but because when the reader, if gifted with second sight, holds the person's palm, he or she is in a more direct relationship with the person, as is the case with somnambulistic consultations.

Seeing mediums may be placed in the category of persons gifted with second sight. Like them, seeing mediums believe they are seeing through their eyes, when it is really the soul that sees; that is why they can see just as well with their eyes either shut or wide open. Hence, it necessarily follows that a blind person could be a seeing medium every bit as well as someone whose vision is intact. It would be an interesting study to see if this faculty is more common in blind persons. We would tend to think – inasmuch as it can be duly verified – that the lack of the ability to communicate with the outer environment due to the absence of certain senses generally confers more power to the faculty of abstraction of the soul. Consequently, there would be more development of the inner sense, through which it is put in relationship with the spirit world.

Seeing mediums can thus be likened to persons with spirit sight, but it would perhaps be too much to consider the latter as mediums. Mediumship consists solely in the intervention of spirits, whereas what one does oneself cannot be considered as a mediumistic action. Those who possess spirit sight see by means of their own spirit, and in the development of their faculty nothing implies the need of the cooperation of an outside spirit.

With that said, let us see how far the faculty of second sight may enable us to discover hidden things and to penetrate the future.

Throughout history, people have longed to know the future, and one could write volumes on the means dreamed up by superstition to lift the veil that covers our destiny. Nature was very wise in hiding it from us; we all have our providential mission in the great human hive and we cooperate in the common toil in our particular sphere of activity. If we knew beforehand how everything would turn out, there could be no doubt that the overall harmony would suffer. Being assured of a happy future would render persons completely idle since they would not have to put forth any effort to reach their main goal: their wellbeing. All physical and moral forces would stand still and humankind's forward progress would grind to a halt. The certainty of unhappiness would have the same result due to discouragement: everyone would refuse to struggle against the unbending decree of fate. Full knowledge of the future would thus be a disaster in the present, which would lead us to the dogma of fatalism, the most dangerous of all dogmas and the most averse to the development of ideas. It is the uncertainty of the moment we are to leave this world that makes us work till our last heartbeat. Travelers who are carried along by a means of transportation surrender to the movement that will take them to their destination. They do not think about taking a different route because they know they are powerless to do so; the same would apply to persons who knew their irrevocable fate. If seers could break this law of Providence, they would be on par with the Divinity; thus it is not their mission.

Since in the phenomenon of second sight the soul is partly disengaged from the material envelope that limits our faculties, there is no longer time or distance for it; embracing time and space, everything becomes one with the present. Freed of its shackles, it determines causes and effects better than we can: it sees the consequences of things happening in the present and can enable us to foreshadow them. It is in this sense that one should understand the gift of foresight attributed to seers. Their foreknowledge is nothing but the result of a clearer awareness of what is, and not a prediction of fortuitous events with no connection to the present. It is a logical deduction of the known to arrive at the unknown, which quite often depends on what our actions are. If we are warned about impending danger, it is up to us to do what is necessary to avoid it: we are free to act or not upon it.

In such cases, seers find themselves in the presence of danger that is hidden from us; they identify it and suggest the means to avoid it; otherwise, the event will follow its course.

Let us imagine a carriage driven along a road that ends at an abyss, a fact the driver does not know about. It is obvious that if nothing makes it detour, the carriage will go over the edge. Now, let us imagine a man who is in a position to be able to see the full length of the road from a bird's eye view; if this man, seeing the inevitable danger, could warn the driver in time, the danger could be avoided. From his position, glancing over a larger space, he sees what the driver, whose line of vision is circumscribed by the shape of the terrain, cannot see; he can see if a fortuitous cause will prevent the fall over the edge. Thus, he knows the outcome of the event beforehand and can foretell it.

If this same man were on top of a mountain and perceived in the distance an enemy troop on the road heading toward a village it planned to burn, it would be easy for him to calculate the distance and speed and foresee the moment the troops would arrive. If coming down to the village he simply said: *At such and such hour your village is going to be burned,* and then afterward it actually happened, he would seem to the ignorant multitude to be a soothsayer or a wizard, when in fact he merely saw what the others could not and thereby deduced the consequences. Like this man, seers capture and follow the course of events; they do not foresee the outcome through the gift of divination – they actually see it! Thus, they can tell you if you are on the right road, indicate a better one, and tell what you will find at the end. For you, it is like the thread of Ariadne[22] showing you the way out of the labyrinth.

As one can see, this is a far cry from prediction per se, as we normally understand it. Nothing is taken away from the free will of humans, who are always in charge of whether to act or not, whether to execute events or let them just happen

---

22 In Greek mythology, daughter of Pasiphae and the Cretan king Minos. She fell in love with the Athenian hero Theseus and, with a thread or glittering jewels, helped him escape the Labyrinth after he slew the Minotaur, a beast half bull and half man that Minos kept in the Labyrinth. www.britannica.com. – Tr.

through either their will or their inertia. The way to arrive at the goal is indicated to them, but it is up to them to make use of it. To suppose that they are at the mercy of an inexorable fatalism regarding the smallest events in life is to disinherit them from their most wonderful attribute: intelligence; it is to put them at the level of the brute. Seers, therefore, are not diviners; they are individuals who perceive what we cannot; for us they are the guide dogs of the blind. Thus, nothing herein contradicts the views of Providence on the secret of our destiny; rather, it is Providence itself that gives us a guide.

Such is the point of view upon which the knowledge of the future in persons gifted with second sight should be contemplated. If the future were fortuitous, if it depended on what we call randomness, if it were not connected at all to present circumstances, no clairvoyant could penetrate it, and all previsions in this case could not offer any certitude. Seers – and we mean true seers, serious seers and not the charlatans that imitate them – veritable seers, we reiterate, do not talk about what is normally called fortunetelling. They foresee the outcome of the present, nothing else, and that is much indeed.

How many errors, how many wrong approaches, and how many futile attempts we would avoid if we always had a sure guide to inform us! How many men and women are out of place in the world for not having set out on the course that nature had traced out for their faculties!

How many failed for having listened to the counsels of a thoughtless obstinacy! Someone could have told them: "Don't pursue such a venture, because your intellectual faculties are insufficient, because it does not fit your character or your physical makeup, or better yet, because you will not be assisted according to need; or, furthermore, because you are mistaken about its scope, for you will run into an obstacle you have not foreseen." In other circumstances, someone could have said: "You will succeed at such a venture if you do it in this or that manner; but if you avoid this approach, you could run into trouble." After probing your disposition and character, someone could have said: "Watch out for the trap that is coming your way"; and then add: "You have been forewarned, my role ends here; I have shown you the dangers; if you succumb, don't blame luck, fatalism or Providence, but only yourself. What can a doctor do when his patient does not heed his advice?"

# INTRODUCTION TO THE STUDY OF THOUGHT PHOTOGRAPHY AND TELEGRAPHY

The physiological action from one individual to another, with or without contact, is an incontestable fact. Obviously, this action cannot be exerted except through an intermediary agent, of which our body is the reservoir, and our eyes and fingers are the main organs of emission and direction. This invisible agent must be a fluid. What is its nature, its essence? What are its inner properties? Is it a special fluid or the modification of electricity or some other known fluid? Is it what was called not long ago the nervous fluid[23]? Or might it be what we nowadays call the cosmic fluid when it is dispersed in the atmosphere and the perispiritual fluid when it is individualized?

Then again, such questions are secondary.

The perispiritual fluid is imponderable like light, electricity and heat. It is invisible to us in its normal state and is revealed only through its effects; however, it becomes visible in the state of lucid somnambulism, and even in the waking state for persons endowed with second sight. In the state of emission, it appears in the form of luminous bands quite similar to electric light diffused in a vacuum; however, the analogy with the latter fluid ends there, for it does not produce – at least obviously – any of the physical phenomena we know of. In the normal state, it reflects various hues according to the individuals from whom it emanates, whether a faint reddish, bluish or grayish color, like a light fog. Most

23 Nervous fluid: the fluid which at one time was supposed to circulate through the nerves and was regarded as the agent of sensation and motion. *Webster's Revised Unabridged Dictionary (1913)*. – Tr.

often, it spreads a more or less pronounced yellowish cloud over nearby objects.

Somnambulists' and seers' reports on this issue are identical; furthermore, we will have an opportunity to return to the matter when we address the qualities impressed on the fluid by the agent that sets them in motion, and by the advancement of the individual who emits them.

No object is an obstacle to it; it penetrates and passes through all of them; so far, we know of no one capable of isolating it. Only the will can expand or restrict its action; in fact, the will is its most powerful principle. By using the will, one directs its emanations through space, accumulates it according to volition at a given point, saturates certain objects with it, or retrieves it from spots where it is overabundant. In passing, we will say that it is upon this principle that the magnetic force is founded. Lastly, it seems to be the vehicle of psychic sight, just as the luminous fluid is the vehicle of normal sight.

Although it emanates from a universal source, the cosmic fluid is individualized, so to speak, in each being and acquires the characteristic properties that permit it to be distinguished from all others. Even death does not erase such characteristics of individualization, which may persist for many years after the cessation of life, as we have seen for ourselves. Hence, we all have our own fluid, which envelops and accompanies us wherever we go, just like the atmosphere accompanies each planet. The expanse of the radiation of these individual atmospheres is highly variable: when the spirit is completely at rest, this radiation may be circumscribed to a few steps, but under the control of the will, it may reach infinite distances. The will seems to expand the fluid in the same way that heat expands gas. Different individual atmospheres meet, cross and mix without ever fusing, exactly like sound waves that remain distinct, in spite of the multitude of sounds that stir the air at the same time. Thus, one could say that each individual is the center of a fluidic wave, the extent of which depends on the person's force and will, just as each vibrating point is the center of a sound wave, the extent of which depends on the force of the vibration. The will is the driving cause of the fluid, just as the shock is the vibrating cause of the air and the driving cause of the sound waves.

The particular qualities of each fluid result in a type of harmony or disharmony among individuals, a tendency to join or to avoid, an attraction or repulsion; in short, the sympathies or antipathies one often experiences without any known cause. If we are within the sphere of an individual's activity, his or her presence is sometimes revealed through the pleasant or unpleasant impression that his or her fluid produces. If we are with persons who do not share our sentiments, whose spiritual fluids do not harmonize with our own, an uncomfortable reaction oppresses us and we feel like we are a dissonant note in a concert! On the other hand, if several individuals are gathered in a commonality of objectives and intentions, each one's sentiments are raised in the same proportion of the mass of the acting forces. Who has not felt the impetus that dominates gatherings where there is a oneness of thought and will? We cannot imagine how many influences we are thus submitted to, unbeknownst to us.

Mightn't such hidden influences be the determining cause of certain thoughts, those thoughts that we have in common at the same time with certain persons, those vague presentiments that make us say: There is something in the air foretelling this or that occurrence? Lastly, mightn't certain indefinable feelings of wellbeing or uneasiness, of joy or sadness be the effect of the reaction of our fluidic environment, of the sympathetic or antipathetic emissions we receive, and which envelop us like the emanations from a fragrant object? We cannot offer an absolutely affirmative answer to these questions, but we must at least agree that the theory of the cosmic fluid, individualized in each being as the perispiritual fluid, opens up a whole new field for solving a multitude of problems that have so far been inexplicable.

Each person, as he or she moves about, thus carries around a fluidic atmosphere, like a snail carries its shell. But this fluid leaves traces of its passage, something similar to a luminous trail inaccessible to our senses in the waking state, but which enables somnambulists, seers and discarnate spirits to reconstruct past events and to analyze the cause that may have been behind them.

Every physical or mental, patent or hidden action of one being upon him or herself or another assumes, on the one hand, an acting force, and on the other, a passive sensitivity. In every case, two equal forces neutralize each other and weakness yields to strength. Thus, since all individuals are not endowed with the same fluidic energy, or to put it another way, since the active force of the perispiritual fluid is not present in all to the same degree, this would explain the reason why in some persons this force is almost irresistible, whereas in others it is nonexistent; why certain persons are highly accessible to its action, whereas others are resistant to it.

This relative higher and lower gradation obviously depends on the organism, but it would be wrong to think that it is due to physical strength or weakness. Experience has proven that sturdier persons sometimes feel the fluidic influences more easily than others of a more delicate constitution, while one may find in the latter a strength that their fragile appearance would not lead one to imagine. This diversity of action may be explained in several ways.

The fluidic force applied to people's reciprocal action on one another, that is, to magnetism, may depend on: 1) the amount of fluid each person possesses; 2) the intrinsic nature of each person's fluid, quantity notwithstanding; and 3) the degree of energy of the driving force – or perhaps even a combination of these three causes. In the first instance, the one who has more fluid would give more of it to the one who has less, and would receive a lesser quantity in return. In this instance, there is a perfect analogy with the mutual exchange of heat between two objects until they each reach the same temperature. Whatever may be the cause of this difference, we can surmise the effect that it produces by imagining three persons whose strength we will represent by three numbers: 10, 5 and 1. 10 will act upon both 5 and 1, but more energetically upon 1 than upon 5; 5 will act upon 1 but will be powerless over 10; and, finally, 1 will not act upon either of the other two. This would explain why certain persons are sensitive to the action of a particular magnetizer but insensitive to that of another.

Once again, we can explain this phenomenon to a certain extent by referring to the preceding considerations. In effect, we have stated that the individual fluids are sympathetic or antipathetic in relation to each other. Thus, could it not be that the reciprocal action of two individuals is due to the sympathy of fluids, that is, their tendency to merge through a sort of harmony, like sound waves produced by vibrating objects? It cannot be doubted that such harmony or sympathy of fluids is a condition that, if not completely indispensable, is at least very preponderant, and which, if there is discord or antipathy, can render the action weak or even nonexistent. This theory does a good job of explaining the preliminary conditions of the action, but it does not tell us on what side this force is. Therefore, all things accepted, we are forced to resort to our first supposition.

Moreover, whether the phenomenon has occurred because of one or another of these causes is irrelevant; the fact exists, and that is what matters. Light phenomena are also explained by the theory of emission and undulations; those of electricity, by the positive and negative, vitreous and resinous fluids.

Based on the preceding considerations, in the next study we will try to establish what we understand by thought photography and telegraphy.

# THOUGHT PHOTOGRAPHY AND TELEGRAPHY

Thought photography and telegraphy are subjects that have just recently emerged. Like all subjects that do not follow laws that, in essence, must be universally spread, they have been relegated to the background even though their importance is crucial, and the elements of study they entail may be called on to explain many problems that have remained unsolvable till now.

When a talented artist paints a picture – the masterful work to which he has devoted all the genius he has progressively acquired thus far – he first establishes the general idea of the work in a way that one understands from the sketch what he intends to do; it is not until he has minutely prepared his overall plan that he proceeds to execute the details; and even though this part of the work perhaps must be treated more carefully than the outline, it would not have been possible if the outline had not come first. The same applies to Spiritism. The fundamental laws, the general principles, whose roots lie in the spirit of every created being, must have been prepared at the beginning. All other matters, whatever they may be, depend on the original ones; that is why, for a certain amount of time, direct study is disregarded.

Actually, one cannot logically talk about thought photography and telegraphy before having demonstrated the existence of the soul, which manipulates the fluidic elements, as well as the existence of the fluids that permit the establishment of the connections between two distinct souls. Even today, we are perhaps barely sufficiently enlightened to definitively address such immense problems! Nevertheless, some considerations in order to prepare a more complete study will certainly not be out of place here.

Because humans are limited in their thoughts and aspirations, and because their horizons are restricted, they must concretize and label all things in order to keep an appreciable memory of them and base their future studies on acquired data. The first notions of understanding come by their sense of sight; it is the image of an object that taught them that the object existed. By knowing various objects and making deductions from the different impressions they produced on their inner being, they fixated the quintessence in their mind through the phenomenon of memory. Thus, what is memory except a sort of more voluminous or less voluminous album that one leafs through to rediscover lost ideas and retrace past events! This album has bookmarks in momentous places; one can recall certain facts immediately, while others need leafing through several pages.

Memory is like a book! One in which we easily read certain passages laid out before our eyes, and whose blank pages, or those rarely perused, must be turned one by one in order to reconstitute a fact that had merited little attention from us.

When the incarnate spirit remembers, its memory presents in some way the photograph of the fact it is looking for. Usually, other incarnates that may be nearby see nothing; the "album" is inaccessible to their sight. However, spirits can see it and leaf through it with us, and in certain circumstances they can even either help our search or hinder it.

What occurs from an incarnate to a spirit also takes place from a spirit to a seer. When one evokes the memory of certain incidents in the life of a spirit, the photograph of these incidents presents itself to the spirit, and the seer, whose spiritual situation is analogous to that of the discarnate spirit, sees it as the spirit does. Moreover, in certain circumstances, it even sees what the spirit does not see by itself, in the same way that a discarnate can leaf through the memory of an incarnate without the latter being aware of it and remind him or her of incidents forgotten for quite some time. As for abstract thoughts that come into existence by this process, they take on a body in order to impress the brain; they must naturally act upon it, somehow imprinting themselves on it. Once again, in this instance as in the first, the similarity between the occurrences on earth and in the spirit world seems perfect.

Since the phenomenon of thought photography has been the subject of a few reflections in the *Revue,* for greater clarity we will reproduce some passages from the article where the subject is addressed, and which we will complete with further remarks.

Since the fluids are the carrier of the thought, the latter acts upon the former as sound acts upon the air. The fluids carry the thought as air brings us sound. Thus, one can truly say that there are thought waves and rays that crisscross in the fluids without mixing, just as there are sound waves and rays in the air.

Furthermore, as thought creates *fluidic images*, it is reflected in the perispiritual envelope like in a mirror, or better, like those images of earthly objects that are reflected in the vapors of the air, taking on a body and somehow photographing themselves. For example, if a man, while his physical body remains impassive, gets the idea to kill another, his fluidic body is set into motion by the thought in which he reproduces all the nuances. He fluidically carries out the gesture, the act he wants to commit. His thought creates the image of the victim and the entire scene is painted like a picture just as it is in his mind.

Thus, the most secret activities of the soul reverberate in its fluidic envelope; a soul can read what is in another soul like a book and see what is not perceptible to the eyes of the body. The body's eyes see the inner impressions that are reflected on the outlines of the face: anger, joy, sadness; but the soul sees on the outlines of the soul the thoughts that are not stamped on the outside.

However, if by seeing the intention, the soul can sense the execution of the subsequent act, it can neither determine the moment in which it will occur nor specify its details, or even affirm that it will actually take place, because ulterior circumstances may modify fixed plans and change dispositions. The soul cannot see what is not yet in the thought; what it does see is the preoccupation of the moment or the habitual worry of the individual, his or her desires, plans and good or bad intentions. That explains the errors in the previsions of certain seers. When an occurrence is dependent on a person's free will, seers can only sense the probability according to the thought they see, but they cannot affirm that it will occur in such and such a manner, at such and such a time. Moreover, the greater or lesser precision of previsions depends on the extent and clarity of the psychic sight. In certain discarnate or incarnate individuals, it is limited to a point or is diffuse, whereas in others it is clear and encompasses all the thoughts and wills that must concur for the realization of an event. But more than anything else, there is always the Higher Will, which, in its wisdom, can either allow a revelation or hinder it; if the latter, an impenetrable veil is cast over even the most incisive psychic sight. (See *Genesis*, the chapter on *Prescience.*)

The theory of fluidic creations and, consequently, of thought photography, is a contribution of modern Spiritism. From now on, it can be considered as being affirmed as a rule, except for its detailed applications, which will be the result of observation. This phenomenon is undoubtedly the source of fantastic visions and must play a great role in certain dreams.

Who on the earth knows how the first means of thought communication were produced? How they were invented, or rather, encountered? For nothing is invented; everything exists in a latent state. It is up to humans to seek the means of putting to work the forces that nature offers them. Who knows how much time was needed for speech to be used in a completely intelligible way?

The first human who let out an inarticulate grunt obviously had a certain awareness of what he or she wanted to express, but those whom he or she addressed did not understand it at first. It was only after a long stretch of time that conventional words came into existence, followed by short phrases, and then finally entire discourses. How many thousands of years were needed to reach the point at which humankind is at today! Each bit of progress in the mode of communication, of human relations, has constantly been marked by an improvement in the social state of human beings. To the extent that relations between individuals become closer and more regular, one feels the need for a new mode of faster language that is more capable of putting people in instant and universal touch with one another. Why could what has occurred in the physical world by means of electric telegraphy not occur in the mental world from incarnate to incarnate by means of human telegraphy? Why could the hidden relations that consciously unite to a greater or lesser degree the thoughts of humans and spirits through spiritual telegraphy not be consciously generalized between humans?

Human telegraphy! That will, of course, bring a smile to the face of those who refuse to believe in anything that does not strike their physical senses. But what does the scorn of the presumptuous matter anyway? All their denials will not impede nature's laws from following their course, nor keep new applications of such laws from being discovered as the human mind finds itself in the condition of being able to feel the effects.

Human beings act directly upon things as well as upon others around them. Persons of little standing often exert a decisive influence on others who have a much bigger reputation. This is because on earth one sees more masks than actual faces and because the eyes are obscured with vanity, personal interest and all the worst passions. Experience has shown that a person can act upon others' minds without their knowing it. According to its strength and elevation, a superior thought that is *strongly thought* – if I may use the expression – can thus travel near or far to reach persons who have no idea as to how it reached them, just as those who emit it often have no idea of the effect of having emitted it. There is a constant play of human minds and their reciprocal action upon one another. Add to this the action of those who are discarnate and try to grasp – if you can – the incalculable power of that force composed of so many gathered forces.

If they could apprehend the immense mechanism that thought puts into play and the effects that it produces from one individual to the next, from one group to another group, and finally, the universal action of people's thoughts upon one another, human beings would be completely dazzled! They would feel powerless before that infinity of details, before those innumerable networks interconnected by a powerful will, acting in harmony to reach a sole objective: universal progress.

Through thought telegraphy, humans would appreciate the law of solidarity in all its worth, realizing that there is no thought – criminal, virtuous or otherwise – that does not exert a real action upon human thoughts as a whole and upon each one in particular. If selfishness has led them to be unaware of the consequences that their malevolent thought has for someone else, through this same selfishness, they will be induced to have good thoughts to elevate the moral level of humankind by pondering the consequences a bad thought from others would have on themselves.

What else but the consequence of human thought telegraphy could be those mysterious shocks that warn us of the joy or suffering of a distant loved one? Is it not due to a similar phenomenon that we owe the sentiments of sympathy or repulsion that draw us to certain spirits but keep us away from others?

This is obviously a huge field for study and observation, but which we cannot yet perceive except the whole. The study of its details will be the outcome of a more complete understanding of the laws that govern the action of the fluids upon one another.

# A STUDY ON THE NATURE OF CHRIST

- Sources of the Proofs regarding the Nature of Christ
- Is Christ's Divinity Proven by His Miracles?
- Is Jesus' Divinity Proven by His Own Words?
- Jesus' Words after His Death
- The Dual Nature of Jesus
- Opinion of the Apostles
- The Predictions of the Prophets regarding Jesus
- The Word Made Flesh
- Son of God and Son of Man

## I – SOURCES OF THE PROOFS REGARDING THE NATURE OF CHRIST

The issue regarding the nature of Christ has been debated since the earliest days of Christianity, and one could say that it still has not been resolved, because it is still argued about to this day. It was the difference in opinion about this issue that gave rise to most of the sects that have divided the Church for eighteen centuries, and it is interesting to note that all the leaders of these sects have been bishops or various other members of the clergy. Consequently, the issue has arisen among educated individuals – mostly talented writers, versed in theology – who have not found conclusive the reasons invoked in favor of the dogma of the divinity of Christ. Both then and now, however, their opinions have been founded on abstractions rather than on facts. Basically, they have tried to figure out what the dogma might contain that is either plausible or irrational, but on whichever side they may be on, they have generally neglected to bring out facts that may cast a decisive light on the issue.

But where are these facts to be found if not in the very actions and words of Jesus himself?

Jesus wrote nothing himself; his sole historians were the apostles, who also wrote nothing down while he was alive; and since no contemporary secular historian spoke of him, there are no other documents that address his life or his doctrine except the Gospels. Thus, one must look for the key to the problem only in the Gospels. All writings thereafter – including St. Paul's – are not, nor could be, anything but commentaries or evaluations, expressions of personal opinions that would not in any case have the authority of the narratives of those who received instructions directly from the Master.

On this issue, as well as on all dogmas in general, the agreement of the Church Fathers and other sacred writers cannot be evoked either as a preponderant argument or as an irrefutable proof in favor of their opinion, since not one of them could cite one single fact concerning Jesus apart from those contained in the Gospels, and not one of them ever discovered any new documents unknown to their predecessors.

The sacred authors could do nothing but return to the same circle, give their personal evaluation, draw consequences from their own points of view, and state in new ways, with more or less breadth, their contradictory opinions. All those of the same persuasion had to write the same way, if not in the same terms, under penalty of being declared heretics, as were Origen and so many others. Of course, the Church only regarded as its Fathers writers who were orthodox from its own point of view; it only praised, sanctified and compiled those who defended it, while it rejected the others and destroyed their writings as much as possible. The agreement among the Church Fathers, therefore, is not at all conclusive, since it is unanimity of choice formed by the elimination of contradictory elements. If everything that was written for and against were to be considered, no one could say to which side the pendulum would swing.

This takes nothing away from the personal merit of the upholders of orthodoxy or their worth as writers and conscientious individuals; they were advocates of one and the same cause, which they defended with incontestable talent, and consequently they had to reach the same conclusions. Far from wanting to disparage them in any way, we merely wish to refute the worth of the conclusions that may be drawn from their agreement.

In our examination of the issue of the divinity of Christ, putting aside scholastic subtleties that would only serve to confuse instead of elucidate, we shall support our argument solely on the facts found in the Gospel texts. Examined coolly, conscientiously and impartially, they furnish superabundantly all the means of conviction that one could wish for. Now, among such facts, there are none weightier or more conclusive than the words of Christ himself – words that cannot be rejected without calling the truthfulness of the apostles into question. One may interpret a parable or an allegory in different ways, but precise, unambiguous statements repeated a hundred times cannot carry a double meaning. No one but Jesus himself could know better what he meant to say, just as no one could claim to be better informed than Jesus himself about his own nature. When Jesus comments on his own words and explains them in order to avoid any mistake, we must rely on him, unless we deny the superiority attributed to him and replace it with our own intelligence. If he was vague on certain points where he made use of figurative language, as far as his person was concerned there was no possible ambiguity. But before examining his words, let us look at his actions.

## II – IS CHRIST'S DIVINITY PROVEN BY HIS MIRACLES?

According to the Church, the divinity of Christ is established primarily by means of the miracles as evidence of a supernatural power. This consideration may have carried a certain weight at a time when the extraordinary was accepted without examination; however, since science today rests its investigations on the laws of nature, miracles find more disbelievers than believers. What has contributed the most to their discredit is the exploitation and abuse of fraudulent imitations. Faith in miracles was destroyed by the very use we made of them, with the result that those found in the Gospels are now regarded by many as pure legend.

Moreover, the Church itself has removed all the impact of miracles as proof of Christ's divinity by stating that the Devil can produce them likewise; consequently, if the Devil has such power, it becomes obvious that phenomena of this type do not have an exclusively divine character. If the Devil can do dazzling things to deceive even the elect, how can mere mortals distinguish good miracles from bad ones? Would it not be cause for concern that upon witnessing similar phenomena they could fail to differentiate between God and Satan?

To give Jesus such a rival in ability was a big blunder. However, as far as contradictions and incongruences are concerned, such things were not closely considered at a time when it would have been a matter of conscience for the faithful to think for themselves and argue over the smallest article imposed on their beliefs. Progress was not taken into consideration and no one ever dreamed that the kingdom of blind and naïve faith – a pleasant, convenient kingdom – could ever come to an end. The highly weighty role that the Church has insisted on giving to the Devil has had disastrous consequences for the faith as people have felt more capable of seeing with their own eyes. The Devil, who was successfully exploited for some time, became the wrecking ball for the old building of beliefs and one of the primary causes of disbelief. One could say that in making the Devil an indispensable auxiliary, the Church nourished within its bosom that which would turn against it and undermine it at its foundation.

A less serious consideration is that miraculous phenomena are not the exclusive privilege of the Christian religion; in fact, there is no idolatrous or pagan religion that does not have its own miracles that are as extraordinary and authentic to its followers as those of Christianity. The Church has claimed the right to judge them, however, attributing the ability to produce them to infernal powers.

The essential quality of a miracle from the theological point of view is that it is an exception to the laws of nature, and thus cannot be explained by those same laws. The moment an incident can be explained by and linked to a known cause, it can no longer be considered a miracle. Thus, the discoveries of science enabled some effects that used to be regarded as miracles as long as their causes remained unknown, to enter the realm of the natural. Later, knowledge about the spiritual principle, the action of the fluids, the invisible world in whose midst we live, the faculties of the soul, and the existence and properties of the *perispirit,* provided the key to phenomena of a psychic order and proved that such phenomena are not, any more than any others, derogations from the laws of nature; quite the contrary, they are often applications of such laws. All the effects of magnetism, somnambulism, ecstasy, double sight, hypnotism, catalepsy, anesthesia, transmission of thought, prescience, instantaneous healings, possessions, obsessions, apparitions, transfigurations, etc., which constitute nearly all of the miracles in the Gospels, belong to this category of phenomena.

It is understood nowadays that these effects are the result of special physiological aptitudes and dispositions; that they have been produced in all times among all peoples, and that they used to be considered as supernatural in the same way as were all other effects whose cause was not understood. This explains why all religions have had their miracles, which were nothing more than natural occurrences nearly always blown out of proportion by credulity, ignorance and superstition to the point of absurdity, and which current knowledge has reduced to their true value by relegating them to the stuff of legends.

Most of the phenomena the Gospels cite as having been produced by Jesus can now be fully demonstrated by magnetism and Spiritism as natural phenomena. Since they are produced right before our very eyes, whether spontaneously or induced, there is nothing abnormal about Jesus possessing faculties identical to those of our magnetizers, healers, somnambulists, seers, mediums, etc. The moment that these same faculties are found in differing degrees in a multitude of individuals that have nothing divine about themselves, that they are found even among heretics and idolaters, they imply nothing at all of a super-human quality.

If Jesus himself qualified his actions as *miracles,* it was because in doing so, as in many other things, he had to accommodate his language to the understanding of his contemporaries. How could they grasp the nuance of a word that was not understood by everyone at the time? To the common folk, the extraordinary things he did, and which seemed supernatural at that time and even much later, were miracles; Jesus could not have called them by any other name. A fact worth mentioning is that, according to what he himself said, Jesus used them to affirm his mission from God, but he never used them to attribute the divine power to himself.[24]

Thus, it is necessary to scratch miracles from the list of proofs upon which the divinity of Christ is claimed to be founded. Let us now see if we can find any such proofs in his own words.

---

24 For a complete discussion of miracles, see *Genesis,* chaps. XIII ff., wherein all the miracles of the Gospels are explained according to natural laws. - Auth.

## III – IS JESUS' DIVINITY PROVEN BY HIS OWN WORDS[25]?

Addressing his disciples, who had gotten into an argument about which of them was the greatest, Jesus took a little child, and standing it beside him said:

"Whoever receives me, receives *the One who sent me*, for he who is the least among you is the greatest." (Lk. 9:48)

"Whoever receives a little child like this one in my name, receives me, and whoever receives me, receives not only me but *the One who sent me*." (Mk. 9:36)

Jesus said to them: "If God were your Father, you would love me because I have come forth from God, *and it is on his behalf that I have come; for I have not come of myself*, but it was He who sent me." (Jn. 8:42)

Jesus said to them: "I will be with you for a little while yet, and then I will go *to the One who sent me*." (Jn. 7:33)

"The one who hears you hears me; the one who scorns you scorns me, *and whoever scorns me, scorns the One who sent me*." (Lk. 10:16)

The dogma of the divinity of Jesus is founded on the absolute equality between his person and God, since he is "very God"[26]: it is an article of faith. Now, these words – *the One who sent me* – so often repeated by Jesus, display not only a duality of persons, but also, as we have stated, exclude the possibility of any absolute equality between them, because the one who is sent is obviously *subordinate* to the one who does the sending; in obeying, he does an act of *submission*. Ambassadors speaking of their sovereign will say: *My superior,*

---

25 Kardec used the Sacy version of the Bible for his line of reasoning. For consistency, translations of biblical citations are from Kardec's original French text. (Louis-Isaac Lemaistre de Sacy (1613 –1684), theologian and French humanist.) – Tr.

26 In the words of the Nicene Creed: "God from God, light from light, *very God* from *very God*, begotten, not made." – Tr.

*the one who sent me;* but if sovereigns come in person, they speak in their own name and do not say: *The one who sent me*, because one cannot send oneself. Jesus spoke to them in no uncertain terms: *I did not come of myself, but it was He who sent me.*

The words "*He who scorns me, scorns the One who sent me*" do not in any way imply equality, much less identity. In all times, an insult against an ambassador has been considered as being made against the very person of the sovereign. The apostles had the word of Jesus, just as Jesus had the word of God. When he said to them: *The one who hears you, hears me,* he did not mean that his apostles and himself were one and the same person, equal in every way.

Moreover, the duality of persons – just like the secondary and subordinate status of Jesus in relation to God – unmistakably stands out in the following passages:

"You are the ones who have always stood firm by me in my temptations. Therefore, I prepare a kingdom for you *just as my Father has prepared one for me* so that you may eat and drink at my table in my kingdom, and that you may sit on thrones to judge the twelve tribes of Israel." (Lk. 22: 28-30)

"I tell you what *I have seen in my Father's house;* you do what you have seen in your father's house." (Jn. 8:38)

"At the same time, a cloud appeared which covered them, and out of the cloud came a voice speaking these words: '*This is my beloved son; listen to him.*'" (Transfiguration, Mk. 9:7)

"When the son of man comes in his majesty in the company of all the angels, he will sit on the throne of his glory; and with all the nations gathered together, he will separate some from others, just as the shepherd separates the sheep from the goats; and he will place the sheep on his right and the goats on his left. Then, the King will say to those who are on his right: 'Come, *you who have been blessed by my Father*, possess the kingdom that has been prepared for you from the beginning of the world.'" (Mt. 25:31-34)

"Whoever confesses me and acknowledges me before men, I will acknowledge and confess before my Father who is in heaven; and whoever denies me before men, *I will deny before my Father who is in heaven.*" (Mt. 10: 32-33).

"I tell you that whoever confesses me and acknowledges me before men, *the son of man will acknowledge before the angels of God;* but if anyone denies me before men, *I will deny him before the angels of God.*" (Lk. 12: 8-9)

"But if anyone is ashamed of me and my words, the son of man will be ashamed of him when he comes in his glory and *in the glory of his Father and the holy angels.*" (Lk. 9:26)

In the two last passages, Jesus seems to place above himself even the holy angels, composing the heavenly tribunal, before which he would be the defender of the good and the accuser of the bad.

"But as for the ones who are to be seated on my right or on my left, *that is in no way mine to give,* but it will be for those for *whom my Father has prepared it.*" (Mt. 20:23)

While the Pharisees were gathered together, Jesus asked them this question: "What do you think about the Christ? Whose son is he?" They answered: "David's." "Then why did David, in the spirit, call him 'Lord' in these words: 'The Lord said unto my Lord: "Sit at my right until I have reduced your enemies to serve as a stepping stone?" *If David then calls him 'Lord,' how can he be his son?*' (Mt. 22:41-45)

But teaching in the temple, Jesus said to them: "Why do the scribes say that the Christ is the son of David, since David himself said to my Lord: 'Sit at my right hand until I have reduced your enemies to serve as a stepping stone?' *Why would David call him 'Lord' if he was his son?*' (Mk. 12:35-37; Lk. 20:41-44)

With such words, Jesus consecrates the principle of the hierarchical difference between the Father and the Son. He could be David's son by corporeal filiation as a descendent of his race, and that is why he was careful to add: How can he *in spirit* call him his Lord? If there is a hierarchical difference between father and son, then Jesus, as God's son, cannot be equal to God.

Jesus confirms this interpretation and acknowledges his inferiority in relation to God in no mistakable terms:

"You heard me say: I am leaving but I will come back to you. If you love me, you would rejoice that I am going to my Father *because the Father* IS GREATER THAN I." (Jn. 14:28)

A young man approached him and asked: "Good teacher, what must I do to have eternal life?" Jesus answered: "Why do you call me good? *Only God is good.* If you desire eternal life, keep the commandments." (Mt. 19:16-17; Mk. 10:17-18; Lk. 18:18-19)

Not only did Jesus in every circumstance not make himself equal to God, but here he positively affirms the opposite, regarding himself as inferior to God in goodness. Now, in stating that God is above him in power and moral qualities, Jesus is saying that he himself is not God. The following passages support those cited above and are also very explicit:

"*I have not spoken for my own sake; my Father, who sent me, has commanded me what to say and how I should say it.* And I know that his commandment is life everlasting. Thus, what I say is according to what my Father *has ordered me to say.*" (Jn. 12:49-50)

Jesus answered them: "*My doctrine is not my own, but his who sent me.* The one who wishes to do the will of God will know if my doctrine is his or if I speak on my own account. The one who speaks on his own account is seeking his own glory, but the one who seeks the glory of the one who sent him is true, and there is no unrighteousness in him." (Jn. 7:16-18)

"The one who does not love me does not keep my word, *and the word that you have heard is not mine but the word of my Father, who sent me.*" (Jn. 14:24)

"Do you not believe that I am in my Father and that my Father is in me? What I have said to you, I have not said of myself; but my Father, who lives in me, He is the One who does the works that I do." (Jn. 14:10)

"Heaven and earth shall pass away but my words shall not. Regarding the day and the hour, no one knows, not even the angels in heaven *nor the Son*, but only *the Father*." (Mk. 13:31-32; Mt. 24:35-36)

Jesus said to them: "When the Son of man has been lifted up, you shall know what I am, since I do nothing of myself; *I only say what the Father instructs me;* and he who sent me is with me and will not leave me alone, because *I always do what is pleasing to him*." (Jn. 8:28-29)

"I have come down from Heaven not to do my own will but to do *the will of the One who sent me.*" (Jn. 6:38)

"*I can do nothing of myself.* I judge according to what I hear and my judgment is righteous *because I do not seek to satisfy my own will but the will of the One who sent me.*" (Jn. 5:30)

"But as for me, I have a testimony greater than John's because the works that *my Father has given me the power to do* bear testimony that it was my Father who sent me." (Jn. 5:36)

"But now you seek to put me to death, for I have spoken the truth *that I have learned from God;* that is what Abraham did not do." (Jn. 8-40)

Since Christ *said nothing of himself;* since the doctrine that he taught *was not his own* but came to him from God, who commanded that he make it known; that he did only what God had given him the power to do; that the truth that he taught *he had learned from God*, to whose will he was subjected, then he himself was not God but only his envoy, his Messiah and subordinate.

It is impossible for Jesus to more positively deny any assimilation to the person of God or to state his main role in more precise terms. In the above passages, there are no veiled allegorical thoughts that can only be discovered by means of interpretations. The meaning is clear, expressed without ambiguities.

If one were to object that God, not having wanted to be acknowledged in the person of Jesus, effected a change in his individuality, then one might ask on what such an opinion is based and who would have the authority to probe the depths of Jesus' thought to give his words a meaning contrary to what they expressed. Since during his lifetime no one regarded Jesus as God, but to the contrary, as the Messiah, if he did not want to be known for what he was, all he had to do was to say nothing. From his spontaneous affirmations, one could conclude that he was not God, or that if he was, he willingly and needlessly said something false.

It is remarkable that St. John, who among the Evangelists is the one whose authority is most called upon to establish the dogma of the divinity of Christ, is precisely the one who contains the most numerous and positive arguments to the contrary. One can be convinced by reading the following passages, which add nothing, it is true, to the proofs already cited, but instead support them, because such passages obviously bring out the *duality* and the *dissimilarity of both persons:*

On account of this, the Jews persecuted Jesus and sought to kill him because he had done these things on the Sabbath. But Jesus said to them: *"My Father works hitherto and I work also."* (Jn. 5:16-17)

"For the Father judges no one, but *gives the Son all the power of judging* so that all may honor the Son just as they honor the Father. Those who do not honor the Son do not honor the Father *who sent him.*

"Verily, verily I tell you that they who hear my word and believe in the One *who sent me* have everlasting life and do not fall into condemnation; rather, they have passed from death to life.

"Verily, verily I tell you that the time is coming and has already come, in which the dead will hear the voice of the Son of God, and those who listen to it shall live; for just as the Father has life in himself, so has he given to the Son to have life in himself – and *has given him the power to judge,* because he is the *Son of man.*" (Jn. 5:22-27)

"And the Father who sent me, he himself has born witness to me. *You have not heard his voice,* nor have you seen his face. And his word shall not remain in you, because you do not believe *in the one whom he sent."* (Jn. 5:37-38)

"Whenever I judge, my judgment shall be worthy of faith because *I am not alone;* my Father, who sent me, is with me." (Jn. 8:16)

"Having said these things, Jesus raised his eyes to heaven and said: 'My Father, the time has come; glorify your Son so that your Son may glorify you. *Just as you gave him power* over all men, may he give life eternal to all whom you have given him. Everlasting life consists in knowing you; that *you are* THE ONE TRUE GOD, *and Jesus Christ, whom you have sent.*

"I have glorified you on the earth; I have finished *the work which you sent me to do.* And you, my Father, glorify me too with that same glory I had with you before the world existed.

"In a little while I will no longer be in the world; but as for them, they are still in the world, and *I return to you.* Holy Father, keep in your name those whom you have given me so that they may be one as we are one.

"I have given them *your word* and the world has hated them because they are not of the world, just as I myself am not of the world.

"Sanctify them in the truth. Your word is truth itself. Just as *you sent me* into the world, I too shall send them into the world. And I sanctify myself for them so that they too may be sanctified in the truth.

"I do not pray for them only, but also for those who will believe in me through their word so that they may all be one, just as you, my Father, are in me and I am in you; that they may be in us *so that the world may believe that you have sent me.*

"My Father, I desire that there where I am, those whom you have given me may be with me so that they may behold my glory, the glory *you have given me,* because *you loved me* before the creation of the world.

"Righteous Father, the world has not known you; I, however, have known you; and these have known that you *sent me.* I have enabled them to know your name, and I continue to enable them to know it *so that the love with which you have loved me* may be in them and I myself may be in them." (Jn. 17: 1-5; 11-14; 17-26 – Jesus' Prayer)

"And this is why my Father loves me: because I lay down my life that I might take it up again. No one takes it from me; I myself lay it down; I have the power to lay it down and I have the power to take it up again. *It is the command that I received from my Father."* (Jn. 10:17-18)

"They took away the stone, and Jesus, raising his eyes to Heaven, said these words: 'My Father, I give you thanks for having heard me. I know that you always hear me. But I say this for these who are around me so that they may believe *that you have sent me.'"* (Jn. 11:41-42 – Death of Lazarus)

"I will not speak to you anymore, because the prince of this world is coming, although *there is nothing in me that belongs to him,* but so that the world may know that I love my Father and that *I am doing what my Father has ordered me to do."* (Jn. 14:30-31)

"If you keep my commandments, you will remain in my love, just as I *have kept my Father's commandments* and remain in his love." (Jn. 15:10)

Then Jesus, after he cried with a loud voice, said, "Father, *into your hands I deliver my spirit.*" And having said these words, he died. (Lk. 23:46)

If at dying Jesus hands over his spirit to the Father, it is because he had a soul that was distinct from God and subject to God. *Thus, he was not God.*

The following words denote a certain human frailty on Jesus' part, a certain apprehension of death and the suffering he was about to endure, and which contradict the essentially divine nature attributed to him. At the same time, they denote the submission characteristic of an inferior to a superior:

Then, Jesus came to a place called Gethsemane and said to his disciples: "Sit here while I go over there and pray." And taking Peter and the two sons of Zebedee with him, *he became sorrowful and greatly afflicted.* He said to them, "*My soul is grieved even unto death;* stay here and watch with me." And going a little farther, he lay face-down on the ground and prayed: *"My Father, if it be possible, let this cup pass from me; nevertheless, not as I will, but as you will."* He then went to his disciples, and finding them asleep, he said to Peter: "What! Could you not watch with me for one hour? Watch and pray that you may not fall into temptation. The spirit is willing but the flesh is weak." He went away a second time to pray, saying, *"My Father, if this cup cannot pass except I drink it, may your will be done."* (Mt. 36-42 – Jesus' prayer in the Garden of Olives)

Then, Jesus said to them, "My soul is sorrowful unto death; stay here and watch. And going a little ways, he laid face-down on the ground, praying that, if possible, *that hour might pass from him.* He said, "Abba, Father, *everything is possible unto you; take this cup far from me;* however, may your will be done and not mine." (Mk. 14:34-36)

Arriving at that place, he said to them, "Pray, so that you may not yield to temptation." And having withdrawn from them about a stone's throw, he kneeled down, saying: "My Father, *if you will, remove this cup from me;* however, not according to *my will* but *yours.*" Then, an angel from heaven came to strengthen him. And being in agony, he prayed more earnestly. Sweat like drops of blood came from him and fell to the ground. (Lk. 22:40-44)

At the ninth hour, Jesus cried with a loud voice, saying: "Eloi! Eloi! Lamma sabachthani?' that is, My God! My God! Why have you forsaken me? (Mt. 27:46)

And at the ninth hour, Jesus cried with a loud voice, saying: "My God! My God! Why have you forsaken me?" (Mk. 15:34)

The following passages could give rise to some doubt and lead one to believe in a oneness of God with the person of Jesus; but besides not prevailing against the precise terms of the passages that precede them, they contain in themselves their own justification:

They asked him, "So, who are you?" Jesus answered, *"I am the beginning of all things,* I who am speaking to you. I have many things to tell you, *but he who sent me* is true and I say only what I have learned from him." (Jn. 8:25-26)

"What my Father has given me is greater than all things, and no one can take it from my Father's hands. *My Father and I are one."* (Jn. 10:29-30)

This means that his Father and he *are one in thought,* since he expresses God's *thought* and since he has God's *word.*

Then, the Jews picked up stones to stone him. Jesus said to them: "You have seen me do many good works *by the power of my Father.* For which of them do you want to stone me?" The Jews answered: "It is not for any of your good works that we will stone you, but because of your blasphemy and because, being a man, you make yourself God." Jesus replied: "Is it not written in your law: *I have said that you are gods?* Thus, if one calls gods those to whom the word of God was spoken, and if the Scriptures cannot be destroyed, why do you say that I blaspheme, I whom my Father sanctified and sent into the world, because I said that I am God's Son? If I do not do the works of my Father, then do not believe in me. But if I do do them, if you do not want to believe in me, then believe in my works so that you may know and believe that my Father is in me and I in him." (Jn. 10:31-38)

In another chapter, he addresses his disciples, saying: "On that day, you shall know that I am in my Father and you are in me and I in you." (Jn. 14:20)

From these words it should not be concluded that God and Jesus were *one sole* entity; otherwise, it should also be concluded from the same words that the disciples and God were *one*.

## IV – JESUS' WORDS AFTER HIS DEATH

Jesus answered her: "Do not touch me, for I have not yet ascended to my Father; but go to my brothers and tell them for me that *I ascend to my Father and your Father, to* MY GOD *and your God."* (Jn. 20:17 – Appearance to Mary Magdalene)

But approaching them, Jesus said, "All power *has been given to me* in heaven and on earth." (Mt. 28:18 – Appearance to the Apostles)

"Thus, you are witnesses of these things. I shall send you *the gift of my Father*, which was promised to you." (Lk. 24:48-49 – Appearance to the Apostles)

Thus, everything in Jesus' words, whether spoken while alive or after his death, show a duality of perfectly distinct persons, as well as a profound sentiment of his inferiority and subordination to the Supreme Being. By his insistence on willingly affirming it without being constrained or provoked by whomever, he seems to have wanted to protest beforehand against the role he foresaw would be attributed to him some day. If he had remained silent about the nature of his person, the field would have been left wide open to all sorts of beliefs and theories. The preciseness of his language, however, annuls all uncertainty.

What greater authority could one have than that of Jesus' own words? When he categorically says: I am or am not such and such, who would dare assume the right to contradict him, even if it were to place him higher than he placed himself? Who could rationally claim to be more knowledgeable than him regarding his own nature? What interpretations could possibly prevail against such definite and multiple statements as the following:

"I have not come of my own will, but the One who sent me is the one true God." "It is on his behalf that I have come." "I tell you what I have seen in my Father's house." "That is in no way mine to give, but it will be for those for whom my Father has prepared it." "I am going to my Father because the Father is greater than I." "Why do you call me good? Only God is good." "I have not spoken for my own sake; my Father, who sent me, has commanded me what to say and how I should say it." "My doctrine is not my own, but his who sent me." "And the word that you have heard is not mine but the word of my Father, who sent me." "I do nothing of myself; I only say what the Father instructs me." "I can do nothing of myself." "I do not seek to satisfy my own will but the will of the One who sent me." "I have spoken the truth that I have learned from God." "My food is doing the will of the One who sent me." "Everlasting life consists in knowing you; that you are the one true God, and [in knowing] Jesus Christ, whom you have sent." "Father, into your hands I deliver my spirit." "My Father, if it be possible, let this cup pass from me." "My God, my God, why have you forsaken me?" "I ascend to my Father and your Father, to my God and your God."

When one reads such words, the question arises as to how it could have come to anyone's mind to attribute a meaning diametrically opposed to what they so clearly express; to conceive of a complete oneness of *nature* and *power* between the Lord and the one who declares himself to be his servant. In this great process, which has lasted fifteen centuries, what are the elements of conviction? The Gospels – there are no others – leave no room for any ambiguity on the issue. What can oppose such authentic documents, established by eyewitnesses, and which cannot be contested without strongly denying the truthfulness of the evangelists and Jesus himself? A purely speculative, theoretical doctrine born three centuries later from a controversy about the abstract nature of the Word, a doctrine vigorously combated for many centuries, and which prevailed only due to the pressure of an absolute civil power.

## V – THE DUAL NATURE OF JESUS

One might object that, due to the dual nature of Jesus, his words are the expression of his sentiment as a man and not as God. Without examining at this time the chain of circumstances that gave rise much later to the theory of this dual nature, let us accept it for a moment and see if, instead of clarifying the issue, it does not complicate it to the point of rendering it unsolvable.

That which would be human in Jesus was the body, the physical part. From this point of view, it is understandable that he could have even suffered as a man. That which would be divine in him would be the soul, the spirit, the mind; in other words, the spiritual part. Thus, while he felt and suffered as a man, he must have thought and spoken as God. So, did he speak as a man or as God? This is an important question due to the exceptional authority of his teachings. If he spoke as a man, his words would be disputable; if he spoke as God, they would be incontestable – we would have to accept them and conform to them under penalty of dereliction and heresy. The most orthodox person would be the one who most closely abided by them.

Could one say that, due to his corporeal envelope, Jesus was not aware of his divine nature? But if that were the case, he would not have *thought like God;* his divine nature would have remained in a latent state and only his human nature would have presided over his mission, his moral actions and his physical actions. Thus, it is impossible to set aside his divine nature during his life without weakening his authority.

But if he *spoke as God,* why such incessant protestations against his divine nature, which in this case he could not have been unaware of? Either he was deceived, which would not be very divine, or he would have knowingly deceived the world, which would be worse yet. To us, it seems difficult to exit this dilemma.

If one says that he spoke at times as a man and at times as God, the issue becomes even more complicated due to the impossibility of distinguishing what came from the man and what came from God.

In case he had reasons to hide his true nature during his mission, the simplest way would have been not to talk about it at all, or to express himself vaguely or in parables as he did on other occasions on topics whose understanding was reserved for the future. However, such is not the case here, since his words display no ambiguity.

If despite all such considerations one were still to believe that while Jesus was alive he was unaware of his true nature, such could not be the case after his resurrection. When he appears to his disciples, it is no longer the man who speaks but the spirit detached from matter, which would have recovered the plenitude of its spiritual faculties and the awareness of its normal state, of its oneness with divinity. And yet, that is when he said, *"I ascend to my Father and your Father, to my God and your God!"*

Jesus' subordination is further indicated by his quality as mediator, implying the existence of a distinct person. He is the one who intercedes before his Father; who offers himself as a sacrifice for the remission of sins. Thus, if he is God himself, or if he were *equal in every way*, he would not have to intercede, because no one intercedes on behalf of oneself.

## VI – OPINION OF THE APOSTLES

Up to this point, we have based ourselves exclusively on Christ's own words as the sole, peremptory element for proof. Beyond that, there are but personal opinions.

Of all such opinions, the most valuable are incontestably those of the apostles. Since they assisted him on his mission, if he did give them secret instruction regarding his nature, traces would be found in their writings. Having lived with him, they must have known him better than anyone else. Therefore, let us see how they regarded him.

"O Israelites! Listen to what I am about to tell you: You know that *Jesus of Nazareth was a man whom God made known among you* by means of wonders, signs and miracles, which God did through him in your midst. Yet you crucified him and put him to death by evil hands after he was delivered to you *by express order of God's will* and decree of his foreknowledge. *But God raised him up*, stopping the pains of hell since it was impossible for him to be held there. Because David said of him: 'I have had the Lord always present before me, for he is at my right hand so that I may not be shaken. Thus, my heart has rejoiced; my tongue has sung songs of joy and my flesh itself shall rest in hope; for you will not leave my soul in hell and you will not allow your Holy One to experience corruption. You have enabled me to know the path of life and you have filled me with the joy of seeing your face.'" (Acts 2:22-28 – Peter's sermon)

"Thus, after he had been exalted by the power of God and had received the fulfillment of the Father's promise to send the Holy Spirit, he poured out this Holy Spirit, which you now see and hear. For David did not ascend into heaven; he himself said, '*The Lord said to my Lord*: Sit at my right hand until I have reduced your enemies and they serve as your stepping stone.' Hence, the whole House of Israel may know with absolute certainty that *God made Lord and Christ that Jesus whom you crucified.*" (Acts 2:33-36 – Peter's sermon)

"Moses said to our forefathers, 'The Lord your God *shall raise up from amongst your brethren a prophet like me.* Listen to everything he tells you. Whoever does not listen to that prophet shall be exterminated from amongst the people.'

"It was for you first of all that *God raised up his Son* and sent him to bless you so that each one of you could turn from your evil life." (Acts 3:22-23, 26 – Peter's sermon)

"We declare to all of you and to all the people of Israel that it is through the name of our Lord *Jesus Christ of Nazareth,* whom you crucified, and whom *God raised from amongst the dead,* that this man is now healed, as you can see right in front of you." (Acts 4:10 – Peter's sermon)

"'The kings of the earth have taken their stand and the princes have united against the *Lord* and against *his Christ.* Herod and Pontius Pilate, with the Gentiles and the people of Israel, truly conspired against your holy *Son Jesus,* whom you consecrated by your unction to do everything that your power and your counsel had ordained him to do." (Acts 4:26-28 – Prayer of the apostles)

Peter and the other apostles answered: "We ought to obey God rather than men. The God of our forefathers *raised Jesus from the dead – whom you killed by hanging him on the cross. It is him that God exalted with his right hand* as being the prince and savior to give Israel the gift of penitence and remission of sins." (Acts 5:29-31 –apostles' answer to the high priest)

"It was this Moses who said to the children of Israel, 'God shall raise up from amongst your brothers *a prophet like me;* listen to him.'"

"But the Most High does not dwell in temples made by the hands of men, according to the word of the prophet: 'Heaven is my throne and earth my stepping stone. What house will you build for me?' says the Lord, 'and where will my resting place be?'" (Acts 7:37, 48-49 – Steven's speech)

But Steven, filled with the Holy Spirit, lifted his eyes to heaven, and seeing the glory of God and *Jesus standing at God's right hand,* he said: "I see heaven open and the *Son of Man* standing *at God's right hand."*

Then, yelling and covering their ears, they rushed at him, and taking him outside the walls of the city, they stoned him. And the witnesses laid their clothes at the feet of a young man named Saul (later Paul). As they were stoning him, Steven called to Jesus, saying, "Lord Jesus, receive my spirit." (Acts 7:55-58 – Steven's martyrdom)

These citations clearly show the nature the apostles attributed to Jesus. The sole idea that stands out is his subordination to God and the constant supremacy of God; there is absolutely nothing in them that reveals any *thought of integration of nature and power.* For them Jesus is a human prophet chosen and blessed by God. Therefore, it was not among the apostles that the belief in Jesus' divinity had its origins. St. Paul, who had not known Jesus personally, but who went from ardent persecutor to being the most zealous and eloquent disciple of the new faith, and whose writings prepared the earliest formulations of the Christian religion, is no less explicit in this regard. The same sense is conveyed of two distinct beings and the supremacy of the Father over the Son:

"Paul, a servant of Jesus Christ, an apostle by divine calling, chosen and destined to proclaim the Gospel of God – the Gospel he had promised beforehand through his prophets in the holy scriptures – *concerning his Son, who, according to the flesh, was born of the blood and race of David,* and who was predestined to be God's Son in sovereign power, according to the Spirit of Holiness through the resurrection from the dead; concerning, I say, Jesus Christ our Lord; through whom we received the grace of apostleship to enable all nations to obey the faith on account of his name; among whose ranks you too are, as those having been called by Jesus Christ; to you who are in Rome, who are beloved by God and called to be saints; *may God our Father and Jesus Christ our Lord give you grace and peace.* (Rom. 1:1-7)

"Thus, being justified by faith, we have peace with *God through Jesus Christ,* our Lord.

"For, while we remained in the indolence of sin, Jesus Christ died for the unrighteous like us at the time *appointed by God.*

"Jesus Christ did not waver in dying for us at the time *appointed by God.* Thus, being justified through his blood, all the more will we be delivered *from God's wrath through him.*

"And we have not only been reconciled but even glorified *in God through Jesus Christ,* our Lord, through whom we have obtained this reconciliation.

"If by the sin of only one many die, the mercy and gift of God are poured out even more abundantly upon many through the grace of *only one man, who is Jesus Christ.* (Rom. 5:1,6,9,11,15,17)

"If we are children, we are also heirs, *HEIRS of God and CO-HEIRS with Jesus Christ,* provided, however, that we suffer with him. (Rom. 8:17)

"If you confess with your mouths that Jesus Christ is Lord, and if you believe in your heart that *God raised him from the dead,* you will be saved. (Rom. 10:9)

"Then, the consummation of all things will come *once he has handed over his kingdom to God, his Father,* after having destroyed all dominion, all authority and all power, for Jesus Christ shall reign until his Father has laid all of his enemies at his feet. Thus, death shall be the last enemy to be destroyed, for the Scriptures say that God has laid everything at his feet and subjected everything to him, and it is indubitable that it must exclude *him who subjected all things.* For when all things have been subjected to the Son, *then the Son himself will be subjected to him who has subjected all things to the Son* so that God may be all in all. (1 Cor. 15:24-28)

"But we see that Jesus, who for a little while was caused to be lower than the angels, has been crowned with glory and honor on account of the death he suffered. God, in his goodness, willing for Him to die for all – because he was well worthy of God, for whom and through whom all things exist; God, willing to lead many children to glory, fulfilled and *perfected through suffering* the one who was to be the leader and author of their salvation.

"Thus, the one who sanctifies and those who are sanctified *all come from one and the same principle;* that is why he is not ashamed to call them *brothers,* saying: "I will proclaim your name to my brothers; I will praise you in the midst of the *assembly of your people.*" And elsewhere: "I will put my trust in him." And elsewhere: "Here I am with the *children whom God has given me.*"

"That is why he had to become like his brothers in every way in order to be *before God* a merciful and faithful high priest in his ministry in order to expiate the sins of the people. For it is by the suffering through which he was tempted that He is worthy to help those who are so equally tempted. (Heb. 2:9-13, 17-18)

"Therefore, my holy brothers, you who have part in the heavenly calling, consider Jesus, who *is the apostle and high priest* of the religion that we profess; who is faithful *to the one who established him in this task,* just as Moses was faithful in all his house; for *He was deemed worthy* of a much greater glory that that of Moses, just as the one who built the house is more worthy than the house itself; for there is no house that was not built by someone, but the one who is the architect *and creator of all things is God."* (Heb. 3:1-4)

## VII – THE PREDICTIONS OF THE PROPHETS REGARDING JESUS

Besides Jesus' own statements and the apostles' opinions, there is one piece of evidence whose worth even the most orthodox believers cannot contest, because they constantly refer to it as an article of faith: God himself; that is, the prophets speaking by inspiration and announcing the coming of the Messiah. Thus, let us take a look at the passages from the Bible considered as predictions of that great event:

"I see him, but not now; I behold him but not up close; a star shall come from Jacob and a scepter shall be raised from Israel and shall smite the leaders of Moab and destroy all the sons of Seth." (Num. 24:17)

"I shall raise up for them a prophet like you *among their brothers* and I shall put my words in his mouth, and he shall say *what I have commanded.* And it shall be that, regarding those who do not listen to the words that *he will have spoken in my name,* I shall demand an accounting from them." (Deut. 18:18-19)

"Thus it shall happen, that when the day comes for you to go to be with your fathers, I shall raise up *one of your own sons,* and I shall establish his kingdom. He shall build me a house and I shall establish his throne forever. *I shall be his father and he shall be my son,* and I shall not take my mercy from him as I took it from the one who preceded you; and *I shall set him* over my house and my kingdom forever, and his throne shall stand fast forever." (1 Chron. 17:11-14)

"Therefore, the Lord himself shall give you a sign: a maiden shall conceive and give birth to a son, and he shall be called Immanuel." (Is. 7:14)

"For unto us a child is born, to us a son is given, and the government shall be placed upon his shoulders; and his name shall be called Wonderful, Counselor, Mighty God, Everlasting Father, the Prince of Peace." (Is. 9:6)

"Here is *my servant;* I shall uphold him; *he is my elect; my soul has put its affection on him; I have put my Spirit on him;* he shall exercise justice among the nations.

"He will not fail or be discouraged until I have established justice on the earth and the peoples have submitted to his law." (Is. 42:1,4)

"He shall delight in the work of his soul and be satisfied with it; and *my righteous servant* shall justify many by the knowledge they shall have of him, and he himself shall bear their iniquities." (Is. 53:11)

"Rejoice greatly, O Daughter of Zion; shout for joy, O Daughter of Jerusalem! Your King shall come to you, a righteous and humble savior riding on a donkey, and upon the foal of a donkey. And I shall do away with the war chariots of Ephraim and the horses of Jerusalem, and the bow of combat shall also disappear; and the King shall speak of peace to the nations. His rule shall extend from sea to sea and from the river to the ends of the earth." (Zach. 9: 9,10)

"And he [the Christ] shall stand and govern with the power of the Eternal One and with the magnificence of the name of the *Eternal One, his God.* And they shall return and he will be glorified unto the ends of the earth, and he shall be the one who makes peace." (Mic. 5:4)

The distinction between God and God's future envoy is most formally characterized in the above passages. God designates him *his servant,* and therefore, his subordinate. There is nothing in God's words that imply the notion of an equality of power or consubstantiality between the two persons. Was God mistaken, and did the men who came three centuries after Jesus Christ see more precisely than God? Such seems to be their claim.

# VIII – THE WORD MADE FLESH

In the beginning was the Word, and the Word was with God, and the Word was God. He was in the beginning with God. All things were made by him and nothing that was made was made without him. In him was life and that life was the light of men. And the light shone in the darkness but the darkness did not comprehend it.

There was a man sent by God, whose name was John. He came to serve as a witness, to give witness to the light so that all may believe through him. He was not the light, but he came to bear witness to the one who was the light.

That one was the true light that illumines everyone who comes into the world. He was in the world, and the world was made through him, but the world did not know him. He came to his own house but his own did not receive him. But to all who did receive him, he gave the power to become children of God; to those who believe in his name, who were born not of blood, nor the will of the flesh or the will of a man, but of God himself.

And the Word was made flesh and dwelled among us; and we beheld his glory, such as the only Son could have received from the Father; and he dwelled among us, full of grace and truth. (Jn. 1:1-14)

This passage from the Gospels is the only one that at first glance seems to implicitly contain a notion of identification between God and the person of Jesus. It is also the one that later served as the basis for controversy regarding the matter. The issue of Jesus' divinity arose gradually. It was born from discussions revolving around the interpretations that some were giving to the words *Word* and *Son.* Only in the 4th century did part of the Church adopt it as a rule. Therefore, this dogma is the result of a human decision and not divine revelation.

It must be noted, before anything else, that the words we cite above are John's and not Jesus' and that, even if we were to admit that they have not been altered, they do not, in reality, express more than a personal opinion, an inference wherein one finds the customary mysticism of the author's language; consequently, they cannot prevail against the repeated statements of Jesus himself.

However, even if accepted as they are, they by no means settle the issue in the sense of divinity, since they also apply to Jesus, God's creature.

In effect, the *Word* is God, because it is the word of God. Having received the word directly from God with the mission of revealing it to humankind, Jesus assimilated it. The divine word, with which he was infused, incarnated in him; that is, he brought it with him upon being born and that is why John can rightly say, *The Word was made flesh and dwelled among us.* Thus, Jesus may have been charged with transmitting the word of God without being God himself, just as an ambassador transmits the words of the sovereign without actually being the sovereign. According to the dogma of divinity, it is God who speaks; in the other hypothesis, God speaks through God's emissary, which takes nothing away from the authority of his words.

However, who authorizes this supposition more than the other? The only authority that is competent enough to decide the issue is Jesus' own words, when he says: "*I have not spoken of my own, but the One who sent me has ordained by his commandment that which I shall say. The doctrine that I teach is not mine but belongs to the One who sent me. The word you have heard is not my word, but that of my Father who sent me.*" It would be impossible for anyone to express it more clearly and precisely.

The quality of *Messiah* or *emissary,* attributed to him throughout the Gospels, implies a subordinate position with respect to the one who orders; the one who obeys cannot be equal to the one who commands. John characterizes this secondary position, and consequently establishes the duality of persons when he says: "*And we beheld his glory, such as the only Son could have received from the Father*"; because the one who receives cannot be the one who gives, and the one who gives glory cannot be the same as the one who receives it. If Jesus is God, he possesses glory in and of himself and does not have to wait for it from someone else. If God and Jesus are one sole being under two different names, there can be neither supremacy nor subordination between them. From the moment that there is no absolute parity of positions, it follows that they are two distinct beings.

The qualification of *Divine Messiah* does not imply that there is any more equality between the one who orders and the one who obeys than that of royal envoy between a king and his representative.

Jesus was a divine messiah because of the two-fold reason that God ordained his mission and that his perfections placed him in direct relationship with God.

## IX – SON OF GOD AND SON OF MAN

Far from implying equality, the title *Son of God* is much more indicative of subjection. In that sense, one is subjected to someone else and not to oneself.

For Jesus to be fully and completely equal to God, he would have had to be like God from all eternity, that is, to have been *non-created.* Well then, dogma states that God *begot* him from all eternity, but whoever says *begot* means *created.* Whether begotten or not from all eternity, he is no less a creature, and as such subjected to his Creator. This idea is implicit in the word *Son.*

Was Jesus born in time? In other words, was there a time in the past of eternity, in which he did not exist? Or, is he co-eternal with the Father? These are the subtleties that have been discussed over the centuries. On what authority rests the doctrine of co-eternity that turned into dogma? On the authority of the opinion of the men who established it.

But on what did these men found such an opinion? Not on Jesus, because he declared himself to be subordinate. Not on the prophets, because they foretold him as being the emissary and servant of God. In what unknown more authentic documents than the Gospels did they find such a doctrine? In the assessment and superiority of their own knowledge, apparently.

Therefore, let us set aside these useless arguments, which will never abate and whose solution, if possible, would never render people any better. Let us say that Jesus is a *Son of God* just like all creatures; that he called God his Father just as he taught us to call God *our Father.* He is the *beloved Son of God,* because having attained the perfection that brings one closer to God, he possesses all of God's trust and love. He said *only Son* not because he was the only being that had attained perfection, but because he was the only one predestined to carry out that mission on the earth.

If the qualification *Son of God* seems to support the doctrine of divinity, the same cannot be said of *Son of Man*, which Jesus applied to himself during his mission, and which has been the object of many commentaries.

In order to grasp the true meaning of the phrase, we must resort to the Bible, where it is bestowed upon Ezekiel by God:

"Such was the likeness of the glory of the Lord that was presented to me. Upon seeing such things, I fell face down on the ground and I heard a voice that spoke to me thusly: '*Son of man,* get up and I shall speak to you.' And having spoken to me like that, the Spirit entered me and I stood up and listened to what he was telling me, saying: '*Son of man,* I am sending you to the children of Israel, to an apostate people who have withdrawn from me. To this day, they and their forebears have continued to violate the covenant that I established with them.'" (Ez. 2:1-3)

"Son of man, they are preparing fetters for you. They will bind you and you will not break free." (Ez. 3:25)

"The Lord then said to me, 'And you, Son of man, hear what the Lord God says to the land of Israel: The end is near; the end is near for the four corners of the land." (Ez. 7:1-2)

"On the tenth day of the tenth month of the ninth year, the Lord said to me, 'Son of man, mark this day, on which the king of Babylon has gathered his troops before Jerusalem.'" (Ez. 24:1-2)

"Furthermore, the Lord said to me, 'Son of man, I will strike you with a wound and take from you what is most pleasing to your eyes; but you will not make any mournful lamentations; you will not weep and tears will not flow down your face. You will moan in secret and not grieve as you would for the dead; you will keep your head covered and your sandals upon your feet; you will not cover your face and you will not eat of the food given to those who mourn.' Thus I spoke to the people in the morning and my wife died that evening. The next day, I did what God had ordered me to do." (Ez. 24:15-18)

"The Lord spoke to me again, saying, 'Son of man, prophesy regarding the shepherds of Israel; prophesy and say to the shepherds: Thus says the Lord God: Woe to the shepherds of Israel, who feed themselves: do the shepherds not feed their flocks?'" (Ez. 34:1-2)

"Then I heard him speaking unto me inside the house; and the man who was next to me said, 'Son of man, this is the place of my throne, the place where I shall put my feet and where I shall remain forever amongst the children of Israel; and the house of Israel shall no longer profane my holy name in the future; neither they, nor their kings with their idolatries and the sepulchers of their kings, or their high places.'" (Ez. 43:6-7)

"For God will not threaten like man, nor be inflamed to anger like the son of man." (The Book of Judith 8:15)

It is obvious that the qualification *Son of man* means this: *that which is born of man*, in opposition to that which is born apart from humanity. The last citation from the book of Judith leaves no doubt about the meaning of this expression, employed in a very literal sense. God designates Ezekiel by this name undoubtedly to remind him that, despite the gift of prophecy bestowed upon him, he does not belong any less to humankind, and that he should not believe himself to be of an exceptional nature.

Jesus gave himself this qualification with remarkable persistency, because only in very rare circumstances did he call himself *Son of God.* Coming from him, it could have no other meaning than to remind them that he, too, belonged to humankind; through it he identifies himself with the prophets who preceded him, and to whom he compared himself by alluding to his death, when he said: *"O Jerusalem, which kills the prophets!"* The insistence with which he called himself the Son of Man seems like an early protestation against the qualification he foresaw bestowed upon him later on, so that it would be well remembered that it did not come from his lips.

It should be noted that, during this interminable argument, which has inflamed individuals in a long succession of centuries and continues to endure to this day, and which has lit the stakes and made rivers of blood flow, the dispute is over an abstraction – the nature of Jesus – which has been made the cornerstone of the edifice, even though he never mentioned it; and that one thing has been forgotten, that which Christ said was *the whole law and all of the prophets:* love for God and for one's neighbor, and charity, which he established as the express condition for salvation. We have dwelt at length on the question of the affinity of Jesus with God and have remained completely silent with respect to the virtues he recommended and of which he gave the example.

Even God has been ignored before the exaltation of the person of Christ. In the symbol of Nicaea, it only states: We believe in one God, etc. But what is this God like? By no means does it mention God's essential attributes: God's supreme goodness and supreme justice. These words would have been the condemnation of the dogmas that consecrate God's bias toward certain individuals, God's inexorability, jealousy, rage and vindictive spirit, upon which authority has rested to justify the cruelties practiced in God's name.

If the symbol of Nicaea, which became the foundation of the Catholic faith, was in conformance with the spirit of Christ, why the anathema with which it ends? Is that not proof that it is the product of human passions? Moreover, to what is its adoption owed? To the pressure of Emperor Constantine, who made it a political rather than a religious issue. Without his orders, the Council of Nicaea would not have taken place; without the intimidation he exerted, it is more likely that Arianism[27] would have prevailed. Thus, it is the result of the sovereign authority of one man – who did not even belong to the church, who realized too late the political error he had made publicly and who futilely sought to retrace his steps in reconciling the parties – that we are not Arians today instead of Catholics, and that Arianism is not nowadays the orthodoxy and Catholicism the heresy.

After eighteen centuries of fighting and unfruitful arguments, during which the most essential part of Christ's teaching has been completely misplaced – the only thing that could guarantee peace for humankind – one is weary of these barren discussions that have brought nothing but trouble,

27 Arianism, a Christian heresy first proposed early in the 4th century by the Alexandrian presbyter Arius. It affirmed that Christ is not truly divine but a created being. Arius's basic premise was the uniqueness of God, who is alone self-existent and immutable; the Son, who is not self-existent, cannot be God. Because the Godhead is unique, it cannot be shared or communicated, so the Son cannot be God. Because the Godhead is immutable, the Son, who is mutable, being represented in the gospels as subject to growth and change, cannot be God. The Son must, therefore, be deemed a creature. www.britannica.com - Tr.

engendered disbelief and whose purpose no longer satisfies reason.

Nowadays, there is a manifested tendency of general opinion to return to the fundamental ideas of the early church and to the moral aspect of Christ's teachings because it is the only thing that can render people better. It is clear, positive and provides no opportunity for controversy. Had the Church taken that route from the beginning, it would now be all-powerful instead of being on its decline. It would have rallied the great majority of humankind instead of having been torn apart by different factions.

When people march under that banner, they will extend fraternal hands instead of anathematizing and condemning each other over issues that, most of the time, they do not understand.

Such a tendency of opinion is a sign that the time has come to take the issue to its true terrain.

# SPIRITIST MUSIC

"Recently, at the headquarters of the Parisian Spiritist Society, the president honored me by asking my opinion about the current state of music and the changes it might undergo due to the influence of Spiritist beliefs. If I did not immediately attend to that benevolent and kind request, you can be sure, ladies and gentlemen, it was only because a pressing issue motivated my abstention.

"Ah! Musicians! They are human just like everyone else – even more human, perhaps – and as such, fallible and sinful. I myself was not exempt from weaknesses, and if God had given me a long life in order to give me time to repent, the intoxication of success, the complacency of my friends and the flattery of my followers often took away the means to accomplish it. Being a maestro is a power in this world where pleasure plays such an important role. Those whose art consists in seducing the ear and touching the heart find many traps under their feet, into which the unfortunate ones fall! They become inebriated with the inebriation of others; applause strikes their ears and they fall straight into the abyss without looking for a point of support to resist the pull.

"Nonetheless, in spite of my errors, I had faith in God. I believed in the soul that vibrated within me, and disengaged from its sonorous prison, it rapidly recognized itself amid the harmonies of creation and blended its prayer with those that rose from nature to the Infinite, from the creature to the uncreated Being!

"I am happy for the sentiment that brought me to be amongst Spiritists because it is sympathy that dictated it. If curiosity attracted me at first, it is to my appreciation that you owe the response to the question you have posed. I was there, ready to speak, thinking I knew everything, when my falling pride revealed my ignorance. I remained silent and I listened. I came back; I learned; and after reflection and meditation were added to the words of truth spoken by your mentors, I said to myself: The great maestro Rossini, the creator of so many masterpieces – according to humans – alas! Unfortunately, he did nothing but glean some of the least perfect pearls from the jewelry chest of music created by the Master of masters. Rossini assembled notes, composed melodies and drank from the chalice that contains all harmonies. He stole a few sparks from the sacred fire, but neither he nor the others created that sacred fire! We invent nothing; we copy from the great book of nature and the crowds applaud – if we have not distorted the score too much.

"A dissertation on celestial music! Who could undertake such a task? What superhuman spirit could make matter vibrate in unison using this enchanting art! What human brain, what incarnate spirit could capture the infinitely varied nuances? ... Who possesses the sentiment of harmony to such an extent? ... No, human beings are not made for such conditions! ... Later, perhaps? ... Much, much later!

"In the meantime, maybe I shall come soon to satisfy your desire and give you my appraisal of the current state of music, and to tell you about the transformations and the progress that Spiritism can introduce into it. For now, it is still too early. The subject is vast; I have studied it but it is still beyond me. When I have mastered it – if that is possible – or rather, when I have glimpsed it as fully as the state of my spirit will allow, I will satisfy you. But for now, I still need a little more time. If a musician is to talk about the music of the future, he should do so as a master, and Rossini does not wish to speak as a schoolboy."

Rossini

*(Medium: Mr. Desliens)*

"I have explained my silence on the question that the instructor of Spiritism asked me. Before addressing this difficult subject, I had to collect myself, recall and condense the elements at hand. I did not have to study music; I only had to classify the arguments methodically in order to present a summary capable of providing an idea about my conception of harmony. That endeavor, which was no easy matter, is finished, and I am now ready to submit it to the evaluation of Spiritists.

"Harmony is hard to define. It is often confused with music, with the sounds resulting from an arrangement of notes and the vibrations of the instruments reproducing this arrangement. But this is not harmony, just as the flame is not the light. The flame results from the combination of two gases; it is tangible. But the light that it projects is an effect of that combination and not the flame itself. The light is not tangible. Here, the effect is superior to the cause. So it is with harmony. Harmony results from a musical arrangement; it too is an effect that is superior to its cause. The cause is coarse and tangible; the effect is subtle and intangible.

"One can conceive of light without a flame, and one can comprehend harmony without music. The soul is capable of perceiving harmony apart from any instrumentation, just as it is capable of seeing light apart from any material combinations. Light is an inner sense that the soul possesses. The more this sense is developed, the better the soul perceives light. Harmony is also an inner sense of the soul and is perceived because of the development of this sense. Apart from tangible causes, light and harmony are of divine essence. We have them due to the efforts we have made to acquire them. If I am comparing light and harmony, it is to make myself better understood, and also because these two sublime delights of the soul are children of God, and therefore sisters.

"Harmony in the spirit world is so complex; it has so many degrees that I know of and so many more that are still hidden from me in the infinite ether that someone who is placed at a certain height of perception is taken with wonder at contemplating those diverse harmonies, which, if they were brought together, would constitute the most unbearable cacophony. On the other hand, if perceived separately, they constitute the harmony particular to each degree. These harmonies are elementary and unrefined in the lower degrees, whereas they lead to ecstasy in the higher degrees. A harmony that is displeasing to a spirit of delicate perception may enchant a spirit of grosser perception; and when a low order spirit is given the chance to revel in the delights of higher harmonies, it is taken by ecstasy and opens up to prayer; the enchantment carries it to the higher spheres of the moral world; it lives a life superior to its own and it would like to continue to live like that forever. But when the harmony ceases to penetrate it, it wakes up, or rather, it goes back to sleep. In any case, it returns to the reality of the situation, and amid the regrets it voices for having had to come back, it utters a prayer to the Eternal One asking for the power to go back. It is for the spirit a great purpose of emulation.

"I will not try to explain the musical effects that the spirit produces when acting on the ether[28]. What is certain is that the spirit produces the sounds it wants to produce, and it cannot want what it does not know. Thus, the spirit who comprehends much, who possesses harmony within itself, who is saturated with it, who rejoices in the inner meaning of this impalpable something, this abstraction that is the conception of harmony, acts whenever it wants upon the universal fluid, which like a faithful instrument reproduces what the spirit conceives and desires. The ether vibrates due to the action of the spirit's will; the harmony the spirit carries within itself concretizes, so to speak; it rises, sweet and soft, like the fragrance of a violet, or it roars like a tempest, explodes like thunderbolt, or wails like the breeze; it is quick like lightning or slow like a cloud; it is broken like a hiccup, or even like a meadow; it is disheveled like a waterfall, or calm

28 In space, in the spirit world. – Tr.

like a lake; it whispers like a brook, or rumbles like a torrent. It is as wildly rugged as a mountain chain, and as fresh as an oasis; by turns, it is sad and melancholy like the night, or joyous and merry like the day; it is capricious like a child, comforting like a mother and protective like a father. It is unruly like the passions, clean like love, and grand like nature. Within this last phase, it fuses with prayer; it glorifies God and leads the one who produces or conceives it to rapture.

"O comparison, comparison! Why is it necessary to use you! Why is it necessary to bend to your degrading needs and borrow from tangible, crude images in order to conceive the sublime harmony in which the spirit delights! And yet, without comparisons, one cannot get an idea of this abstraction, which is a sentiment when it is cause and a sensation when it becomes effect.

"The spirit who has the sentiment of harmony is like the spirit who has intellectual acquisition: both continually enjoy the inalienable asset they have acquired. The learned spirit who teaches its knowledge to those who are unlearned feels the happiness of teaching because it makes those whom it instructs happy. The spirit who makes the chords of its inner harmony resound in the ether experiences the happiness of seeing those who hear it happy.

"Harmony, knowledge and virtue are the three grand conceptions of the spirit. The first enraptures it, the second enlightens it and the third uplifts it. Possessed in all their fullness, they fuse and constitute purity. O pure spirits who do possess them! Descend into our darkness and illumine our way. Show us the road you have taken so that we may follow in your footsteps!

"And when I think that such spirits – whose existence I can comprehend – are finite beings, mere atoms in comparison with the Eternal Lord of the Universe, my mind becomes confused as it ponders the grandeur of God and the infinite happiness he enjoys in himself due to the mere fact that his purity is infinite, since everything the creature acquires is but a speck that emanates from the Creator. Well then, if this speck is able to fascinate through its will, captivate and dazzle through its softness, and gleam through its virtue, what can the eternal and infinite fount from which it was taken produce? If the spirit, being created, gets to draw such happiness from its purity, what idea should one have about the happiness that the Creator draws from his absolute purity? This is the eternal question!

"The composer who conceives the harmony translates it into the coarse language called music; he concretizes his idea; he writes it down. The artist apprehends the form and takes hold of the instrument, which enables him to express the idea. The air, brought into play by the instrument, carries it to the ear that transmits it to the soul of the listener. But the composer is powerless to transmit entirely the harmony he conceives for lack of an adequate language. The performer, in turn, does not comprehend the entire written idea, and the untamed instrument he uses does not allow him to translate everything he has understood. The ear is struck by the coarse air that surrounds it, and the soul receives, finally, through a rebellious organ, the horrible translation of the idea that bloomed in the soul of the maestro. The maestro's idea was his inner sentiment; although marred by the agents of instrumentation and perception, it nevertheless produced sensations in those who tried to translate it. These sensations are the harmony. The music has produced them; they are the effect of the music. The music is put in service of the sentiment to produce the sensation. The sentiment within the composer is harmony. The sensation within the listener is also harmony, but with the difference that it is conceived by one and received by the other. Music is the *medium* for harmony, it receives it and gives it, just as the reflector is the *medium* for light, and just as you are the *medium* for spirits. Music transmits harmony that is more marred, or less so, depending on how well or badly it is played, just like the reflector reflects the light better or worse depending on how well it is polished, and just like the medium expresses well or poorly the thoughts of the spirit, depending on how flexible he is.

"And now that the meaning of harmony is well understood; now that it is known that it is conceived by the soul and transmitted to the soul, one can comprehend the difference between harmony on earth and harmony in the spirit world.

"With you, everything is rudimentary: the instrument of translation and the instrument of perception. With us, everything is subtle. You have the air; we have the ether; you have the organ that obstructs and veils; we have direct, unveiled perception. For you, the author is translated; for us, the author speaks without intermediary and in the language that expresses all conceptions. Nonetheless, these harmonies have the same source. Just as the light of the moon has the same source as that of the sun, the harmony of the earth is but the reflection of the harmony of the spirit world.

"Harmony is as indefinable as happiness, fear or anger: it is a sentiment. One does not understand it unless one possesses it, and one does not possess it unless one acquires it. Joyous persons cannot explain their joy; fearful persons cannot explain their fear. They can state the facts that provoke such sentiments, and they can define and describe them, but the sentiments remain unexplained. What causes joy in one produces nothing in another; the object that causes fear in one produces courage in another. The same causes are followed by different effects. This does not happen in physics but does in metaphysics because sentiment is the property of the soul and souls differ from one another in sensitivity, impressionability and liberty.

"Music, which is the secondary cause of the harmony perceived, penetrates and transports one but leaves another cold and indifferent. This is because the former is in a state to receive the impression produced by the harmony, whereas the latter is in an opposite state. He hears the air that vibrates but does not comprehend the idea that is conveyed to him.

The latter gets bored and sleepy; the former, enthusiastic and tearful. Obviously, the person who enjoys the delights of harmony is more advanced, more purified than the person it cannot penetrate; his soul is more capable of feeling; it disengages more easily and harmony helps it to do so; harmony transports it and enables it to see the moral world better. From this, one must conclude that music is essentially moralizing because it carries harmony to souls, and that harmony uplifts and develops them.

"The influence of music on the soul and on its moral progress is acknowledged all over the world. But the reason for this influence is usually unknown. Its explanation lies entirely in this fact: harmony puts the soul under the power of a sentiment that dematerializes it. This sentiment exists to a certain degree by itself, but it develops under the action of a similar, more elevated sentiment. Those who lack this sentiment are brought to it gradually. They end up allowing themselves also to penetrate and enter the ideal world, where, for an instant, they forget the coarse pleasures they prefer to the divine harmony.

"Thus, if one considers that harmony comes from the spirit, we may deduce that if music exerts a blissful influence on the soul, the soul that conceives it also exerts an influence on music. The virtuous soul that is passionate about goodness, beauty and excellence, and has acquired harmony, will produce masterpieces capable of penetrating, touching and moving the most hardened souls. If the composer is trite, how can he express the virtue that he disdains, the beauty he is unaware of, and the excellence he does not comprehend? His compositions will be the reflection of his sensual tastes, his frivolousness, his unconcern. They will be licentious, obscene, comical or burlesque. They will communicate to the listeners the sentiments they express and will pervert them rather than uplift them.

"By moralizing persons, Spiritism will therefore exert a great influence on music. It will produce more-virtuous composers, who will communicate their virtues through the understanding of their compositions.

"One will laugh less and weep more; hilarity will give way to emotion, ugliness to beauty and comedy to grandeur.

"On the other hand, the listeners whom Spiritism will have prepared to receive this harmony easily will feel truly enchanted at listening to serious music. They will disdain the frivolous and licentious music that corrupts the masses. When the grotesque and the obscene are replaced by the beautiful and the good, composers of this sort will disappear; without listeners, they will gain nothing, and it is for gain that they corrupt themselves.

"Oh yes! Spiritism will have an influence on music! How could it be otherwise? Spiritism's coming will change art and purify it. Its source is divine and its power will take it everywhere where there are people to love, uplift and comprehend. It will become the ideal and objective of artists. Painters, sculptors, composers and poets will request its inspiration, and it will furnish it because it is plentiful, because it is inexhaustible.

"The spirit of Maestro Rossini will come in a new existence to continue the art that he considers foremost of all. Spiritism will be his symbol and the inspirer of his compositions."

ROSSINI
*(Medium: Mr. Nivart)*

# THE ROAD OF LIFE

The matter of the plurality of existences has concerned philosophers for ages, and more than one has acknowledged the preexistence of the soul as being the only possible solution to the most important problems of psychology. Without this principle, they find themselves halted at each step and caught in a deadlock they cannot escape except with the aid of the plurality of existences.

The main objection one might pose to this theory is the lack of the memory of former existences; in effect, a string of existences unaware of each other; to leave one body behind to take up the next without the remembrance of the past would be the same as nothingness because it would be the nullity of thought. It would be a multiplicity of new departure points without any connection with the previous ones. It would be the continual rupture of all the affections that make one's present life charming, the sweetest and most consoling hope for the future. Lastly, it would be the negation of all moral responsibility. Such a doctrine would be as unacceptable and incompatible with God's justice as a sole existence with the perspective of an absolute eternity of punishment due to a few short-term wrongs. One can thus understand why those who have such an idea about reincarnation reject it; however, that is not the way that Spiritism presents it to us.

The soul's life in the spirit world – Spiritism tells us – is its normal existence, wherein the soul has an unlimited retrospective remembrance. Corporeal existences are nothing but breaks, short seasons in the spirit's overall existence; and the sum of all such seasons is only a tiny speck of its normal existence, just like on a journey of many years a traveler stops from time to time for a few hours. If during its corporeal existences there may seem to be a break in continuity due to the lack of memories, the connection, in reality, is established during the spirit life, which suffers no interruption. The break in continuity actually exists only for the outward corporeal life and the life of relationships, and the absence of memory during that time demonstrates the wisdom of Providence, which in this way prevents people from being too distracted in life, because they have tasks to fulfill. But when the body is resting during sleep, the soul takes partial flight to reestablish the chain that is broken only during the waking state.

One might object to this by asking how anyone could learn from their previous existences in order to improve themselves if they cannot remember the wrongs they have committed. First of all, Spiritism responds that the remembrance of unfortunate existences, combined with the miseries of the present life, would make living even more painful. It is therefore an addition of sufferings that God has willed to spare us. Without this forgetfulness, how great our humiliation would often be when we contemplated who we had been! As far as our betterment is concerned, such memory would be useless. During each existence, we always take a few steps forward, acquire a few qualities and rid ourselves of a few imperfections. Each such existence is thus a new starting point, where we are what we have made of ourselves and where we see ourselves for who we are without concern with what we have been. If in a previous existence we were cannibals, what would it matter as long as we are not cannibals any longer? If we had a certain defect, but show no trace of it now, it is a settled account and we do not have to concern ourselves with it anymore. On the other hand, let us suppose it is a defect that we have only partially managed to correct: the residue will carry over into the next life and our focus should be to correct it at that time.

Let us take an example: a man was a murderer and a thief. He was punished either during the corporeal life or the spirit life. He repented of and corrected the former tendency but not the latter. In his next existence, he will be only a thief

– maybe a big one – but he will no longer be a murderer. One more step forward and he will be merely a petty thief; a little later and he will no longer steal but may have the desire to, which his conscience will neutralize. A final effort, with every vestige of moral infirmity gone, he will be a model of probity. What will it matter to him what he used to be? Would not the memory of having been hanged be a constant torment and humiliation? Apply this rationale to all vices, to all deviations, and you will see how the soul grows morally by passing and re-passing through the sieve of reincarnation. Was not God more just by making humans the arbiters of their own fate through their efforts at self-improvement than by having created their souls at the same time as their bodies, condemning them to everlasting torment for their short-term wrongs without giving them the means to purify their imperfections? Due to the plurality of existences, their future is in their own hands. If they take a long time to improve themselves, they will have to endure the consequences; this is supreme justice, but hope is never closed to them.

The following comparison can help make the experiences of the soul understandable.

Let us imagine a long road, along which at unequal intervals one encounters forests that have to be crossed, and upon entering each one, the long, beautiful road comes to an end, only to continue again upon exiting. A traveler follows this road and enters the first forest. However, there are no trails to follow, only an inextricable maze in which he gets lost. The light of the sun has disappeared beneath the canopy of trees. He wanders around without knowing where he is going. At long last, after unprecedented fatigue, he reaches the end of the forest, but he is exhausted, cut by thorns and bruised by rocks. There, he finds the road again and follows its path seeking to get healed from his wounds.

Further along, he comes to the next forest, where the same difficulties are waiting for him, but he already has some experience and exits it less bruised. In yet another forest, he meets a logger who points out the direction he must take and this keeps him from getting lost at all. With each new forest, his skills are increased to the point where the obstacles are gradually easier to overcome. Reassured that he will find the good road upon exiting, this confidence sustains him; moreover, he knows what direction to take to find it more easily. The road ends at the top of a very high mountain, where he can see the whole journey from the very beginning. He can also see the many forests he crossed and can remember the vicissitudes he experienced, but this memory is not painful because he has arrived at the goal. He is like an old soldier, who, in the tranquility of his home, remembers the battles he has seen. The forests scattered along the road are for him like black spots on a white strip, and he says to himself: "When I was in those forests, especially the first ones, how long it seemed to take to cross them! It seemed like I would never reach the end; everything around me seemed so huge and insurmountable. Just think: if not for that brave logger who set me on the good road, I might still be in there! Now that I consider those same forests from where I now stand, how small they seem! As if with one little step I could have gotten through all of them. What is more, my sight penetrates them and I can make out the smallest details, to the point of seeing the wrong steps I took."

Then, an old man says to him: "My son, you have come to the end of the journey; however, endless rest would cause you lethal boredom and you would soon miss the vicissitudes you experienced, and which set your hands, feet and mind in motion. From here, you can see a large number of travelers on the road you yourself have traveled; like you, they run the risk of getting lost en route. You have the experience and no longer have anything to fear. Go, meet them and endeavor to guide them with your advice so that they may arrive more quickly."

"I will go with joy," replies our man. "But let me ask you: why isn't there a road that runs directly from the starting point to here? That would save travelers from having to go through those abominable forests."

"My son," replies the old man, "pay close attention and you will see many travelers that avoid some of the forests. They are the ones who acquired the necessary experience earlier and knew how to take a more direct and shorter road to arrive. This experience, however, is the result of the labor the first forests imposed on them, to the extent that they would not get here but for their own merit. What would you yourself know if you hadn't gone through those forests? The activities you had to initiate, the resources of the imagination you had to use to clear your pathway, have increased your knowledge and developed your intelligence; without it, you would be as inexperienced as when you first set out. Furthermore, by seeking to rid yourself of problems, you contributed to improving the forests you passed through. What you did was little, imperceptible; but think of the thousands of travelers who did as much and who, by working for themselves, worked for the common good without realizing it. Isn't it just that they receive recompense for their woes with the repose they enjoy here? What right would they have to it if they hadn't done anything?"

"My father," responds the traveler, "in one of those forests I met a man who said to me: 'On the edge of the forest there is an immense abyss that has to be crossed in just one leap. Only one in a thousand can do it; all the others fall into the abyss, into a blazing furnace and are lost forever; they can never get out.' But I never saw such an abyss."

"My son, that is because such an abyss does not exist; otherwise, it would be an abominable trap set for all the travelers that come to me. I know full well that they need to surmount difficulties, but I also know that, sooner or later, they will all overcome them. If I had created impossibilities for a single traveler, knowing that he or she would succumb, that would have been a cruelty – even more so if I had done it for a large number. That abyss is just an allegory, whose explanation you will know. Look at the road, at the gaps between the forests. Among the travelers, you can see those who proceed slowly with a joyous demeanor; you can see friends who lost track of each other in the mazes of the forest, and how happy they are to meet again at the exit. But alongside them there are others who proceed painfully. They are impaired and beg for the pity of those who pass by because they suffer cruelly from wounds that, due to their own fault, they acquired when crossing the brambles. Even so, they will be healed, and it will be a lesson that will benefit them in the next forest they traverse and from which they will emerge less bruised. The abyss symbolizes the ills they experience, and in saying that only one in a thousand can cross it, that man was right because the number of imprudent travelers is quite large. But he was wrong in saying that once they fell in they would never get out. There is always an exit in order to come to me. Go, my son, go and show this exit to those who are at the bottom of the abyss. Go and help the wounded on the road and show the way to those who are crossing through the forests."

The road is an allegory for the spiritual life of the soul, whose journey is happier or less happy as it travels it. The forests are corporeal existences, during which the soul works for its advancement while at the same time working for the common good. The traveler that arrived at the goal and then returns to help those who came afterwards symbolizes guardian angels, the missionaries of God, who find their happiness not only in seeing God, but also in carrying out their activities to do the good and obey the Supreme Lord.

# HUMANKIND'S FIVE ALTERNATIVES

The Materialist Doctrine
The Pantheist Doctrine
The Deist Doctrine
The Dogmatic Doctrine
The Spiritist Doctrine

Very few people can live without worrying about tomorrow. Thus, if one is concerned about what will happen after a twenty-four hour day, there is all the more reason to be concerned about what will happen after "the biggest day" of one's life, because it does not entail only a few minutes but eternity. Will we continue living or not? There is no middle ground; it is a matter of life or death; it is the supreme alternative! ...

If we were to question the great majority of people about their innermost sentiment on the matter, they would answer: "We go on living." Such hope is a consolation to them. On the other hand, a small minority, especially of late, has endeavored to prove to them that they will not go on living. There is no denying the fact that this school has been gaining followers, principally among those who, fearing the responsibility of the future, find it more comfortable to enjoy the present without limit and without bothering themselves with the consequences. But that is the opinion of a small number.

If we do go on living, how will we live? What will our situation be? Here, the theories vary according to religious and philosophical beliefs. However, all the opinions about people's future may be reduced to five principal alternatives.

We will summarize them so that comparison is easier, and so that a choice can be made with full knowledge of the facts as to which one seems the most rational and corresponds best to one's personal aspirations and the needs of society. The five alternatives are those resulting from the doctrines of *materialism, pantheism, deism, dogmatism, and Spiritism.*

## I – THE MATERIALIST DOCTRINE

According to this doctrine, human intelligence is a property of matter; it is born and dies with the body. The human being is *nothing before and nothing after* corporeal life.

*Consequences:* Since human beings are only matter, only material pleasures are real and desirable; moral affections have no future; death forever breaks any moral bonds; there is no compensation for life's miseries; suicide becomes the rational and logical choice in life when suffering is without any hope of relief; it is useless to impose any restraints to conquer one's bad inclinations; living for oneself is the best way possible while here; it is foolish to inconvenience oneself and sacrifice one's rest and well-being for others, that is, for others who will be annihilated in turn and whom one will not see anymore; social duties have no basis; one needs not concern oneself with them, and good and evil are mere conventions; social restraint is reduced to the material power of civil law.

*Remark: Perhaps it would be worthwhile to remind our readers about a few passages from an article we published on materialism in the August 1868 issue of Revue Spirite:*

"We have stated that, by flaunting itself more than at any other time, and by posing as the ultimate regulator of humankind's moral destiny, materialism has had the effect of frightening the masses due to the unavoidable consequences of its doctrines for the social order; consequently, in favor of spiritualist ideas it has provoked a strong reaction, which should prove to materialism that it is far from enjoying the widespread sympathy it has imagined, and that it possesses a strange delusion if it expects its laws to be imposed on the world someday.

"Of course, the spiritualist beliefs of the past are insufficient for this century: they are not at the intellectual level of our generation; on many points, they are in conflict with the indubitable data of science; they leave the spirit with ideas that are incompatible with the positive need that dominates modern society. Furthermore, they make the big mistake of imposing themselves through blind faith and proscribing free examination; hence, without a doubt, the increase of disbelief among so many. It is obvious that, if people were nourished from infancy with ideas that can be confirmed later through reason, there would be no disbelievers. However, brought back to faith through Spiritism, many have said to us: 'If we had been told about God, the soul and the future life in a rational manner, we would never have doubted!'

"Just because a principle has been wrongly or falsely applied, does that mean it should be rejected altogether? The same thing applies to spiritual matters as applies to legislation and all social institutions: they must be adapted to the times so as not to die out. But instead of presenting something better than old spiritualism, materialism prefers to suppress everything, which has kept it from searching and which seems more comfortable to those inconvenienced by the idea of God and the future. What would one think of a doctor who, upon finding the diet of a convalescent not substantial enough for his temperament, orders him not to eat anything at all?

"What is most surprising to find in most materialists of the modern school – those that constantly assert the right of freedom of conscience – is the spirit of intolerance taken to the ultimate degree! …

"…At this moment, there is a general outcry on the part of a certain group against spiritualist ideas in general, including, of course, Spiritism. What this group wants is not a greater or more just God, but a materialistic and less significant God, because then there will be no accountability to him. No one is contesting this group's right to its opinion or its right to argue opposing opinions. What should not be granted, however, is these persons' intention – which is most striking for persons who pose as apostles of liberty – to keep others from believing as they see fit and to argue over doctrines they do not share. Intolerance for intolerance, one is not worth any more than the other…"

## II – THE PANTHEISTIC DOCTRINE

The intelligent principle, or soul, apart from matter, is extracted at birth from the universal whole; it is individualized in each person during his or her life and at death it returns to the common mass like raindrops to the ocean.

*Consequences:* *Without individuality and self-awareness, it is as if the person never existed at all. The moral consequences of this doctrine are exactly the same as those of the materialist doctrine.*

*Remark:* *Some pantheists believe that the soul, taken at birth from the universal whole, retains its individuality for an indefinite length of time and only returns to the mass after having reached the ultimate degree of perfection. Nonetheless, the consequences of this variety of belief are exactly the same as those of the pantheist doctrine per se, since it would be completely useless for anyone to work to acquire a little knowledge that will be lost after a relatively short amount of time. If the soul, in general, refuses to accept such a concept, how much more of a painful shock it will feel when, thinking that at the moment it attained ultimate knowledge and perfection, it would be condemned to losing the fruit of its labors and its individuality.*

## III – THE DEISTIC DOCTRINE

Deism entails two very distinct categories of believers: *independent deists* and *providential deists.*

Independent deists believe in God; they accept all of God's attributes as Creator. God, they say, has established the general laws that govern the universe, but once established, they function by themselves and their author is no longer concerned with them. Individuals do what they want or what they can without God being bothered by it. There is no providence. Since God is not concerned about us, we have nothing to thank God for and nothing to ask for.

Those who deny any intervention of providence in people's lives are like children who deem themselves reasonable enough to be free of the guardianship, counsels and protection of their parents, or who think that their parents should no longer be concerned about them after having brought them into the world.

Under the pretext of glorifying God – who is too big, they say, to stoop to the level of the creature – they make God out to be a big egotist and they lower God to the level of the animals that abandon their offspring to the elements.

This belief is the result of pride; it is the idea that we are subject to a higher power, and that fact wounds our self-esteem; therefore, we should seek to free ourselves from it. While some completely deny this power, others admit its existence but sentence it to nullity.

There is an essential difference between the *independent deist* we have just described and the *providential deist.* In fact, the latter believes not only in the existence and creative power of God at the beginning of things but also in God's incessant intervention in creation. They pray to him, but they do not believe in outward worship or the dogmatism of nowadays.

## IV – THE DOGMATIC DOCTRINE

The soul, independent from matter, is created at the time of the birth of each person. It survives and retains its individuality after death; its fate at that moment is irrevocably set. It makes no subsequent progress; consequently, throughout eternity it is intellectually and morally what it was during its lifetime. The wicked, sentenced to everlasting and irredeemable punishment in hell, are left with the complete uselessness of repentance. Consequently, God refuses to grant them the possibility to repair any wrongs they committed. Good souls, on the other hand, are rewarded with seeing God and with perpetual contemplation in heaven. The cases that merit either heaven or hell for all eternity are left to the decision and judgment of fallible human beings, who are given the ability to absolve or condemn.

*Remark:* *If one objects to this last proposition and says that God has the final say, one must ask what the value of the human decision entails since it can be invalidated.*

Separation of the condemned from the elect is final and absolute. Moral help and consolation for the condemned are useless. Angels or privileged souls are created exempt from all efforts to reach perfection, etc.

*Consequences: This doctrine leaves the following grave problems unsolved:*

1. Where do the innate intellectual and moral leanings that cause people to be born good or bad, intelligent or mentally impaired come from?
2. What is the fate of children who die very young? Why do they enter the blessed life without the effort others are subjected to for long years? Why are they rewarded without having been able to do the good, or deprived of perfect bliss without having done anything evil?
3. What is the fate of the severely mentally impaired, who have no awareness of their actions?

4. Where is the justice of congenital disorders and diseases since they are not the result of any action in the present life?
5. What is the fate of primitives and all those who inevitably die in a state of moral infancy – in which they were placed by nature itself – if they are not given the chance to progress thereafter?
6. Why does God create some souls more gifted than others?
7. Why does God call prematurely those who could have become better persons if they had lived longer, since they are not allowed to progress after death?
8. Why did God create angels in a state of perfection without effort, whereas other creatures are subjected to harsh trials in which there is a greater possibility to succumb than to emerge victorious? etc.

## V – THE SPIRITIST DOCTRINE

The intelligent principle is independent of matter. The individual soul preexists and survives the physical body at death. The starting point is the same for all souls without exception; all are created simple and ignorant and are subject to continuous progress. No creatures are more privileged or gifted than others; angels are beings who have reached perfection after having passed through all the lower degrees just like all other creatures. Souls or spirits progress at different speeds because of their free will, their own efforts and their willingness. The spirit life is the normal life; corporeal life is a temporary stage in the spirit's life, during which it is momentarily clothed in a physical envelope, which it rids itself of at the time of death.

The spirit progresses both in the corporeal and the spirit state. The corporeal state is necessary for the spirit until it has reached a certain degree of perfection. While incarnate, it develops itself through the labor to which it is subjected due to its own needs, and it acquires special practical knowledge. Because one single corporeal existence is insufficient for the spirit to acquire perfection in all areas, it retakes a body as many times as it needs, each time bringing with it the progress it made in its previous corporeal existences and in the spirit world. Once it has acquired all it can on a particular world, it leaves it to go to other worlds that are intellectually and morally more advanced and less and less material; it continues to do so successively until it reaches the perfection possible for human beings.

The happy or unhappy state of spirits is inherent to their moral advancement. The punishment they suffer is the consequence of their hardness in evil; thus, if they persevere in evil, they are only punishing themselves. Nonetheless, the door of repentance is never shut, and whenever they want to they can return to the path of the good and over time make all the progress possible.

Children who die very young may be spirits who are more advanced or less so because they have already had other existences in which they practiced the good or committed wrongful acts. Death does not free them from the trials they must endure, and in due time they return to a new existence on the earth, or on more advanced worlds, according to their degree of elevation.

The soul of the severely mentally impaired is of the same nature as any other incarnate soul; their intelligence is often quite high, and they suffer from the deficiency of means they have available to them to relate to their fellow incarnate spirits, just as the speech impaired suffer from not being able to speak. They abused their intelligence in previous lives, and have willingly accepted the situation of being reduced to powerlessness in order to expiate their wrongs.

# SPIRITUAL DEATH

The issue of *spiritual death* is one of the new principles that mark the progress of Spiritist science. The manner in which it used to be presented in a particular individual theory caused it to be rejected right away because it seemed to imply the loss of the *self* at some point in time and it seemed to treat the transformations of the soul like those of matter, whose elements disaggregate to form new bodies. Blessed, perfected individuals would actually be new individuals altogether, which is unacceptable. The equity of future punishments and joys is only evident with the perpetuity of the same individuals climbing the ladder of progress and purifying themselves by means of labor and the efforts of their own will.

Such were the consequences derived *a priori* from that theory. However, we concede that it was not presented with the arrogance of a proud person bent on imposing his own beliefs. The author modestly stated that he only wanted to sow an idea in the soil of discussion, and that such an idea might give rise to a new truth. According to our eminent spirit guides, he would have sinned less regarding the main point than regarding the form, which lent itself to a false interpretation. This is what led us to seriously study the matter, and that is what we shall try to do based on the observation of the facts that point to the situation of the spirit at two crucial times: its return to the corporeal life and its reentry into the spirit life.

At the time of corporeal death, the spirit enters a state of confusion and loses consciousness of itself, such that it never witnesses the last breath of its body. This confusion dissipates little by little and the spirit regains its self-awareness, much like someone awakening from a deep sleep. Its first sensation is that of being free of its corporeal burden; then it is startled by its new environment. It is in the situation of someone who had been chloroformed for an amputation and was then taken somewhere else while asleep. Upon awakening, he feels free of the limb that made him suffer, but he frequently looks for it, shocked that he no longer possesses it. In the same way, the spirit looks for its body at first. It sees it lying close by and is astonished at being separate from it; only gradually does it perceive its new situation.

This phenomenon entails only a change of material situation. Morally, the spirit is exactly the same as it was a few hours ago and it has not gone through any noticeable change. Its faculties, ideas, tastes, inclinations and character are still the same. The transformations it may experience take place only gradually through the influences that surround it. In sum, there was death only for the body; for the spirit, there was only sleep.

In reincarnation, the process is the exact opposite.

At the moment of the conception of the body that is destined for it, the spirit is gripped by a fluidic current, which, like a cord, attracts it and pulls it toward its new dwelling. From then on, it belongs to the body, just as the body will belong to it till death. However, complete union, true possession, will take place only at birth.

From the instant of conception, confusion grips the spirit. Its ideas become cloudy; its faculties are nullified; the confusion increases as the cords tighten and becomes complete during the last stages of gestation, such that the spirit is no more a witness of the birth of its body than it is of its death. It is completely unaware of it.

From the moment the child starts breathing, the confusion begins to dissipate little by little; ideas return gradually, but under conditions different than those at the time of death.

In the act of reincarnation, the spirit's faculties are not simply numbed by a sort of momentary sleep, as happens when it returns to the spirit life. All spirits, without exception, go through a state of *latency*. The purpose of corporeal life is to develop the faculties through exercise. However, not all of them develop simultaneously because the exercise of one may harm the development of another, whereas through successive development they support one another. Thus, it is useful for some to remain at rest while others develop. This is why the spirit, in its new existence, may present itself under a completely different aspect, especially if it is more advanced than in its previous existence.

In one spirit, for instance, the musical faculty may be more active; it conceives, perceives and thus does everything necessary to develop this faculty. In another existence, it will be the turn for painting, the exact sciences, poetry, etc. While these new faculties are being exercised, the music faculty will remain latent, retaining the progress it has made. Consequently, someone who was an artist in one existence may be a scholar, a statesman or a strategist in another and display no artistic abilities whatsoever, and vice-versa.

The latent state of the faculties during reincarnation explains the forgetfulness of previous lives. At the death of the body, however, because these faculties are only in a state of sleep of small duration, the memory of the life just departed is complete as the spirit awakens in the spirit world.

The faculties that manifest naturally are related to the position that the spirit must occupy in the world and the trials it has chosen. However, it often happens that social prejudices displace it, which is why certain persons are intellectually and morally above or below the position they occupy. Due to the hindrances it presents, this repositioning is part of the spirit's trials and should cease with progress. In a socially advanced order, everything is regulated according to natural law, and persons who are only capable of making shoes are not called by birthright to govern peoples.

Let us go back to the child. Prior to birth, while all its faculties are in a latent state, the spirit has no awareness of itself. At the moment of birth, the faculties it must develop do not blossom all of a sudden; their development accompanies the organs that will serve for their manifestations. By their inner activity, they put into motion the corresponding organ, like the sprouting shoot triggers the development of the bark. Consequently, in the early stages of infancy, the spirit does not enjoy the fullness of any of its faculties, either as an incarnate or as a spirit. It is truly a child, just like the body to which it is attached. However, it does not find itself painfully restrained in an imperfect body; otherwise, God would have made incarnation a torment for all spirits whether good or bad. Such is not the case with severely mentally impaired persons, however. Because the organs have not developed in step with the faculties, the spirit ends up in the situation of someone bound by ropes that deprive it of freedom of movement. That is why one may evoke the spirit of a mentally impaired person and receive sensible answers, whereas the spirit of an infant or one that has not yet been born is incapable of responding.

All faculties, all aptitudes lie in seed form within the spirit at its creation. They are in a rudimentary state like all the organs in the first outline of the unformed fetus, like all the parts of a tree within the seed. Primitives who later become civilized persons thus possess within them the seeds that someday will make them a scholar, a great artist or a great philosopher.

As these seeds reach maturity, Providence gives them *for earthly life* a body suitable to their new aptitudes. Hence, the brain of a European is more completely organized and equipped with a larger number of keys than the brain of a primitive. *For the spirit life,* Providence gives them a fluidic body, or perispirit, which is subtler and more impressionable for new sensations. As the spirit evolves, nature provides it with the instruments it needs.

As for disorganization, the disaggregation of the parts and the dispersal of the elements, there is no death except for the material envelope and the fluidic envelope; the soul or spirit does not die in order to progress; otherwise, it would lose its individuality, which would be the equivalent of nothingness. In the sense of transformation, of regeneration, one could say that the spirit dies with each incarnation in order to be resuscitated with new attributes without ceasing to be itself; for example, a peasant enriches himself and becomes a wealthy landowner: he exchanges his hut for a palace and his peasant's shirt for an embroidered coat. Everything is changed concerning his habits, his tastes, his language – even his character. In sum, the peasant is dead, he has buried the homespun clothing to be reborn a man of society, yet it is always the same individual, albeit transformed.

Therefore, each corporeal existence is for the spirit an opportunity to progress. Upon returning to the spirit world, it brings new ideas with it; its moral horizon has broadened; its perceptions are more acute, more refined; it sees and understands what it did not see or understand previously. Its sight, which at first did not go beyond its last existence, grasps successively its past lives, like a person who climbs a mountain and for whom the fog dissipates, allowing him or her to successively grasp a wider view of the horizon.

With each new stopover in the errant state[29], new wonders of the invisible world unwind before its eyes, because at each stopover a veil is rent. At the same time, its fluidic envelope is purified; it becomes lighter, more radiant, and later, it will become resplendent. It is almost a new spirit; it is the peasant refined and transformed. The old spirit is dead, and yet it is always the same spirit.

This is what we believe is to be understood by spiritual death.

---

29 Existence in the spirit world. – Tr.

# THE FUTURE LIFE

The future life is no longer a problem. It is a fact proven by reason and demonstration to nearly all people; its deniers comprise an insignificant minority in spite of all the noise they have endeavored to make. Thus, it is not its reality that we intend to demonstrate here – that would be repeating ourselves without adding anything to the general conviction. With the principle accepted as the premise, what we propose to do is examine its influence on the social order and morality according to the way in which it is envisioned.

The consequences concerning the opposite principle, that is, nihilism, are also too well-known and understood for it to be necessary to delve into them again. We will only say that if it were demonstrated that the future life does not exist, the present life would have no other purpose except maintaining a body that tomorrow, or in an hour, may cease to exist, and everything, in that case, would be over forever. The logical consequence of such a condition for humankind would be the concentration of all thoughts on increasing material pleasures without concern for harming others; so why deprive ourselves or impose sacrifices? What would be the need to compel ourselves to evolve, to correct our defects? Furthermore, remorse and repentance would be completely useless because there would be nothing to expect. In sum, it would be the consecration of selfishness and of the maxim: *The world belongs to the strongest and the most cunning.* Without the future life, morality is nothing more than a constraint, a conventional code imposed arbitrarily with no roots in the heart. A society founded on such a belief would have no other bond than force, and would quickly fall into dissolution.

One cannot deny the fact that among the deniers of the future life there are honest persons incapable of knowingly harming others, and who are susceptible to great devotion! First, we must point out the fact that, among many disbelievers, the denial of the future is more bragging and boasting, and the pride of coming across as a strong character, than the result of absolute conviction. In the depths of their being, there is a nagging doubt, and that is why they try to stifle it. However, it is not without mental reservation that they proclaim the dreadful *nothingness* that deprives them of the fruit of all their intellectual endeavors and forever wrecks the dearest affections. More than one of those who shout the loudest are the first to tremble before the idea of the unknown; moreover, when the fatal moment approaches for them to enter that unknown, very few of them sleep their last sleep firmly convinced that they will not awaken somewhere else, because nature never abdicates its rights.

Hence, we can say that disbelief is highly relative for a large number of such persons; their reason is not satisfied with dogmas or religious beliefs, and thus not having found anything to fill the void within them, they have concluded that there is only nothingness, and have developed theories to justify their denial. Consequently, they are disbelievers for lack of something better. Absolute disbelievers are very rare, if they exist at all.

A latent and unconscious intuition of the future could, therefore, hold back a certain number from the cliff of evil; there are many examples, even on the part of the most hardened, evidencing this secret sentiment that dominates them without their knowledge.

It must also be added that whatever the degree of disbelief, persons of a certain social condition are restrained by human respect. Their position forces them to hold to a line of highly reserved conduct; what they fear more than anything else is disgrace and contempt, which could cause them to lose the world's consideration due to the fall from the rank they occupy, and that would be something that would deprive them of the pleasures they seek there. If they do not yet have the core of virtue, at least they have the varnish of it. But as for those who have no reason to be concerned about the opinion of others, who scorn what others might say – and they comprise the majority – what keeps them from the overflowing of their base passions and coarse appetites? On what should they base the theory of good and evil, the need to reform their bad inclinations, the duty to respect others' possessions, if they themselves possess nothing? What could encourage honor in persons who are persuaded that they are nothing more than animals? The law – we say – is there to restrain them. But the law is not a code of morality that touches the heart; it is a force they subject themselves to and elude if they can. If they fall under its blows, they attribute it to bad luck or ineptitude, which they seek to remedy the first chance they get.

Those who claim that disbelievers deserve more merit for doing the good without the hope of recompense in a future life they do not believe in rest such claim on an equally ill-founded sophism. Believers, too, say that doing good with an eye on any recompense one might garner is less meritorious. They go even further, persuaded that, depending on the intent that motivates it, merit could be completely annulled.

The prospect of the future life does not exclude disinterestedness in good deeds, because the happiness it provides is, above all, dependent on the degree of moral advancement. In this aspect, the prideful and the ambitious are among the least endowed. But disbelievers who practice the good: are they as disinterested as they say they are? If they expect nothing in the other world, do they expect nothing from this one either? Does vanity really have nothing to do with it? Are they really insensitive to the approval of others? That would be a rare degree of perfection, and we do not believe that there are many who would be led to it by the sole worship of material things.

A more serious objection is this: If belief in the future life is a moralizing factor, then why is humankind, which has been preached to about it ever since its appearance on the earth, so evil?

First of all, who is to say that humankind would not be even worse without it? There is no doubt that it would be, considering the unavoidable results of the popularization of nihilism. On the contrary, in observing the different gradations of humankind from primitivism to civilization, can we not see the progress of intellectual and moral advancement, the refinement of customs and a more rational idea of the future life? This idea, however, is still very imperfect and cannot yet exert the influence that it necessarily will as it becomes better understood, and as we acquire more exact notions about the future that is reserved for us.

No matter how firm their belief in immortality may be, people are concerned only about their soul from a mystical point of view. The future life, defined with an extreme lack of clarity, impresses them only vaguely. It is no more than an objective that is lost in the distance; it is not a means, because their fate is irrevocably set and no aspect of it has been presented to them as being progressive. This leads to the conclusion that we will be for eternity what we are when we depart this earth. Moreover, the picture of the future life and the determining conditions for happiness or unhappiness that we experience in it are far from fully satisfying one's reason, especially in a time of examination such as ours. Furthermore, it is not connected very directly with earthly life; there is no solidarity between the two, but rather an abyss, such that those who concern themselves principally with one almost always lose sight of the other.

Under the domain of blind faith, this abstract belief was sufficient for the inspirations of humankind when it allowed itself to be led; nowadays, in an age of free examination, people want to lead themselves, to see with their own eyes and understand. Those vague notions of the future life are not in tandem with the new ideas, and they no longer meet the needs created by progress. With the development of ideas, everything must progress around humankind because everything is connected, everything is reciprocal in nature: sciences, beliefs, worship forms, legislation, and means of acting. Forward progress is irresistible because it is the law of existence. Those who lag behind, beneath the societal level, are set aside like garments that no longer fit, and they are finally swept away by the mounting tide.

The same applies to the childish ideas about the future life that satisfied our ancestors. To continue to impose such ideas nowadays would be to encourage disbelief. In order to be accepted by everyone's opinion and to exert its moralizing action, the future life must be presented as something positive, somewhat tangible, capable of being scrutinized, and satisfying to reason, without leaving anything in the dark. It was at the moment when the insufficiency of notions about the future opened the door to doubt and disbelief that new means of investigation were given to humankind to penetrate the mystery, enabling it to comprehend the future life in its reality, its positivism and its close relationship with corporeal life.

Why do people, in general, care so little about the future life? Is it a reality after all, since thousands of men and women depart for that unknown destiny every day? Since each one of us must depart when our turn comes, and since the hour for our departure may sound at any moment, it would seem natural for all of us to be concerned about what happens next. But why is that not the case? Precisely because the destination is unknown, and because, until now, there has been no way to know it. Inexorable science has dislodged it from the places to which it used to be circumscribed. It is nearby? Far-off? Is it lost in the infinite? The philosophies of the past had no answer, because they themselves did not understand it. So they said, "It will be what it will be"; hence the indifference.

We are taught that we will be either happy or unhappy according to whether we have lived well or badly. But that is so vague! What constitutes that happiness or unhappiness? The picture that is drawn for us about one or the other is so much in disaccord with our idea about God's justice, so full of contradictions, incongruences, and radical impossibilities that we are involuntarily seized by doubt, if not complete disbelief. Furthermore, those who are mistaken regarding the places assigned for future habitation may also have been led to err regarding the conditions assigned for happiness and suffering. After all, what will we actually be like in that other world? Will we be concrete or abstract beings? Will we have a form, an appearance? If there will be nothing physical about us, how can we experience physical suffering? If the blissful have nothing to do, then instead of being a reward, eternal idleness will be a punishment, unless we believe in the nirvana of Buddhism, which is no more enviable than idleness.

Humankind is not concerned about the future life unless it sees in it a clearly defined purpose, a logical situation that corresponds to its aspirations, which solves all its present problems and in which it finds nothing that reason cannot accept. If humankind is concerned about tomorrow, it is because life tomorrow is closely connected with life today; they are reciprocal. People know that their situation tomorrow will depend on what they do today, and that what they do tomorrow will determine their situation the day after tomorrow, and so on.

The same should apply to the future life when it is no longer lost in the nebulousness of abstraction but is a palpable actuality, the necessary complement to the present life and *one of the phases* of life in general, just as days are phases of the corporeal life. When they can see that the present impacts the future by necessity, and especially when they understand that *the future impacts the present;* when, in sum, they can see that the past, present and future are linked together through an inexorable necessity, just as yesterday, today and tomorrow in the present life, then oh! their ideas will change completely because they will see the future life not only as an end but also as a means; not as a distant effect but a present one. Then such belief will unavoidably exert a preponderant action, as a fully natural consequence, on the social state and the moralization of humankind.

Such is the point of view from which Spiritism enables us to consider the future life.

# QUESTIONS AND PROBLEMS

## Collective Expiations

**Question:** *Spiritism perfectly explains the cause of individual suffering as being the immediate consequence of wrongs committed in the present existence or as expiation for the past. But since each person is only responsible for his or her own wrongs, that does not satisfactorily explain the collective misfortunes that strike groups of individuals: frequently an entire family, city, nation or race, including the good and the bad, the innocent and the guilty.*

**Answer:** *All the laws that govern the universe, whether physical or moral, material or mental, have been discovered, studied and comprehended, starting with the study of the individuality and the family and proceeding to that of the collectivity, thus gradually generalizing the laws and demonstrating the universality of the results.*

Today, the same occurs with respect to the laws that the study of Spiritism is making known to you. Without fear of erring, one can take the laws that govern the individual and apply them to the family, nation, races, all the inhabitants of the many worlds, and those who form collective individualities. There are wrongs committed by the individual, the family and the nation, and each wrong, whatever it may be, is expiated according to the same law. Cruel persons expiate the wrongs they inflicted on their victims, whether upon meeting them in the spirit world or in several subsequent existences until they have righted all the evil they did to them. The same applies to crimes committed by a certain number of persons together;

they expiate their wrongs together, but this does not nullify the simultaneous expiation of individual wrongs.

Regarding every person, there are three characters: that of the individual (the being per se), that of the member of the family, and lastly, that of the citizen. And regarding each of these three aspects, the person may be either criminal or virtuous, that is, virtuous as the head of the family, but criminal as a citizen, and vice-versa. Hence the special situations the person experiences in subsequent existences.

Barring exceptions, one can therefore accept as a general rule that all those who in one existence are brought together for a common purpose have already lived together to work with the same objective in mind, and that they will be brought together again in the future until they have achieved that purpose, that is, until they have expiated the past or have completed their mission.

Thanks to Spiritism, you can now understand the justice of trials that do not result from actions during the present life, because you realize that they are the quittance for debts from the past. Why wouldn't the same apply regarding collective trials? You say that widespread misfortunes strike both the innocent and the guilty, but don't you know that the innocent of today may have been the guilty of yesterday? Whether they are struck individually or collectively, it is what they deserve. Moreover, as we have stated, there are wrongs of both the individual and of the citizen; expiating some wrongs does not exempt the individual from expiating others, for every debt must be paid to the last cent. The virtues of private life are different than the virtues of public life. One person who is an excellent citizen may be a terrible father; another who is a good father and who is upright and honest at his job may be a bad citizen, stoking the fire of discord, oppressing the weak, and drenching his hands in corruption. Collective wrongs are those that are expiated collectively by the individuals who contributed to them, who meet up again to suffer together the punishment of talion or to have the opportunity to right the wrong they committed by helping and assisting those whom they mistreated in the past. Thus, what is incomprehensible and inconceivable in light of God's justice without the preexistence of the soul becomes clear and logical by understanding that law.

Solidarity, which is the true social bond, does not apply therefore only to the present. It extends to the past and the future because the same persons have met before, meet now, and will meet again in the future to climb the ladder of progress together while mutually helping each other. This is what Spiritism makes comprehensible through the equitable law of reincarnation and the continuity of relationships involving the same persons.

Clelie Duplantier

**Remark:** *Even though this communication encompasses the known principles of responsibility for the past and the continuity of relationships among spirits, it contains an idea that is somewhat new and of great importance. The distinction it establishes between responsibility for individual or collective wrongs, for those of private or public life, explains certain events that are not yet understood very well and shows very precisely the interdependence that connects individuals and generations.*

Thus, often one is reborn into the same family, or at least members of the same family are reborn together to make up a new family in a different social position, in order to strengthen the bonds of their affection or to right reciprocal wrongs. For considerations of a more general order, we are often reborn into the same environment, nation and race, whether out of sympathy or whether to continue, with the elements already established, the endeavors we had begun, thus perfecting ourselves and pursuing works started before and whose completion was not allowed due to the brevity of life or circumstances. This reincarnation into the same environment is the determining cause of the distinct character of peoples and races. Although continuing to evolve, individuals retain the original nuance until progress has transformed them completely.

Consequently, the French of today are those of the last century, the Middle Ages, and the times of the Druids. They are the enforcers and the victims of feudalism. Those who have subjected other peoples and those who have worked for their emancipation meet again in transformed France, where some expiate in humiliation their race pride, and where others enjoy the fruit of their labors. When one remembers all the crimes of those times when the lives of individuals and the honor of families were not taken into account; when fanaticism employed burnings at the stake in honor of the divinity; when one recalls all the abuses of power, all the injustices that were committed in utter disregard for the most sacred rights, who could be sure of not having participated to some degree in them and be astonished at witnessing large and dreadful collective expiations?

Such social turmoil, however, always results in improvement; spirits are enlightened by the experience; the misfortune is the stimulus that drives them to look for its remedy; they reflect and make new resolutions in the errant state, and when they return, they do things in a better way. This is how progress is accomplished from generation to generation.

One cannot doubt the fact that there are guilty families, cities, nations and races, because, dominated by the instincts of pride, selfishness, ambition and greed, they walk the path of error and do collectively what an individual does by him or herself. One family grows wealthy at another's expense; one nation subjugates another, leading it to desolation and ruin; one race endeavors to wipe out another. This is why the punishment of talion falls on families, peoples and races.

"Whoever kills with the sword shall die by the sword," said Christ, words that may be translated as: Those who spill blood will have their own blood spilt; those who set fire to the belongings of others will see fire set to their own belongings; those who plunder will be plundered; those who enslave and mistreat the weak will be enslaved and mistreated in turn, whether as an individual, a nation or a race, because the members of a collective individuality are in solidarity regarding both the good and the bad they practiced in common.

While Spiritism broadens the field of solidarity, materialism restricts it to the miniscule proportions of a single, ephemeral existence, rendering solidarity a baseless social responsibility with no other sanction except the good will and personal interest of the moment. It is merely a theory, a philosophical maxim that no one practices. For Spiritism, solidarity is a fact based on a universal law of nature, connecting all the individuals of the past, present and future, and no one can escape its consequences. Everyone can understand this no matter how uneducated they are.

When everyone understands Spiritism, they will also understand true solidarity, and consequently, true fraternity. Solidarity and fraternity will no longer be mere circumstantial duties that everyone obeys more out of self-interest than the interests of others. The reign of solidarity and fraternity will by necessity be the reign of justice for all, and justice will be the reign of peace and harmony among individuals, families, peoples and races. Will this reign be implemented some day? To doubt it would be to deny progress. If we compare today's society in civilized nations with society in the Middle Ages, the difference is obviously enormous. If people have advanced thus far, why would they stop? Looking at the progress they have made after only one century, one can imagine what they will do over the next.

Social upheavals are the insurgencies of incarnate spirits against the evils that constrain them, an indication of their longing for that kingdom of justice for which they yearn without clearly perceiving what they want and the means of reaching it. This is why they keep moving about, hustling and bustling, knocking things down right and left, creating theories, proposing more or less utopian remedies and committing thousands of injustices supposedly in the spirit of justice, in the hopes that something will result from the turmoil. Later, they will better define their aspirations, and the way to realize them will become clearer.

Whoever probes the principles of philosophical Spiritism and considers the horizons it opens up, the ideas it inspires and the sentiments it develops, will have no doubts about the preponderant role it will play in the regeneration of humanity, because it leads precisely and decisively to the objective to which humankind aspires: the reign of justice through the extinction of the abuses that have made progress difficult, and also through the moralization of the masses. If those who dream about the preservation of the past did not judge it as such, they would not go about it so wholeheartedly; they would let it die in peace, just like so many other utopias. This fact alone should lead certain scoffers to reflect and make them realize that perhaps there is something more serious about Spiritism than they had thought. But there are people who laugh at everything; they would laugh at God if they were to actually see God while on the earth. Moreover, there are also those who are afraid of seeing the soul before them, the soul that they so stubbornly deny.

Whatever may be the influence that Spiritism someday exerts on the future of societies, that does not mean it will substitute one autocracy for another, nor that it will impose laws; first, since it proclaims the absolute right to freedom of conscience and free examination in the matters of faith; then, as a belief system itself, it wants to be freely accepted through conviction and not through coercion. By its very nature it cannot, nor should it, exert any pressure; proscribing blind faith, it wants to be comprehended. For Spiritism, there are no mysteries but rather a rational faith based on facts, and which seeks the light. It does not repudiate the discoveries of science, given that science is the collection of the Laws of Nature; and since these laws come from God, to repudiate science would be to repudiate the work of God.

Second, since Spiritism's action lies in its moralizing power, it cannot assume any autocratic form, because it would then be doing what it condemns. Its influence will be mostly felt through the modifications it brings to ideas, opinions, people's character, their customs and their social relations. And this influence will be all the greater because it will not have been imposed. As a powerful philosophy, Spiritism will only fail in this age of reason if it becomes a temporal power. Thus, Spiritism per se will not regenerate the world's social institutions – people will, under the reign of the ideas of justice, charity, fraternity, and solidarity, which are better understood thanks to Spiritism.

Essentially positive in its beliefs, Spiritism rejects all mysticism as long as one does not apply this word – as do those who do not believe in anything at all – to all spiritualist ideas, the belief in God, the soul, and the future life. Of course, Spiritism compels people to take a serious look at the spirit life because that is the normal life and that is where they must fulfill their destiny, since earthly life is only transitory and temporary. Through the proofs it gives regarding the spirit life, it teaches people to ascribe only a relative importance to the things of this world, thus giving them the strength and courage to patiently endure the vicissitudes of earthly life. It teaches them that when they die they will not leave this world behind forever; that they may return to it in order to perfect their intellectual and moral education, unless they are already sufficiently advanced to merit going to a better world; that the endeavors and progress they accomplish personally or contribute to on the earth will be advantageous for them, improving their condition in the future. It shows them that they have a vested interest in not neglecting it. If they find returning to the earth repulsive, since they have free will, it is up to them to do what is necessary to go somewhere else! But let them not be mistaken about the conditions required for meriting their change of residence! It is not with the aid of some formulas in words or actions that they will obtain it, but with a serious and radical reform of their imperfections;

it will be through self-change and ridding themselves of their lower passions by acquiring new qualities, by teaching everyone, with their example, the line of conduct that will lead all people together towards happiness through fraternity, tolerance and love.

Humankind is composed of personalities that constitute individual existences and of generations that constitute collective existences. Both advance on the path of progress through various phases of trials – individual for persons, collective for generations. Just as each existence is a step forward for an incarnate spirit, each generation marks a period of progress for the whole. It is this progress of the whole that is uncontainable and pulls the masses along with it, at the same time modifying and transforming into an instrument of regeneration the errors and prejudices of a past destined to disappear. Thus, because generations are composed of individuals that have already lived during previous generations, it follows that the progress of generations is the result of the progress of individuals.

One might ask, however: Who can demonstrate the connection between today's generation and those that preceded it or those that will come after it? For example, how can it be proven that I lived during the Middle Ages and that I will return to take part in the events of the future?

The principle of the plurality of existences has been sufficiently demonstrated in *Revue Spirite* and the fundamental works of Spiritism, so we will not dwell on the subject. Experience and observation of the incidents of everyday life are swarming with physical proofs of an almost mathematical demonstration. We will thus invite thinkers to only consider the moral proofs that result from reasoning and induction.

Is it absolutely necessary to see something in order to believe in it? By observing the effects, can we not acquire the material certainty of the cause?

Apart from experimentation, the only legitimate course open to this investigation consists in following the effect back to its cause. Justice offers us a noteworthy example of this principle when it endeavors to uncover the *pieces of evidence* about how a crime was committed, and the *intent* that contributes to the culpability of the wrongdoer. Even if the wrongdoer was not caught in the act, he or she may be found guilty because of the evidence.

Science, which intends to progress only through experimentation, affirms principles every day that are nothing but inductions of causes of which it had seen only the effects. For example, in geology one determines the age of mountains. But did geologists witness their rising? Did they witness the formation of the sedimentary layers that determines their age?

Astronomical, physical and chemical knowledge enables the weight of the planets, their orbits, volumes, speed and the nature of the elements that compose them to be determined; nonetheless, scientists have not performed any direct experiments on them, and it is through analogy and induction that we owe so many beautiful and invaluable discoveries.

Based on the testimony of their senses, early humans believed that the sun orbited around the earth; however, such testimony was mistaken and reason has prevailed.

The same would apply to the principles advocated by Spiritism, if one would be willing to study them without prejudice. Humankind would then truly and quickly enter an age of progress and regeneration because individuals would no longer feel caught between two abysses – the unknown past and the uncertain future – and they would work fervently to perfect and increase the elements of the happiness that comes from their own efforts. They would realize that the position they occupy in the world is not by chance, and that in the future and under better conditions, they will enjoy the fruits of their labors and industriousness. Lastly, Spiritism would teach them that, if wrongs committed collectively are expiated collectively, progress communally reached is also a collective accomplishment; based on this principle, race, family and individual dissentions will disappear, and humankind, free of the characteristics of infancy, will advance rapidly and vigorously toward the conquest of its true destiny.

# SELFISHNESS AND PRIDE

## Their Causes, Effects and the Means of Eradicating Them

It is well known that most of life's miseries are the result of human selfishness. Since all think of themselves before thinking of others and seek first of all to satisfy their own desires, they naturally provide themselves this satisfaction at whatever cost, unscrupulously sacrificing the interests of others in the most insignificant as well as the most significant moral or material matters. This results in all social antagonisms, all struggles, all conflicts and all miseries, since everyone wants to despoil their neighbor.

Selfishness finds its source in pride. Exalting the personality leads people to consider themselves better than others; considering their rights to be superior, they are offended by anything which, in their opinion, is an affront to such rights. The importance they attribute to themselves out of pride naturally renders them selfish.

Selfishness and pride arise from a natural sentiment: the self-preservation instinct. All instincts have their reason to be and their usefulness since God could do nothing useless. God did not create evil; human beings caused it by abusing the divine gifts in virtue of their free will. This sentiment, if contained within proper limits, is good per se. It is its amplification that renders it evil and pernicious. The same applies to all the passions that so often lead people away from their providential objective. God did not create people selfish and prideful; God created them simple and ignorant;

people made themselves selfish and prideful by exaggerating the instinct that God gave them for their self-preservation.

Human beings cannot be happy if they do not live in peace, that is, if they are not animated by a sentiment of benevolence, indulgence and mutual tolerance; in other words, while they seek to crush one another. Charity and fraternity sum up all conditions and social duties; however, they presuppose selflessness. We know that selflessness is incompatible with selfishness and pride; therefore, true fraternity is impossible when these two vices exist, and neither represent liberty and equality, because the selfish and proud want everything for themselves. They will always be the gnawing worms of all progressive institutions, and as long as they dominate, the most generous and wisely conceived social systems will fall to their blows. Of course, it is wonderful to proclaim the kingdom of fraternity, but how can this be done if there is a destructive cause? That would be building on unwholesome soil. In such a kingdom, if one desires people to fare well, it is not enough to send them doctors, because doctors will die like everyone else; one must destroy the causes of unhealthiness. If one desires that they live like brothers and sisters, it is not enough to given them lessons on morality; it is necessary to destroy the causes of antagonism, to attack the root of the evil: pride and selfishness. That is where the open sore lies; that is where all attention needs to be focused by those who seriously desire the good of humankind. As long as such an obstacle persists, they will see all their efforts paralyzed, not only by the resistance of inertia, but by an active force that will incessantly endeavor to destroy their work, since every grand, generous and emancipating idea ruins personal pretense.

One may say that it is impossible to destroy pride and selfishness, because they are vices inherent to the human species. If that were the case, there could be no moral progress at all; however, if one considers humankind down through history, one cannot deny that there has been obvious progress. Thus, if humankind has progressed, it can progress further still. Moreover, do we not find persons lacking pride and selfishness? Do we not see naturally generous individuals, in whom the sentiments of humility, devotion, self-denial and love for one's neighbor seem inborn? Of course, their number is smaller than that of the selfish; otherwise, the latter would not lay down the law. Nevertheless, there are more of the former than one might think, and if there seems to be so few of them, it is because pride puts itself in more conspicuous positions, whereas modest virtue remains in obscurity. Hence, if selfishness and pride were necessary conditions for humankind, just as nourishment is necessary for life, there would be no exceptions. The essential point is, therefore, for the exception to become the rule, and for that to happen, the causes that produce and encourage evil have to be destroyed before anything else.

Of such causes, the main one is obviously the result of the wrong idea people have with regards to their nature, their past and their future. Not knowing where they came from, they believe themselves to be more than they are, and not knowing where they are going, they focus all their thoughts on earthly life, and they want it to be as pleasant as possible. They long for every satisfaction, for every delight, and that is why they unscrupulously step on their neighbors if they become an obstacle. But for that to happen, they have to dominate – equality would give others rights that they want only for themselves; fraternity would impose sacrifices in detriment to their well-being; and they want liberty only for themselves and will only grant it to others if it does not put their own prerogatives at risk. Everyone wanting the same thing results in perpetual conflicts that lead them to pay dearly for the few pleasures they do acquire.

If people would acknowledge the future life, their way of seeing things would change completely, similar to individuals who have to live in a bad location but for a little while, knowing that upon leaving, they will live in a wonderful place for the rest of their days.

The importance of the present life, so sad, so short, so ephemeral, vanishes before the splendor of the infinite future that unfolds to their view. The natural and logical consequence of this certainty is to sacrifice a fleeting present for a lasting future, whereas before they sacrificed everything for the present. With the future life as their objective, having a little more or a little less in this one matters little to them. Worldly interests become accessories instead of the main thing, and they labor in the present with a view to mitigating their situation in the future, especially because they know the conditions that will make them happy.

People can hinder worldly interests; they must avoid them, yet they become selfish by necessity. However, if they would glance upward at a happiness that no one can impede, they would not be interested in oppressing others; selfishness would lose its purpose. But even so, the stimulus of pride will always remain.

The cause of pride lies in people's belief in their own individual superiority; furthermore, it is there that the influence of the concentration of their thoughts on the earthly life is felt. For persons who see nothing before, behind or above them, the sentiment of individuality is predominant and pride has no counterweight.

Disbelief not only has no means for combating pride, it encourages it and gives it a reason for being by denying the existence of a power superior to humanity. Disbelievers believe only in themselves, so of course they are prideful; so much so that they see the blows that strike them as nothing but an accident from which to recover, whereas those who have faith see the hand of God and submit. Believing in God and the future life is, consequently, the first condition for mitigating pride, but it is not enough. In addition to the future, one must look to the past to get a precise idea of the present.

For prideful persons to drop their belief in their own superiority, they must be shown that they are no better than others and that others are as important as they themselves are; that equality is a fact and not only a fine philosophical theory; that such truths result from the preexistence of the soul and reincarnation.

Without the preexistence of the soul, people are led to believe that God – if they believe there is one – has conferred exceptional advantages on them. If they do not believe in God, they give thanks to chance and their own merit. Initiating them into the previous life of the soul, preexistence teaches them to distinguish the transitory life of the physical body from the never-ending life of the spirit. They realize that all souls leave the Creator's hands as equals; that all have the same departure point and that all will reach the same goal in a shorter or longer amount of time, depending on their efforts; that they have not come to be who they are except after having lengthily and painfully drifted along like everyone else in the lower degrees of evolution; that between the most advanced and the most un-advanced, it is only a matter of time; that advantages at birth are purely corporeal and independent of the spirit; that in another existence the humble commoner may have been a monarch, and that the most powerful monarch may have been a commoner.

Those who take only the life of the physical body into account see only the social inequalities of the moment because these impress them the most; however, if they would look at the whole life of the spirit and its past and future from its departure point until the present, such inequalities would disappear and they would realize that God has not granted any advantages to some to the detriment of others; that God has given an equal share to everyone and has not smoothed the way for some more than for others; that those who appear to be less advanced than others can take the lead if they work harder to perfect themselves. Lastly, they would realize that, since none can arrive except through their own efforts, the principle of *equality* is a principle of justice and a law of nature, before which the pride of privilege topples over.

By showing that spirits can be born into different social conditions, whether for expiation or for trial, reincarnation teaches that those whom we treat with disdain may be someone who used to be our superior or our equal, a friend or a family member in another existence. If people knew this, they would treat such individuals with consideration, but in that case there would be no merit; on the other hand, if they knew that their current friend used to be their enemy, servant or *slave,* they would spurn that person. However, God did not will it to be like that, which is why a veil is cast over the past. Consequently, people are led to see everyone as their brothers, sisters and equals, resulting in a natural basis for *fraternity;* knowing that they could be treated in the same way that they used to treat others, *charity* becomes a duty and a necessity founded on nature itself.

Jesus established the principle of charity, equality and fraternity as an express condition for salvation; however, it was reserved for the third manifestation of God's will, i.e. for Spiritism, through the knowledge it gives of the spirit life, the new horizons it discloses and the laws it reveals, to sanction this principle by showing that it does not imply a mere moral doctrine but a law of nature, and that it is in people's best interests to practice it. People will practice it when they stop looking at the present as the beginning and the end and understand the cohesion that exists between the present, the past and the future. In the immense field of the infinity that Spiritism enables them to glimpse, their personal importance is annulled; they understand that by themselves they are nothing and can do nothing; that everyone needs everyone else and no one is better than anyone else: a double blow to their pride and selfishness.

However, for that they need faith; otherwise, they will inevitably remain in the rut of the present; not blind faith, which flees from the light, restrains ideas and thus feeds selfishness, but intelligent, rational faith, which seeks the light and not the darkness, and which fearlessly rends the veil of the mysteries and broadens the horizon. It is this faith, the essential element of all progress, that Spiritism brings them; a robust faith because it is based on experience and facts, because it furnishes palpable proofs of the immortality of the soul and shows people where they have come from, where they are going and why they are here; and lastly, because it strengthens their uncertain ideas about their past and future. Once they have entered this pathway, selfishness and pride will no longer stimulate them and will disappear little by little for lack of objective and sustenance, and all social relations will change under the influx of rightly understood charity and fraternity.

Will this happen abruptly? No. That would not be possible, since nothing is abrupt in nature. Health never returns suddenly to a sick person; between sickness and health there is always convalescence. Therefore, people cannot instantly change their point of view and turn their eyes to heaven instead of earth; the infinite confuses and overwhelms them. They need time to assimilate new ideas. Spiritism, without a doubt, is the most powerful moralizing element there is; it weakens selfishness and pride at their bases, and by providing a point of support for morality, it has worked miracles of conversion. It may be true that they were only individual and frequently partial healings, but what it has done with respect to individuals is a guarantee as to what it will do someday with respect to the masses. It cannot uproot the harmful weeds all at once. It provides faith, and faith is the good seed; but the seed needs time to germinate and to produce fruit, and this is why all Spiritists are not yet perfect. Spiritism seizes people in the middle of life, in the fire of their passions, and in the fullness of their prejudices; and if in such circumstances it works wonders, what will it do when it seizes them at birth, unblemished by any noxious impressions; when they nurse on the milk of charity and fraternity that lulls them to sleep; when, finally, an entire generation is educated and nourished with ideas that their developed reason strengthens rather than falsifies? Under the domain of such ideas, which will render faith common for everyone, progress will no longer be hindered by selfishness and pride; institutions will reform themselves and humankind will advance rapidly toward the destiny promised to it on earth as it waits for that of heaven.

# LIBERTY, EQUALITY, FRATERNITY

*Liberty, equality, fraternity.* By themselves, these three words represent the plan for an entire social order that would accomplish humankind's most complete progress if the principle they stand for were fully applied. Let us take a look at the obstacles that, in the state of today's society, might oppose it, and alongside the ill, let us seek the remedy.

Fraternity, narrowly defined, sums up all of people's duties toward one another; it means devotion, self-denial, tolerance, benevolence and indulgence. It is evangelical charity par excellence, and the application of the maxim: "Do unto others as you would have them do unto you." The opposite is *selfishness.* Fraternity says: "One for all and all for one." Selfishness says: "Every man for himself." Since these two qualities are opposites, it is as impossible for a selfish person to act fraternally toward others as it is for a miser to be generous, or a short person to grow into a tall one. Since selfishness is the predominant plague of society, as long as it reigns supreme the reign of true fraternity will be impossible. Everyone wants to use fraternity to their own advantage, but they do not want to practice it on behalf of others. If they do, it is only after they are sure they will not lose anything because of it.

Considered from the point of view of its role in accomplishing social happiness, fraternity is of first importance, it is the foundation. Without it there can be neither serious equality nor liberty. Equality proceeds from fraternity, and liberty is the result of both.

Let us imagine a society of highly selfless, good and benevolent people who live together fraternally without any of them having any privileges or exceptional rights, a fact which without fraternity would be impossible. Treating someone as a brother or sister is to treat that person as an equal; it means wanting for that person what one would want for oneself. In a culture of brothers and sisters, equality will be the consequence of their sentiments and the way they deal with one another, and it will be established through the force of things. But what is the enemy of equality? Pride: pride, which wants to control and dominate everywhere; pride, which lives on privileges and exceptions. It may actually tolerate social equality, but it will never sanction it and will destroy it the first chance it gets. Thus, because pride is one of the plagues of society, as long as it is not destroyed, it will erect a barrier to true equality.

As we have stated, liberty is the child of fraternity and equality. We mean legal liberty and not natural liberty, which is by right indefeasible for every human being, from the primitive to the civilized person. Living as brothers and sisters with equal rights animated by a sentiment of mutual benevolence, people will practice justice toward one another and not try to harm one another; consequently, they will not have to fear one another. Liberty will not entail any peril, because no one would even think about abusing it to the harm of others. But how could selfishness, which wants everything for itself, and pride, which always wants to dominate, ever shake hands with liberty, which wants to dethrone both of them? Selfishness and pride are thus the enemies of liberty, as well as of equality and fraternity.

Liberty presupposes mutual trust. There can be no trust among people motivated by the exclusivist sentiment of the personality. Unable to satisfy themselves except at others' expense, they are constantly on their guard against one another. Constantly in fear of losing what they believe to be their rights, domination is the condition of their existence, which is why they will continually lay traps for liberty and will suffocate it for as long as they can.

As we have stated, these three principles are interconnected and mutually support each other; without all three of them together, the social edifice cannot be complete. Fraternity cannot be practiced in all its purity if the other two are left out, since without equality and liberty there can be no true fraternity. Liberty without fraternity gives free rein to all the lower passions, which then have nothing to hold them back. With fraternity, people do not make ill use of their liberty – there is order; without fraternity, they use liberty to indulge in all their turpitudes – there is anarchy and licentiousness. This is why freer nations feel obligated to put restrictions on liberty. Equality without fraternity leads to the same result, since equality entails liberty. Under the pretext of equality, the lowly bring down the higher-ups in order to take their place, but they then become tyrannical in turn – nothing but one form of despotism replacing another.

Are we to conclude from this that until people are imbued with the sentiment of true fraternity, they are to be kept in slavery? That institutions founded upon the principles of equality and liberty are of no use? Such an opinion would be more than erroneous – it would be absurd. No one waits for a child to completely grow up before teaching him or her to walk. Moreover, who most frequently keeps the guardianship of true fraternity? Is it individuals with lofty and generous ideas, guided by the love of progress? Individuals who use the obedience of their inferiors to develop their moral sense and raise them little by little to the status of free persons? No. For the most part, they are individuals jealous of their power, whose ambition and cunningness use others as instruments that are little more intelligent than animals, and who, to that end, instead of emancipating them, keep them subjugated and ignorant for as long as possible.

This order of things, however, changes by itself thanks to the irresistible power of progress. Sometimes the reaction is violent and all the more terrible when the sentiment of fraternity, imprudently suffocated, does not interpose its moderating power. There is struggle between those who want to take and those who want to hold on to, which results in a conflict that often drags on for centuries. Finally, an artificial balance is established; things are somewhat better; but one can sense that the social bases are not solid; the ground shakes with each step because liberty and equality do not yet reign under the auspices of fraternity, because pride and selfishness are always there to cause the failure of the efforts of individuals of the good.

All of you who dream about that golden age for humankind, work, before anything else, on laying the foundation of the edifice before you even think about the dome; for its foundation, give it fraternity in its purest acceptation. But to do so, it is not enough to proclaim it and inscribe it on a banner; it must be in the heart, and people's hearts are not changed by means of decrees. In the same way that one works to make a field produce a crop by removing the stones and the bramble, in this endeavor one has to toil tirelessly to extract the virus of pride and selfishness, for therein lies the cause of all evil, the real obstacle to the kingdom of the good. Eliminate from laws, institutions, religions and education the last vestiges of the times of barbarity and privilege, as well as all the causes that maintain and develop those eternal obstacles to true progress, with which we nurture ourselves and exhale, so to speak, through all the pores of the social atmosphere. Only then will people understand the duties and benefits of fraternity; and only then will the complementary principles of equality and liberty be established without disturbance or peril.

Is it actually possible to destroy selfishness and pride? We will respond with a resounding YES! Otherwise, the progress of humankind will have to be suspended. Human beings have grown in intelligence – that is an incontestable fact; but have they reached the culminating point beyond which they cannot go? Who would dare support such an absurd notion? Will they progress in morality? To respond to that question, one need only compare the eras of one particular country. Why would it reach the peak of moral progress but not of intellectual progress? Its yearning for a better order of things is a sign of the possibility of reaching it. It is up to progressive individuals to activate that movement through study and to put in practice the most effective means.

# ARISTOCRACIES

The word *aristocracy* comes from the Greek *aristos,* meaning the best, and *kratos,* meaning power. Literally, therefore, aristocracy means *power of the best.* One must agree that the original meaning has sometimes been remarkably distorted, but let us see what influence Spiritism might have on its application. To do so, let us take things at their starting point and follow them through the ages in order to deduce what will happen later on.

At no time, nor in any culture, can people in a society do without leaders, which is why we find them even in the most primitive tribes. This is because, due to the diversity of aptitudes and characters inherent to the human species, there are incapable individuals that need to be guided, weak ones that require protection, and passions that need to be repressed; hence the need for authority. It is well known that in primitive societies such authority was conferred on heads of families and elders; in other words, on patriarchs. This was the first of all aristocracies.

As societies became more numerous, patriarchal authority became powerless in certain circumstances. Quarrels between neighboring tribes gave way to wars, and elders were no longer needed to lead tribes, but strong, energetic and intelligent men; hence military leaders. When victorious, these leaders were invested with authority, and those under their command thought that their courage would be a guarantee against enemy attacks. However, many abused their position and seized power. Afterwards, the victors imposed themselves on the vanquished or reduced them to servitude; hence the authority of brute force, which was the second aristocracy.

The strong, with their possessions, naturally transferred their authority to their children, and the weak and repressed, not daring to say anything, gradually got used to considering them as heirs of the rights that their fathers had won and regarded them as their superiors. Hence the division of society into two classes: upper and lower; those who ordered and those who obeyed. This gave rise to the aristocracy of birth, which became as powerful and preponderant as the aristocracy of might, because if it did not have might itself – as in earlier times when everyone was expected to pay with their own sacrifice – it could use mercenary might. Having complete power, it naturally gave itself all privileges.

In order to maintain such privileges, it had to give them the prestige of legality; thus, it made laws to its own advantage, which was quite easy because it alone made the laws. That, however, was not always sufficient; it added the prestige of divine right in order to render its privileges respectable and inviolable. And in order to ensure the respect of the subjected classes, which were becoming more and more numerous and difficult to control even with force, there was but one other thing to do: keep them from seeing things for what they really were; that is, keep them in ignorance.

If the upper class could have fed the lower class with idleness, it would have kept it low for a long time; however, since the lower class was obliged to work in order to survive – and the more it was oppressed, the more it had to work – the need to constantly find more resources, to struggle against pervasive competition, and to find new outlets for its products developed its intelligence and enlightened it by means of the same causes that the upper class used to subject it. Do we not see in this the hand of Providence?

Thus, the subjected class saw matters more clearly; it saw the weak consistency of the privilege that was suppressing it, and feeling stronger because of its numbers, it abolished such privilege and proclaimed itself equal before the law. In certain cultures, this principle marked the end of the reign of the aristocracy of birth, which became merely nominal and honorific, since it no longer conferred any legal rights.

Subsequently, a new power arose – money – because with money one can avail oneself of people and things. Money was a rising sun before which everyone bowed, just as in the past one bowed before a coat-of-arms, and much lower for that matter. What one's title did not confer, wealth did, and wealth had its own legal privileges. However, it was soon realized that, if a certain amount of intelligence was needed to acquire wealth, it was not needed to inherit it; that heirs were often more skilled at spending it than acquiring it, and that the means for becoming affluent were not always irreprehensible. Consequently, money gradually lost its moral prestige, and this power tended to be replaced with another power, a more just aristocracy: that of intelligence, before which everyone could bow without debasing themselves, because intelligence belongs to the poor as well as to the wealthy.

Will intelligence be the last? Will it be the highest expression of civilized humankind? No.

Intelligence is not always a guarantee of morality and the most intelligent persons can make the worst use of their faculties. On the other hand, morality by itself can often be inept. The union of these two faculties, *intelligence* and *morality,* is thus necessary to create a legitimate preponderance to which the masses will submit blindly, as it will inspire them with complete confidence due to its light and justice. This will be the ultimate aristocracy, which will be the consequence, or rather, the sign of the advent of the kingdom of the good on earth. It will appear very naturally through the very force of things. Once persons of this category are sufficiently numerous to form a powerful majority, the masses will entrust their interests to them.

As we have seen, all aristocracies have had their reason for being; they were born from the state humankind was in at the time; the same will occur with that aristocracy that will become a necessity. All have had or will have had their time, according to the country, because none have been based on the moral principle. Only this principle can constitute a lasting supremacy because it will be animated by the sentiments of justice and charity. Let us call it the *intellectual-moral aristocracy*.

But is such a state of things possible with the selfishness, pride and greed that reign supreme? Let us respond forthrightly: Yes; not only is it possible, but it will happen because it is inevitable.

Today, intelligence dominates; it is sovereign; no one can contest it. This is so true that one can see ordinary people attaining high ranking jobs. Is not this aristocracy more just, more logical and more rational than brute force, aristocracy of birth or aristocracy of money? Then why would it be impossible to add morality to it? Because, say the pessimists, evil still dominates the earth. Does that mean that the good will not ever supplant it? Are not customs, and consequently, social institutions, a hundred times better today than in the Middle Ages? Has not each century been characterized by some progress? Then why would humankind hold itself back when it still has so much to do? Due to a natural instinct, people seek their own well-being; if they cannot find it fully in the kingdom of intelligence, they will look for it elsewhere; and where will they find it but in the kingdom of morality? For that to happen, morality must take over numerically. Of course there is much to do; but again, it would be foolish to say that humankind has already reached its apogee when one can see it marching incessantly ahead on the road of progress.

Most importantly, let us say that good persons are not as scarce as one might think. Bad persons are numerous; that, unfortunately, is true. However, what makes them seem even more numerous is the fact that they are more audacious because they believe such audacity is necessary to succeed. Still, they understand the preponderance of the good to the extent that, unable to practice it, they wear it as a mask.

Good persons, on the other hand, do not parade their good qualities; they do not make themselves obvious and that is why they seem less numerous. However, probe their unostentatious private actions, and in every social class you will find quite enough individuals of a good and loyal nature to reassure your heart and not fill humankind with despair. Furthermore, we must state that among all the bad persons, there are many who are only bad because they have been dragged into it, and that they would become good if they were submitted to a good influence. Let us say that out of 100 individuals, there are 25 good ones and 75 bad; that of the latter, 50 are bad out of weakness and would be good if they had good examples to follow, especially if given good guidance in childhood; and that of the 25 who are actually bad, not all of them are incorrigible.

As it now stands, bad people are in the majority and dictate the law to the good ones. Let us suppose that something happens that converts 50 of them: good people will then be in the majority and will dictate the laws to the bad ones; of the remaining 25 who are downright bad, many will experience the influence of the good; a few incorrigible ones will remain but they will have no influence.

Let us take an example for comparison: There are societies where murder and robbery are the norm; the good is the exception. On the other hand, among the most advanced and best governed nations in Europe, crime is the exception; restrained by laws, it exerts no influence on society. What still hold sway in these countries are the vices of character: pride, selfishness, greed and their derivatives.

So, as these nations progress, why would vices not become the exception, just as crime now is, and why would less advanced cultures not be capable of reaching their level? To deny this possibility would be to deny progress.

Of course, arriving at such a state of things cannot happen overnight, but if there is a cause capable of speeding up its advent, such cause is without a doubt Spiritism. A factor of human solidarity par excellence because it shows that the trials of the present life are the logical and rational outcome of acts committed in previous existences, and because it makes all individuals the willing artisans of their own happiness, the universal dissemination of Spiritism will necessarily result in a perceptible rise in today's moral level.

Although they have just begun to be prepared and coordinated, the general principles of our philosophy have already brought together in a powerful communion of ideas millions of adherents scattered throughout the world. The progress realized by their influence, the individual and local transformations that they have elicited in less than fifteen years, enables us to ascertain the immense and radical changes that will occur in the future.

However, if thanks to the development and widespread acceptance of the teachings of the Spirits the moral level of humankind is continuously tending to rise, one would be sadly mistaken to suppose that morality will hold sway over intelligence. In fact, Spiritism does not want to be blindly accepted. It calls for discussion and enlightenment.

"Instead of blind faith, which annihilates freedom of thought, Spiritism says: *Unshakable faith is only that which can meet reason face to face in every human epoch. Faith requires a foundation, and such foundation is the perfect understanding of that which is to be believed; in order to believe, it is not enough simply to see; it is essential above all to understand."*(*The Gospel according to Spiritism*[30]) Therefore, we are fully justified in regarding Spiritism as one of the strongest precursors of the aristocracy of the future, that is, the *intellectual-moral aristocracy.*

---

30 See *The Gospel according to Spiritism*, International Spiritist Council, EDICEI of America, 2008 – Tr.

## DESERTERS

If it is a fact that all great ideas have ardent and devoted followers, it is no less a fact that even the best ideas have their deserters. Spiritism could not escape the consequences of human weakness. It too has had its deserters and a few remarks in this regard might be quite useful.

Early on, many were mistaken about the nature and purposes of Spiritism, and they did not grasp its scope. At first, it aroused curiosity; many saw spirit manifestations as nothing more than objects of entertainment. They amused themselves with spirits as long as spirits wanted to amuse them. It was a pastime and was often included at soirees.

This initial way of presenting it was a tactic spirits found useful. In the form of entertainment, the idea spread far and wide and sowed its seed without frightening timorous consciences. The child was played along with, but the child had to grow up.

When serious, moralizing spirits replaced the frivolous ones, when Spiritism became a science and a philosophy, frivolous persons no longer found it entertaining. For those who were mostly preoccupied with material life, it was an inopportune and embarrassing censor, which more than one of them laid aside. One should not lament such deserters, because frivolous individuals are poor aides at any time or place. Nevertheless, that first phase was not time wasted – far from it. Thanks to that disguise, the idea became a hundred times more popular than if it had assumed an austere form from the very start. Thinkers of great worth would appear from the midst of that frivolous, undisciplined milieu.

Made fashionable by the curiosity they attracted, the phenomena became a craze, tempting the greed of those who look for what is new in the hopes of finding an open door. The manifestations seemed to be something wonderfully exploitable, and a lot of people thought of making themselves party to it. Others saw a variant of the art of fortunetelling, possibly a surer way than card reading, coffee ground reading, etc. to know the future and to discover hidden things, since according to the opinion at the time, spirits knew everything.

When these people saw that speculation was slipping through their fingers and was turning into deceit, that the spirits had not come to help them get rich or to provide them with winning lottery numbers, to give them private readings, to lead them to buried treasures, to collect inheritances, to bring them some useful and patentable invention, or to supplement their ignorance and keep them from making an intellectual and material effort, spirits became good for nothing and their manifestations were regarded as mere illusions. Just as they had placed Spiritism on a pedestal while hoping to get something from it, they decried it when disappointment ensued. More than one critic that ridicules it would have raised it to the clouds if it had revealed a rich uncle in America to him or helped him profit from the stock market. That makes up the largest category of deserters, but one has to realize that they cannot consciously be qualified as true Spiritists.

This phase was useful as well. By showing that one should not wait for the help of spirits, it made the serious objective of Spiritism known and it purified the Doctrine. The Spirits knew that the lessons of experience are the most profitable. If at the start they had said: "Don't ask about this or that because we won't tell you," perhaps no one would have believed in them at all. That is why they let things take their course so that the truth could be gleaned from observation. These disappointments discouraged the exploiters and contributed to their decreasing numbers. They were parasites that disappointments removed from Spiritism; they were not sincere adherents.

Certain people were more perceptive than others. They caught a glimpse of the adult in the child that had just been born and they feared it, just as Herod feared the child Jesus. Not daring to attack Spiritism head on, they had their moles embrace it in order to suffocate it; moles who disguised themselves in order to gain entrance everywhere and skillfully incite disaffections at Spiritist centers, furtively spreading the poison of slander while at the same time lighting the torch of discord, driving compromising actions and trying to derail the Doctrine by rendering it ridiculous or hateful, thus inciting defections. Others were even more skillful: preaching unity, they sowed schism. They adroitly brought up for discussion irritating and hurtful issues; they awakened the jealousy of preponderance among the different centers, and would have been quite delighted to see the pointing of fingers and banner against banner due to some difference in opinion regarding certain issues of form or essence, most of the time intentionally provoked. Every doctrine has had its Judases; Spiritism could not avoid having its own, and they have not been lacking.

They are not legitimate Spiritists, but even they have proven useful: they have taught true Spiritists to be prudent, circumspect, and not to trust in appearances.

In principle, one should be wary of overly feverish zeal, which is almost always a straw fire or a sham, or of fleeting enthusiasm, which replaces deeds with an abundance of words. True conviction is calm, thoughtful, motivated; it reveals itself, as true courage, through facts; that is, through firmness, perseverance, and above all, selflessness. Moral and material disinterestedness is the real touchstone of sincerity.

Sincerity has a *sui generis* nature; it shows itself through nuances quite often easier to understand than to define; it is felt through the effect of the transmission of thought, the law of which Spiritism has revealed to us, and which falsehood can never simulate completely, because it cannot change the nature of the fluidic currents it projects. Falsehood wrongly believes it can deceive through a shallow and servile flattery that can only seduce prideful souls, but it is through this flattery that it betrays itself to elevated souls.

After all, ice could never imitate heat.

If we go to the category of Spiritists per se, even there we run up against certain human weaknesses, over which the Doctrine never triumphs immediately. The hardest to overcome are selfishness and pride, the two original human passions. Among true believers there are no deserters in the true meaning of the word, because the one who would desert due to self-interests or any other reason would never have been a sincere Spiritist in the first place; however, failings can occur. Courage and perseverance can weaken as the result of a disappointment, a frustrated ambition, a prominence not reached, a crumpled self-esteem, or a difficult trial. One can lose heart when faced with sacrificing one's well-being, the fear of compromising one's material interests and the fear of "what they will say"; one can become disconcerted for having been deceived. Some do not give up, but cool down. Some live for themselves and not for others; some want to benefit from their beliefs, but on the condition that it does not cost anything. Of course, those who act this way can be believers, but they are definitely selfish believers, in whom faith has not yet lit the sacred fire of devotion and self-denial; it is hard for their soul to detach from matter. Nominally they are believers, but one cannot count on them.

All the others are Spiritists who truly deserve the label. By themselves, they accept all the consequences of the Doctrine and are recognized by the efforts they make to improve themselves. Without disdaining their material interests more than what is reasonable, they regard them as accessories and not the main thing; earthly life is but a crossing that is more painful or less so; the future will depend on its beneficial or unbeneficial utilization; its pleasures are insignificant when compared to the splendid objective that can be glimpsed up ahead; they do not lose heart because of the obstacles they meet along the way, as vicissitudes and disappointments are trials that are no cause for discouragement, since repose is the reward for toil. That is why there are neither desertions nor failures amongst them.

That is also why good spirits visibly watch over those who struggle courageously and perseveringly, those whose devotion is sincere and without ulterior motives. They help them overcome obstacles and mitigate the trials they cannot avoid, whereas they abandon no less visibly those who abandon them and who sacrifice the cause of the truth for their personal ambitions.

Must we include amongst the deserters of Spiritism those who abandon its ranks because they find our way of seeing things to be unsatisfactory? Those who, finding our method to be too slow or too fast, intend to reach more quickly and under better conditions the objective that we propose to accomplish? No, if sincerity and desire to spread the truth is their sole guide; yes, if their efforts tend solely to call public attention to themselves in order to satisfy their vanity and personal interests!

Your way of looking at things is different that ours; you do not sympathize with the principles we believe in! But that does not mean that you are any closer to the truth than we are. There can be differences of opinion regarding matters of knowledge; investigate from your own standpoint just as we investigate from ours; the future will show which of us is right or wrong. We do not pretend to be the only ones apart from whom serious and worthwhile study is not possible; what we have accomplished, others can surely accomplish as well. Whether intelligent people associate with us or gather far from us matters little! So much the better if study centers increase; it will be an incontestable sign of progress and we will applaud it with all our might.

As for rivalries and attempts to supplant us, we have an infallible way not to fear them. May we endeavor to understand, to enrich our minds and our hearts; may we face conflicts, but with charity and selflessness. May love toward our neighbor be written on our banner, be our motto, and may the study of the truth, wherever it comes from, be our sole objective! With such sentiments we shall brave the mockery of our enemies and the attempts of our competitors. If we err, we will not wear the robe of vanity by remaining stuck in wrongful ideas. There are principles, however, upon which we are sure to never be wrong: love for the good, self-denial, and the renunciation of every sentiment of envy and jealousy. Such are our principles; we see in them the ties that will bind all people of the good together, whatever their differences of opinion may be. Only selfishness and falsehood can set up unsurpassable obstacles to them.

But what will the consequences of such a state of things be? Of course, the maneuvers of false brothers and sisters may temporarily bring some partial disturbances, which is why we must use every effort to outmaneuver them as much as possible. However, they will last but for a little while and will not harm the future, primarily because they are maneuvers of opposition that will fail due to the force of things; moreover, whatever one may say or do, one cannot remove from the Doctrine its distinctive character, its rational and logical philosophy, its consoling and regenerative morality. Today, the bases of Spiritism are firmly set; the books written without ambiguity, which have been placed within reach of all inquiring minds, will continue to be the clear and precise expression of the Spirits' teachings and will transmit them intact to those who come after us.

We must not lose sight of the fact that we are living in a time of transition, and that no transition takes place without conflict. Therefore, one should not be surprised at seeing certain passions stir: unsuccessful ambitions, crumpled interests and thwarted pretense. However, little by little this will all disappear; the fever will cool down; people will come and go; but the new ideas will remain. Spiritists! If you want to be invincible, be benevolent and charitable; the good is a breastplate against which the maneuvers of malevolence will always be dashed to bits!

Therefore, let us be fearless: the future is ours. Let our adversaries writhe in the grip of the truth that makes them unworthy. All opposition is powerless against the evidence, for it inevitably triumphs by necessity. The universal popularization of Spiritism is only a matter of time, and in this century, time is taking gigantic steps under the impulse of progress.

ALLAN KARDEC

*Remark:* *As a supplement to the above article, we have published an instruction given by Allan Kardec on the same topic as soon as he returned to the spirit world. We thought it would be interesting to our readers if we would add to the above eloquent and compelling pages the current thoughts of the organizer par excellence of our philosophy.*

*Paris, November, 1869*

*While I was with you in body, I often said that a history of Spiritism should be outlined in an interesting way. This is still my opinion, and the elements I have compiled toward that end might someday serve to fulfill my idea. Actually, I was better positioned than anyone else to appreciate the curious spectacle provoked by the discovery and popularization of a great truth. I sensed then, and I know now, what a wonderful order and inconceivable harmony preside over the concentration of all the documents destined to give birth to the new endeavor. Benevolence, goodwill, the full devotion of some; the falsehood, the hypocrisy, the malevolent schemes of others – everything concurs to guarantee the stability of the edifice that is being built. In the hands of the higher powers that preside over all progress, the unconscious or simulated resistances, the attacks seeking to sow discredit and ridicule become the means of expansion.*

*What steps have not been taken to smother the child in its crib!*

*Charlatanism and superstition wanted to usurp our principles in order to exploit them for their own use. The press hurled all sorts of thunderbolts at us. The most respectable things were mocked. The teachings of the Spirits most worthy of universal admiration and veneration were attributed to the spirit of evil. And yet, all these accumulated efforts, this coalition of crumbled interests, did nothing but proclaim the powerlessness of our adversaries.*

*It is in the midst of this incessant struggle against entrenched prejudices and believed-in errors that one gets to know humankind. When I consecrated myself to the work of my predilection, I knew that I would be exposing myself to hatred, envy and jealousy. My pathway was sown with problems that recurred incessantly. Since nothing could be done against the Doctrine, the man was attacked; but in this respect, I was strong because I had renounced my personality. What did the attempts at slander matter to me, after all? My conscience and the grandeur of the objective enabled me to ignore the briars and thorns along the way. The proofs of sympathy and esteem I received from those who knew how to appreciate me were the kindest reward I could ever have wished for. However, how many times I would have buckled under the weight of my task if the love and recognition of so many had not enabled me to ignore the ingratitude and injustice of so few. If the attacks against me always found me impervious, I must confess that I was deeply wounded every time I discovered false friends amongst those I counted on the most.*

*If it is right to cast blame on those who have tried to exploit Spiritism or to distort it in their writings without having studied it beforehand, how much more guilty are those who, after having assimilated all its principles, were not content with stepping aside and turned their efforts against it! It is especially for the deserters of this type that we should ask for divine mercy, because they have willfully extinguished the flame that once enlightened them, and with which they could have enlightened others. They quickly lost the protection of good spirits, and it was our sad experience to watch them quickly fall into the direst situations!*

*Since my return to the spirit world, I have seen quite a few of these unfortunate souls! They are now repenting; they regret their inaction and their ill-will, but they cannot make up for lost time! … They will soon return to the earth with the firm purpose of actively cooperating for progress, and they will find themselves struggling with their former tendencies until they finally triumph over them.*

*One would like to believe that today's Spiritists, enlightened by such examples, would avoid falling into the same errors. But that is not the case. There will be false brothers and sisters and unfit friends for a long time to come; but like their previous brothers and sisters, they will not succeed in diverting Spiritism from its path. Even though they may cause some momentary and purely local trouble, the Doctrine will not collapse. Quite the contrary, delinquent Spiritists will soon realize their mistake. They will more fervently cooperate in the work they briefly forsook, and acting in harmony with the high order spirits who guide humankind's transformations, they will advance in rapid strides toward the blissful times promised to a regenerated humanity.*

*Allan Kardec*

# BRIEF RESPONSE TO SPIRITISM'S DETRACTORS

The right to examine and criticize is an inviolable right that Spiritism has no more intention of denying than it has of pleasing everybody. Everybody is therefore free to approve of or reject it, but it should be discussed with full knowledge of the facts. Criticism, however, has only too often proven that it is ignorant of Spiritism's most elementary principles, causing it to say the exact opposite of what it actually says, attributing to it what it actually disowns, confusing it with the crude and frivolous imitations of charlatanism, thereby presenting, in sum, the eccentricities of a few individuals as the general rule. Even more frequently, malevolence has wanted to render it responsible for reprehensible or ridiculous acts, in which its name was involved incidentally, and has used this as a weapon against it.

Before blaming a doctrine for inciting any condemnable act, reason and fairness require an examination to determine if it contains maxims that would justify such an act.

There is a very simple way to find out Spiritism's responsibility in any given circumstance: conduct a detailed investigation with *good faith,* not amongst its adversaries but at the source itself, as to what it approves or condemns. This is very easy to accomplish since Spiritism holds no secrets; its teachings are right out in the open and no one can control them.

Therefore, if books on the Spiritist Doctrine explicitly and formally condemn an act that is justly disapproved; moreover, if they only entail instructions that lead to the good, one must conclude that they did not inspire a wrongdoer to commit a wrong even if that person owned a few of them.

Spiritism does not support those who love calling themselves Spiritists any more than Medicine supports the charlatans that exploit it, or religion the abuses and crimes that are committed in its name. It acknowledges as adherents only those who practice its teachings; that is, those who work to improve themselves morally, who make an effort to overcome their bad tendencies, to be less selfish and proud, to be kinder, more humble, patient, benevolent and charitable toward their neighbor, and more moderate in all things, because that is the characteristic sign of the true Spiritist.

The object of this brief discourse is not to refute all the erroneous allegations that have been leveled against Spiritism, or to develop and prove all of its principles, and even less to try to convert to its principles those who profess opposing opinions. It is meant to say in a few words what it is and what it is not, what it accepts and what it rejects.

Its beliefs, tendencies and purpose are summed up in the following propositions:

1. The *spiritual element* and the *material element* are the two principles, the two living forces in nature. They mutually complement each other and constantly react to each other. Both are indispensable to the workings of the universe.

From the reciprocal action between these two principles originate the phenomena that each cannot explain by itself.

The special mission of science per se is to study the laws of matter.

The objective of Spiritism is to study the *spiritual element* and how it is related to the material element; Spiritism finds in the unity of these two principles the cause of a huge number of phenomena that used to be unexplainable.

Spiritism progresses in tandem with science in the realm of matter: it accepts all the truths that science has proven; however, where scientific investigations stop, Spiritism goes on to conduct its research in the field of spirituality.

2. Since the spiritual element is an active state in nature, the phenomena connected to it are subject to laws and are thus as natural as those connected with inert matter.

Some of these phenomena used to be considered *supernatural* only because the laws that govern them were unknown. Due to this principle, Spiritism does not accept the miraculous character attributed to certain phenomena, although it does acknowledge their reality or possibility. In Spiritism there are no miracles in the sense of derogation from the laws of nature; consequently, Spiritists do not perform miracles and their qualification as magicians, given by some people, is improper.

Knowledge of the laws that govern the spiritual principle is directly connected to the question of people's past and future. Are people's lives limited solely to their current existence? When they come into this world, do they bring nothing with them and take nothing with them when they leave? Have they lived before and will they live again? *How will they live and in what conditions?* In other words, where have they come from and where are they going? Why are they here and why do they have to suffer? Such are the questions everyone asks themselves because they are of great interest for every individual, and no doctrine has yet given a rational answer to them. The answers given by Spiritism, based on the facts and satisfying the requirements of logic and the most rigorous justice, are one of the main reasons for its rapid spread.

Spiritism is not the brainchild of one person or the result of a preconceived theory. It is the result of thousands of observations made all over the world, and which have converged on a central point, where they have been compiled and coordinated. All their constitutive principles, without exception, have been deduced by means of experimentation. Experimentation has always preceded theory.

Thus, from the beginning, Spiritism began laying down roots far and wide. History offers no other example of a philosophical or religious doctrine that in ten years won over such a large number of followers. Spiritism has not used any of the means normally employed to make itself known; it has spread by itself because it has been so favorably received.

Another fact no less constant is that in no country has the doctrine come into being via the lower classes of society; in all of them it has spread from the higher to the lower social levels; it is in the enlightened classes that it is nearly exclusively diffused, with the illiterate classes being a very small minority.

It is also been proven that ever since it began, the spread of Spiritism has followed an ever ascending march of progress, in spite of all that has been done to hinder it and distort its character so as to discredit it in the public's eye. It should also be noted that all the efforts in this objective have only helped its spread. The noise they made when it appeared brought it to the knowledge of people who had never even heard of it; the more they tried to smear or ridicule it, the fiercer they ranted and raved, the more people's curiosity was piqued. And since it could but gain with any examination, the result was that its enemies, without wanting to, became its ardent propagators. If the diatribes did it no harm, it was because by studying Spiritism at its true source, they discovered it to be quite different than previously represented.

In the struggles that it has had to endure, impartial individuals have testified to its moderation; it has never employed reprisals against its adversaries, nor has it ever responded to insult with insult.

Spiritism is a philosophical doctrine with religious consequences just like any other spiritualist philosophy, which is why it necessarily touches on the fundamental bases of all religions: God, the soul, and the future life. But it is not an organized religion, because it has no worship services, rites or temples, and none of its adherents have taken or received the title of priest or high priest. Such labels are the pure invention of detractors.

Individuals are Spiritists solely because they agree with the Doctrine's principles and shape their conduct according to them. It is an opinion just like any other, which anyone has the right to profess, like that of being Jewish, Catholic, Protestant, Fourierist, Simonist, Voltairian, Cartesian, Deist, and even materialist.

Spiritism proclaims freedom of conscience as a natural right; it requests it for its adherents, as well as everybody else. It respects all sincere convictions and asks the same in return.

From freedom of conscience follows the right of *free examination* in matters of faith. Spiritism combats the principle of blind faith as imposing on individuals the abdication of their reason; it states that all imposed faith is without roots. That is why it inscribes among its maxims: *Unshakable faith is only that which can meet reason face to face in every human epoch.*

In keeping with its principles, Spiritism does not impose itself on anyone; it wishes to be freely accepted and by conviction. It makes its doctrines known and welcomes all who willingly come to it.

It does not seek to divert anyone from their religious convictions; it does not address those who have a faith that is sufficient for them, but those who, dissatisfied with what they have been given, seek something better.

# POSTHUMOUS WORKS OF ALLAN KARDEC

## PART TWO

# PART TWO

# SELECTED PASSAGES *IN EXTENSO* FROM THE BOOK ON

Previsions

CONCERNING SPIRITISM

A manuscript carefully written

by

ALLAN KARDEC

and of which no chapter has yet been published

# MY INITIATION INTO SPIRITISM

It was in 1854 that I first heard about the turning tables. One day, I ran into the magnetizer Mr. Fortier, whom I had known for quite some time. He asked me, "Have you heard about the remarkable property that has just been discovered regarding magnetism? It seems that it isn't just individuals who can be magnetized, but tables as well. They can be made to turn and move about at will." "That is indeed remarkable," I responded, "but I don't see anything radically impossible about it. The magnetic fluid is a kind of electricity and can certainly act upon inert objects and make them move. Accounts published in newspapers about experiments performed in Nantes, Marseilles and other cities leave no room for doubt about the reality of such phenomena."

Sometime later, I met Mr. Fortier again and he said, "There is something even more remarkable: not only can a table be made to move by magnetizing it, but it can also talk. If it is asked a question, it answers it." "Now, that is a different matter altogether," I responded. "I will only believe it when I see it, and when it is proven to me that a table has a brain that thinks and nerves that feel, and that it can become somnambulistic. Until then, forgive me for looking at it as nothing but a fairy tale."

This line of reasoning was logical. I could conceive of the possibility that a table could move due to a mechanical force, but since I was unaware of the cause and the law governing the phenomenon, it seemed absurd to attribute intelligence to something that was purely material. I found myself in the situation of today's disbelievers, who deny a fact simply because they cannot understand it. Fifty years ago, if someone had flatly stated that a telegram could be sent five hundred leagues and that a response could be received in less than an hour, he would have been laughed at, and there would have been no lack of excellent scientific reasons to prove that such a thing was materially impossible. But now that everyone knows about the law of electricity, no one is surprised – not even peasants. The same applies to all spirit phenomena. To anyone who does not know about the law that governs them, they seem supernatural, extraordinary, and consequently, impossible and ridiculous. Once the law is known, however, the extraordinary disappears; the phenomena cease to be objectionable to one's reason because their possibility is understood.

So, at the time, I had before me an unexplained phenomenon which apparently went against the laws of nature, and which my reason therefore rejected. I still hadn't seen or observed anything. Experiments, performed in the presence of reputable persons worthy of being believed, confirmed the possibility of a purely physical effect, but the idea of a *talking* table had not yet found entrance to my mind.

The following year (it was the beginning of 1855), I ran into Mr. Carlotti, my friend of 25 years. He talked to me about the phenomena for almost a whole hour with the enthusiasm he always showed toward all new ideas. He was a native of Corsica and had a passionate and energetic temperament. I had always appreciated in him the qualities that indicate a great and wonderful soul, but I did not trust his excitability. He was the first person to speak to me about the intervention of spirits, and he told me such surprising things that, rather than being convinced, my doubts increased. "Someday you will be one of us," he said to me. "I'm not saying I won't be," I answered; "We shall see."

Sometime later, around May of 1855, I was in the home of the somnambulist Mrs. Roger with Mr. Fortier, her magnetizer. There I met Mr. Patier and Mrs. Plainemaison, who told me about the phenomena that Mr. Carlotti had spoken of, but in a much different tone. Mr. Patier was a public employee, older, well-educated, of a serious nature, unflappable and calm. His composed speech, exempt of any enthusiasm, made a deep impression on me, and when he invited me to witness the experiments that were being conducted in Mrs. Plainemaison's home at 18 Grange-Bateliere St., I eagerly accepted. The meeting was set for the coming Tuesday at 8:00 p.m.

It was there that for the first time I witnessed the phenomenon of the turning, jumping and moving tables in such a way that no doubt was possible. I also saw some very imperfect attempts at mediumistic writing[31] on a slate with the aid of a little basket. My mind was far from having reached a conclusion, but there was an effect there that had to have a cause behind it. In those apparently insignificant incidents and the entertainment the phenomena inspired, I saw something serious, like the revelation of a new law, which I promised myself I would probe more deeply.

I was soon given the opportunity to observe the phenomena more closely in a way I had not been able to do before. At one of Mrs. Plainemaison's meetings, I was introduced to the Baudin family, who then resided on Rochechouart Street. Mr. Baudin invited me to the weekly séances at his house, which from that time on I attended on a regular basis.

These meetings were quite frequent, and besides the usual attendees, anyone who asked to participate was freely admitted. The two mediums were the Baudins' daughters, who would write on a slate using a basket called a *spinning top* (described in *The Mediums' Book*). This method, which required the concourse of two persons, ruled out any possibility of one of the mediums interjecting her own ideas. Thus, I was able to witness ongoing communications and answers to formulated questions – sometimes even mental questions, which obviously pointed to the intervention of an outside intelligence.

---

31 Also called automatic writing or psychography – Tr.

The topics addressed during the meetings were usually frivolous, mainly matters concerning material life and the future; in other words, nothing really serious. Curiosity and entertainment were the main motivation of the participants. The spirit who usually showed up called himself *Zefiro*[32], a name that was perfectly in keeping with his character and that of the meeting. Nevertheless, he was a good spirit and declared himself to be the protector of the family. If he often made everyone laugh, he also knew how to offer valuable advice if need be, and on such occasions, he would forgo spirited and mordant comments. We soon got to know each other and he gave me constant proof of a great friendship. He was not a highly evolved spirit, but later, aided by high order spirits, he assisted me in my initial endeavors. Sometime later, he said he had to reincarnate and I did not hear from him again.

At these meetings I began my first serious studies of Spiritism, still more by observation than revelation. As I had always done up to that point, I applied the experimental method to this new science; I never developed preconceived theories; I observed attentively, compared, and deduced the results. From the effects, I sought to go back to the causes through deduction and the logical chain of events, never accepting an explanation as valid until I could resolve all the aspects of the issue. This had always been my procedure in previous endeavors ever since the age of 25 or 26. First of all, I grasped the gravity of the exploration I was about to undertake; I perceived in those phenomena the key to the highly obscure and controversial issue of humankind's past and future, the solution to which I had been looking for my entire life. In other words, it was an entire revolution of ideas and beliefs; consequently, I had to proceed with the greatest circumspection and not superficially – to be a positivist and not an idealist so as not to go adrift with illusions.

One of the first results from my observations was that spirits, being nothing more than the souls of human

32 Literally, Zephyr - Tr.

beings, possessed neither sovereign wisdom nor complete knowledge; that their knowledge was limited to their degree of advancement, and that their opinion only held the value of a personal opinion. This truth, realized from the very start, kept me from falling into the serious error of believing in their infallibility, and kept me from formulating immature theories on what was said by one or a few of them.

The simple fact that spirits communicated at all – whatever they said – proved the existence of a surrounding invisible world. That alone was a crucial point; an immense field opened up to our explorations, the key to innumerable inexplicable phenomena. The second point, and no less important, was that of being able to know about the state of that world and its customs – if we may say so. I soon saw that each spirit, in virtue of its personal situation and knowledge, revealed an aspect of that world, in the same way that we get to know about a particular country by questioning the inhabitants of all its classes and conditions, each one being able to tell us something and no one individually being able to tell us everything. It was up to the observer to do the compilation with the aid of documents collected from various parts, and to collate, coordinate and compare them with one another. Thus, I dealt with spirits as I would have dealt with regular human beings. They were to me, from the least of them to the greatest, a means of informing myself; they were not *predestined revelators.*

Such were the dispositions with which I undertook and continued to pursue my Spiritist studies. Observe, compare, judge: such was the rule I always followed.

Until then, the séances at Mr. Baudin's house had had no set purpose. I endeavored to get the answers to resolve the problems that interested me from the philosophical and psychological point of view and from the nature of the invisible world. I arrived at each séance with a series of questions prepared and methodically arranged beforehand. They were always answered with precision, depth and logic. From then on, the séances took on a much different character. Among the attendees were serious individuals who took a lively interest in it, and if I didn't make it to the séance, they didn't know what to do. For the great majority, pointless questions had lost all their appeal. At first, I had only my own learning in mind; later on, when I saw that the questions were forming a whole and assuming the proportions of a doctrine, I got the idea of publishing them for everybody's instruction. They were the same questions that, subsequently developed and completed, became the basis for *The Spirits' Book*.

The following year – 1856 – I also attended the Spiritist meetings held on Tiquetone Street in the home of Mr. Roustan and the somnambulist Miss Japhet. These meetings were serious and orderly. The communications were transmitted through the medium, Miss Japhet, with the help of a *corbeille à bec*[33], a basket with a long arm that held a writing instrument at the end.

My work was nearly complete and had assumed the proportions of a book, but I made it a point to submit it to the examination of other spirits with the help of different mediums. I thought of making it the object of study at Mr. Roustan's meetings. Toward the end of a few séances, the Spirits said that they would prefer to revise it in private, and to that effect they assigned certain days to work privately with Miss Japhet in order to do so more serenely and also to avoid premature public indiscretions and comments.

I was not happy about this arrangement, but the Spirits had recommended it. Since the circumstances had put me in contact with other mediums, every time I got the chance I would pose some of the questions that seemed the thorniest. In this way, more than ten mediums helped with the endeavor. From the comparison and harmonization of all the coordinated answers, classified and often rehashed in the silence of meditation, I prepared the first edition of *The Spirits' Book*, published on April 18, 1857.

33 Literally "basket with a beak" – Tr.

Toward the end of that same year, the two Baudin daughters got married. The meetings ended and the family scattered. But my relationships began to grow and the Spirits increased the means of instruction for my subsequent works.

******

## MY GUARDIAN SPIRIT

(In Mr. Baudin's home; medium: Mrs. Baudin)
*December 11, 1855*

*Question (to the spirit Z): In the spirit world, might there be a spirit that is my good genius?*
*Answer: Yes.*

*Q:* Is it the spirit of some relative or friend?
*A:* Neither.
*Q:* Who was it while on the earth?
*A:* A righteous and wise man.
*Q:* What must I do to win his benevolence?
*A:* All the good possible.
*Q:* By what signs may I recognize his intervention?
*A:* By the satisfaction you will feel.
*Q:* Is there some means of evoking him, and if so, what would it be?
*A:* Have living faith and call to him persistently.
*Q:* After I die, will I recognize him in the spirit world?
*A:* No doubt about it. He will be the one who congratulates you if you have accomplished your tasks.

*Remark: One can see by these questions that I was still very inexperienced regarding matters of the spirit world.*

*Q:* Has my mother's spirit come to visit me at times?
*A:* Yes, and she watches over you as much as possible.

*Q:* I often see her in my dreams. Is it just a memory and a figment of my imagination?
*A:* No. She really does appear to you; you know it to be true because of the emotion you feel.

*Remark:* *This is perfectly accurate. Whenever my mother appeared in one of my dreams, I felt an indescribable emotion, something that the medium would not have known about.*

*Q:* A while back, when we evoked S. and asked him if he was the guardian spirit of one of us, he answered: "Show me one of you who is worthy of it and I will be with that person. Z will tell you." Do you think I might deserve that favor?
*A:* If you'd like.
*Q:* What do I have to do?
*A:* Do all the good you can and bravely bear the sorrows of life.
*Q:* By the nature of my mind, am I capable of grasping, as far as a man may be permitted, the great truths regarding our future destiny?
*A:* Yes, you have the capability, but the result will depend on your perseverance in your endeavors.
*Q:* Will I be able to take part in spreading such truths?
*A:* Undoubtedly.
*Q:* By what means?
*A:* You'll find out later; meanwhile, work.

## MY SPIRIT GUIDE

(In Mr. Baudin's home; medium: Miss Baudin)
*March 25, 1856*

At that time, I was living on Martyrs Street, in apartment 8 on the second floor in the back. One night, while working in my office, I heard light raps in the wall that separated me from the adjacent room. At first, I didn't pay any attention to it; however, when the noises grew louder and changed places, I made a detailed examination of both sides of the wall, listening to see if they were coming from a different floor; but I didn't find anything. What was so unusual was that, each time I tried to investigate, the noise would stop and then would start up again as soon as I went back to work. My wife came home around 10:00 p.m. She came into my office and upon hearing the raps asked me what they were. I told her I didn't know, but they had been going on for about an hour. We investigated together without much success. The noises continued until midnight, when I went to bed.

The next day, there was a séance in Mr. Baudin's home. Recounting the incident, I asked for an explanation.

*Q:* Without a doubt you must have understood what I have just described; could you tell me the cause of those raps that were heard so persistently?

*A:* It was your familiar spirit.

*Q:* What was the reason for rapping like that?

*A:* He wanted to communicate with you.

*Q:* Could you tell me who he is and what he would like from me?

*A:* You can ask him yourself because he is here right now.

*Remark:* *At that time, I had not yet made a distinction between the various categories of kindly spirits. They were all grouped under the general classification of familiar spirits.*

*Q:* My familiar spirit, whoever you may be, I thank you for having come to visit me. Would you be willing to tell me who you are?

*A:* For you, I shall be called *Truth,* and every month, for 15 minutes, I shall be here at your disposal.

*Q:* Yesterday, when you made rapping noises while I was working, did you have something in particular to tell me?

*A:* What I wanted to tell you had to do with the work you were doing. I was displeased with what you were writing and I wanted you to stop.

*Remark:* *What I was writing was precisely relative to my studies regarding spirits and their manifestations.*

*Q:* Were you displeased with the chapter I was writing or with the work in general?

*A:* Yesterday's chapter. I submit it to your judgment. Read it again tonight. You will see your mistakes and correct them.

*Q:* I myself was not very happy with that chapter and I re-wrote it today. Isn't it better now?

*A:* It is better, but it still isn't right. Read it from line 3 to 30 and you will find a serious mistake.

*Q:* But I tore up what I wrote yesterday.

*A:* That doesn't matter. Tearing it up did not keep the mistake from continuing. Reread it and you will see.

*Q:* The name *Truth* that you have adopted – does it allude to the truth I'm seeking?

*A:* Perhaps; at least it is a guide that will watch over you and help you.

*Q:* May I evoke you in my home?

*A:* Yes, to assist you through thought. But as for written answers in your home, it will be a long time before you receive them.

*Remark:* *In fact, for nearly a year I did not receive any written communications in my home, and every time a medium was present – and through whom I hoped to receive something – an unforeseen circumstance would prevent it. I only received communications away from home.*

*Q:* Could you come more often than month to month?

*A:* Yes, but I can promise no more than once a month until I receive new orders.

*Q:* Have you animated a known person on the earth?

*A:* I have told you that *for you* I am *Truth;* this *for you* means discretion regarding this information as well. You shall not know any more than that.

*Remark:* *When I got home that evening, I hurried to reread what I had written. Both on the copy I had thrown into the wastebasket as well as on the new one, I discovered on line 30 a serious mistake that I was surprised at having made. Since then, no further manifestations of the same kind have occurred. Once I established the connection with my protector spirit, such manifestations were no longer necessary, and therefore stopped. The one-month interval that he had set for his communications was rarely maintained at first, and later, not at all. Undoubtedly, it was a warning that I had to do the work myself and not to constantly resort to him when the smallest difficulty came up.*

(In Mr. Baudin's home; medium: Miss Baudin)
*April 9, 1856*

*Question (asked of Truth):* *The other day, you criticized the work I had done and you were right. I reread it and on line 30 I found a mistake that you had protested by using raps. That led me to find other problems and to redo the work. Are you happier with it now?*

*Answer:* *I find it better, but would advise you to wait one month before publishing it.*

*Q:* What do you mean by publishing it? I have no intention of publishing it yet, if it is to be published at all.

*A:* I mean: do not show it to any third parties. Find a pretext to refuse it to those who ask you to see it. Meanwhile, you can improve it. I'm making this recommendation to save you from criticism; I'm looking out for your self-esteem.

*Q:* You said you would be a guide who would help and watch over me. I conceive this protection and its objective within a certain order of things, but could you tell me if this protection also applies to the material things of life?

*A:* In this world, material life is a part of it; not helping you to live your life would be like not loving you at all.

*Remark:* *The protection of that spirit, whose superiority I was far from imagining, in fact was never lacking. His solicitude and that of the good spirits who acted under his orders manifested in every circumstance of my life, whether smoothing out my material problems, helping me carry out my endeavors, or saving me from the effects of the malevolence of my antagonists, who were always rendered powerless. If the tribulations inherent to my mission could not be avoided altogether, they were always at least mitigated and largely compensated for by truly rewarding moral satisfactions.*

## THE FIRST REVELATION OF MY MISSION

(In Mr. Roustan's home; medium: Miss Japhet)
*April 30, 1856*

For quite some time I attended the séances in Mr. Roustan's home, and there I began the verification of my work, which would later comprise *The Spirits' Book*. During one of the closed séances, involving only seven or eight persons, various matters were addressed relative to events that could lead to a transformation of society, when the medium, grabbing the basket, spontaneously wrote the following:

"When the great bell tolls, you are to let it; only you can provide relief to others. Individually, you are to magnetize them in order to heal them. Then, may everyone be at their post – for everyone will be needed – since everything will be destroyed, at least temporarily. There will be no more religion, yet one will be needed; but one that is true, grand, beautiful and worthy of the Creator … Its first foundations have already been laid … As for you, Rivail, your mission lies there. (Released, the basket clearly turned to me, as would a person pointing to me with a finger). For you, M…, the sword that does not wound, but kills; against everything that is, it is you who will be first. Rivail will be second. He will be the worker that rebuilds that which has been demolished."

*Remark:* *This was the first positive revelation of my mission, and I must confess that when I saw the basket brusquely turn towards me and designate me by name, I could not avoid a certain emotion.*

Mr. M…, who was at the meeting, was a young man who had extremely radical opinions, was involved in political matters, and was obliged not to be put in a prominent position. Believing in an approaching political upheaval, he was in a hurry to take part in it and devise plans for reform. Otherwise, he was a kind, inoffensive man.

## MY MISSION

(In Mr. Roustan's home; medium: Miss Japhet)
*May 7, 1856*

*Question (asked of Hahnemann):* The other day, the Spirits told me that I had an important mission to fulfill and indicated its objective. I would like to know if you could confirm it.

*Answer:* *Yes, and if you would look into your aspirations, your inclinations and the almost constant object of your thoughts, it should not surprise you. You shall fulfill what you have dreamed about for a long time now. It is necessary that you work tirelessly to get ready for it, for the day is closer than you might think.*

*Q:* To carry out this mission as I conceive it, the modes of execution are still beyond my grasp.

*A:* Let Providence do its work and you will be satisfied.

## EVENTS

*May 7, 1856*

*Question:* *The communication received the other day seems to foretell very serious events. Could you give us some explanations in this regard?*

*Answer:* *We cannot specify the facts. What we can say is that there will be much ruin and desolation because the time predicted for a renewal of humankind has come.*

*Q:* What will cause this ruin? A cataclysm?

*A:* Not a physical cataclysm, as you understand it; but afflictions of all sorts will devastate nations; wars will decimate peoples; outdated institutions will sink in streams of blood. The old world must collapse in order to open up a new era of progress.

*Q:* So war will not be limited to just one country?

*A:* No. It will encompass the whole earth.

*Q:* But nothing at this time seems to presage such an impending storm.

*A:* Things are hanging by a spider's thread that is about to snap.

*Q:* Without being indiscreet, may we ask where the first spark will occur?

*A:* In Italy.

## EVENTS

(Private séance in Mr. Baudin's home)
*May 12, 1856*

*Question (asked of Truth):* *What do you think of Mr. M…? Is he someone who will influence events?*

*Answer:* *A lot of noise. He has good ideas; he is a man of action, but not of thought.*

*Q:* Should we take what was said literally, i.e. that his role is to destroy what exists?

*A:* No. It was only meant to use him to personify the party whose ideas he represents.

*Q:* May I maintain a friendship with him?

*A:* Not for now; you would be running a needless risk.

*Q:* Mr. M, who has a medium, said that he was told about the chain of events leading to a set date, so to speak. Is that true?

*A:* Yes, he was told of precise times, but by frivolous spirits who do not know any more than he does, and who exploit his enthusiasm. You know that we should not be specific about future things. The foretold events will certainly take place in the near future, but the exact time cannot be determined.

*Q:* Spirits have said that the time has come when such things must happen; how should these words be interpreted?

*A:* When dealing with such serious things, what are a few more or a few less years? They never happen all of a sudden, like a bolt of lightning. They are prepared for a long time through partial events that act as their precursors, like the tremors that precede a volcanic eruption. So, one could say that the times have come without it meaning that things will happen tomorrow. It means that you are living within the timeframe in which they will take place.

*Q:* Would you confirm what was said about there not being a cataclysm?

*A:* Certainly. You do not have to fear a flood, the conflagration of your planet, or any other events of that sort, since one cannot label as cataclysms the local disturbances that have occurred in all epochs. Instead, it will be a cataclysm of a moral nature, of which human beings themselves will be the instruments.

## THE SPIRITS' BOOK

(In Mr. Roustan's home; medium: Miss Japhet)
*June 10, 1856*

*Question (asked of Hahnemann): Since we will soon finish the first part of the book, I thought of asking B… to help me as a medium in order to speed things up; what do you think?*
*Answer:* *I think it would be better not to use him.*

*Q:* Why not?
*A:* Because the truth cannot be interpreted through falsehood.
*Q:* Even if B…'s familiar spirit is given to lying, that shouldn't keep a good spirit from communicating through the medium as long as we do not evoke the other one.
*A:* No, it shouldn't, but in this case the medium aids the spirit, and when the spirit is deceitful, the medium takes part in it. Aristo, his interpreter, and B… will end up badly.

*Remark:* *B… was a highly versatile young writing medium, but assisted by a prideful, despotic and arrogant spirit who took the name Aristo, and who flattered B…'s natural tendency to pride. Hahnemann's predictions did in fact occur. This young man, believing to have found in his faculty a means to riches, either through medical consultations or by inventions and profitable discoveries, reaped nothing but disappointment and deceit. After a while, no one ever heard from him again.*

## MY MISSION

(In Mr. C…'s home; medium: Miss Aline C…)
*June 12, 1856*

*Question (asked of Truth):* *Goodly Spirit, I would like to know what you think about the mission designated to me by a number of other spirits. Tell me, I ask of you, if it was to test my pride. As you know, I have the deepest desire to contribute to the propagation of truth, but there is a great distance from the role of a humble worker to that of head missionary. I do not understand what could justify my receiving such a favor when there are so many others who have talents and qualities that I do not.*

*Answer:* *I can confirm what you were told, but I suggest that you be very discreet if you want to succeed. Later on, you will understand things that will explain to you what surprises you at the moment. Don't forget that you can succeed, just as you can fail. In the latter case, someone else will replace you, because God's designs do not rest on the head of one person only. Never talk about your mission; that would be the way to make it founder. It can only be justified by the work accomplished, and you have done nothing yet. If you do fulfill it, people will know how to recognize it sooner or later, because it is by its fruits that one recognizes the quality of the tree.*

*Q:* I certainly have no desire to boast about a mission I barely believe in myself. If I am in fact destined to serve as an instrument for the designs of Providence, may it make use of me. In that case, I would ask for your assistance and that of the good Spirits to aid me and uphold me in my task.

*A:* You will not lack our assistance, but it will be useless if you don't do what is necessary on your part. You have your free will; it is up to you to use it as you wish. No one is unavoidably forced to do anything.

*Q:* What could cause me to fail? The insufficiency of my abilities?

*A:* No. But the mission of a reformer is wrought with pitfalls and perils. I must warn you that yours will be hard because it is meant to stir and transform the entire world. Don't think that it will be enough just to publish one, two or ten books and then rest peacefully at home. No. You will have to make sacrifices. You will arouse terrible hatred against you; obstinate enemies will plot your downfall; you will be the target of malevolence, slander and even betrayal by those who will seem the most devoted to you. Your finest teachings will be misjudged and falsified. More than once you will succumb under the weight of fatigue; in sum, you will have to endure an almost constant struggle, as well as the sacrifice of your repose, your tranquility, your health and even your life since without all that, you would live much longer. More than a few turn back when, instead of a path of flowers, they find only briars, sharp stones and serpents under their feet. For such missions, intelligence is not enough. First of all, to please God, one needs humility, modesty and detachment, for God strikes down the proud, the presumptuous and the ambitious. To struggle against others, one needs courage, perseverance and unshakable firmness. Prudence and tact are also needed to conduct things appropriately and not compromise their success by intemperate words or measures. In sum, devotion, selflessness and readiness for every sacrifice is necessary.

As you can see, your mission is subordinate to conditions that depend on you yourself.

The spirit *Truth*

*Me: Truth*, thank you for you wise counsels. I accept everything, without restriction and without preconceived ideas.

O Lord! If you deign to set your eyes on me for the fulfillment of your designs, may your will be done! My life is in your hands; as your servant, I am at your disposal. I acknowledge my weakness before such a great endeavor. My goodwill will not fail, but perhaps my strength will give out. Supplement my deficiencies; give me the physical and mental strength I will need. Sustain me in the difficult moments, and with your aid and the help of your heavenly messengers, I will use every effort to comply with your designs.

*Remark:* *I am writing this remark on January 1, 1867, ten and a half years after I received the above communication, and I realize that every bit of it was true because I have experienced all the vicissitudes that were announced to me. I have been the target of the hatred of obstinate enemies, of offense, slander, envy and jealousy. Vile libels have been published against me. My best teachings have been distorted. I have been betrayed by those I trusted and paid with ingratitude by those whom I rendered services. The Parisian Society*[34] *has been a focal point of continuous intrigues hatched against me by those who said they were on my side and who, all smiles in my presence, stabbed me in the back when I turned. It also has been said that those who took my side were bribed by me with money I collected from Spiritism. I have never had a moment of repose. More than once, I have succumbed to excessive work; my health has been shaken and my life compromised. But thanks to the protection and assistance of the good Spirits, who incessantly gave me manifest proofs of their solicitude, I am pleased to realize that I have never felt a moment of feebleness or discouragement, and that I have always pursued my task with the same fervor, without*

34 *Parisian Society for Spiritist Studies*, founded on April 1, 1858. – Tr.

*concerning myself with the malevolence aimed at me. According to the communication by the Spirit Truth, I was to expect all this and indeed it all really did happen.*

Even so, along with these vicissitudes, how much happiness I have felt at seeing the work grow so prodigiously! With what sweet compensation have my tribulations been paid for! What blessings, what proofs of real sympathy I have received from so many afflicted, whom the Doctrine has consoled! This result was not mentioned to me by the Spirit *Truth*, who without a doubt, intentionally pointed out only the difficulties of the way. Thus, how ungrateful I would be if I complained! If I said that there is compensation between good and evil, I would not be truthful, because the good – and by *good* I refer to moral satisfactions – has prevailed much over evil. Whenever confronted with a disappointment or an annoyance, I would lift my thought above humanity and put myself in advance in the spirit realm. And from that high point, from where I could see my endpoint, the miseries of life slid right over me without affecting me. I made such a habit of it that the shouts of the malevolent never troubled me.

## THE SPIRITS' BOOK

(In Mr. Baudin's home; medium: Miss Baudin)
*June 17, 1856*

*Question (asked of Truth): One part of the book has already been reviewed. Would you kindly tell me what you think of it?*

*Answer: What has been reviewed is fine, but when the work is finished, you should reread it in order to lengthen it on certain points and shorten it on others.*

*Q:* Do you think it should be published before the foretold events have happened?

*A:* Part of it, yes; all of it, no; because I can assure you there are going to be some chapters that are very thorny indeed. As important as this first endeavor may be, *it is in a certain way no more than an introduction.* It will take on proportions that you cannot even imagine right now. You yourself will understand that certain parts can only be published much later and gradually as new ideas are developed and take root. Making everything available at once would be imprudent. Opinion needs time to take shape. You will run into impatient persons that will try to hurry you up: don't listen to them. Watch, observe, probe the terrain, know how to wait, and do as the prudent general who attacks only when the time is right.

*Remark (written in January 1867):* At the time of the above communication, I only had *The Spirits' Book* in mind, and as *Truth* stated, I was far from imagining the proportions the entire work would assume. The predicted events would not take place for many years, and they still have not. The books that have appeared so far have only been published sequentially, and I was led to compile them *as new ideas developed.* Of those yet to be written, the most important, the one that will be regarded as the capstone of the edifice, and which, in fact, contains *the thorniest* chapters, could not be published without harm before the time of the disasters. Thus, I saw only one book in detail and could not see how it could be split up, whereas *Truth* was alluding to the books that would follow, and whose premature publication would be inappropriate.
"Know how to wait," he said. "Don't listen to the impatient people that will try to hurry you up." There was, in fact, no lack of them, and if I had listened to them, the ship would have crashed on the reef. A strange thing: while some pushed me to go faster, others criticized me for not going slower. I did not listen to either one; I constantly used the progress of ideas as a compass.
I felt such confidence in the future as I saw the things predicted being accomplished, and as I recognized the depth and wisdom of the teachings of my invisible protectors.

## THE SPIRITS' BOOK

(In Mr. Baudin's home; medium: Miss Baudin)
*September 11, 1856*

After I had given a reading of a few chapters from *The Spirits' Book* concerning the moral laws, the medium wrote spontaneously:

"You have grasped the purpose of your endeavor very well. The plan is well-thought out. We are satisfied with you. Continue, but above all remember that when the book is finished, we recommend that you have it printed and disseminated. It is of widespread usefulness. We are content and will never forsake you. Believe in God and press on!"

Several Spirits

## THE SPIRITUAL TIARA

(In Mrs. Cardonne's home)
*May 6, 1857*

I had the opportunity to meet Mrs. Cardonne at one of Mr. Roustan's séances. Someone told me – I think it was Mr. Carlotti – that she had the remarkable talent of reading palms. I had never believed in the significance of the lines on the palm, but I had always thought that, for certain persons gifted with a sort of second sight, it could be a way to establish a connection that enabled them, just like somnambulists, to sometimes say things that were true. The signs of the hand would be but a pretext, a way to focus the attention, to develop lucidity, similar to cards, coffee grounds, and so-called magic mirrors for persons who have such a faculty. Experience often confirmed the veracity of that opinion. Be it as it may, I accepted the invitation to pay her a visit and the following is a summary of what she said:

"You were born with a great abundance of intellectual resources and means … an extraordinary power of discernment … Your taste is cultured; governed by your mind, you moderate inspiration with reason; you subordinate instinct, passion and intuition to method, to theory. You have always had a penchant for the moral sciences … a love for absolute truth … a love for defined art.

"Your style has weight, measure and rhythm; but sometimes, you would trade a bit of your precision for some poetry.

"As an idealist philosopher, you have been subjected to the opinion of others; as a believing philosopher, you now experience the need to form a sect.

"You possess thoughtful benevolence; an imperative need to relieve, to help, to console; a need for independence.

"You correct yourself very gently from your quick temper.

"You are remarkably suitable for the mission entrusted to you because your character is more suited to make you the center of immense undertakings than isolated endeavors … Your eyes have the look of thought.

"I see here the sign of the *spiritual tiara* … It is highly visible … Look." (I looked, but did not see anything special.)

"What do you mean by *spiritual tiara?*" I asked. "Do you mean that I will be a Pope? If so, it certainly won't be in this lifetime."

*Answer:* *"Notice that I said spiritual tiara, which means moral and religious authority, and not actual sovereignty."*

I have reproduced purely and simply this woman's words, which she herself transcribed for me. It is not up to me to judge if they are precise on every point. I acknowledge that some of them are true because they are in harmony with my character and the dispositions of my spirit. However, there is one passage that is obviously wrong, where she says that with regard to my style, I sometimes would trade a bit of my precision for some poetry. I have no poetic instinct whatsoever. What I seek above all, what pleases me, what I value in others, is clarity, clearness, precision, and far from sacrificing all that to poetry, what I could be criticized for, somewhat, is that I sacrifice poetic sentiment for the dryness of the positive style. I have always preferred what speaks to the intelligence to what speaks only to the imagination.

As for the *spiritual tiara, The Spirits' Book* had just come out. The Doctrine was just forming and one could not yet predict its subsequent results. I gave little importance to that revelation and limited myself to noting it as just a bit of information.

The following year, Mrs. Cardonne left Paris and I did not see her again until eight years later, in 1866, during which interval things had already progressed quite a bit. She said to me, "Do you recall my prediction regarding the *spiritual tiara?* It has been fulfilled."

"What do you mean fulfilled?" I replied. "As far as I know, I'm not sitting on St. Peter's throne."

"No, but that is not what I told you. Aren't you, in fact, the head of the Doctrine, recognized by Spiritists all over the world? Don't your writings set principles? Aren't your adherents in the millions? Is there another man whose name actually carries more authority than yours in matters of Spiritism? Aren't the titles of high priest, pontiff and even Pope willingly given to you? It is mainly by your adversaries and out of sarcasm, I know, but it is no less an indication of the type of influence they recognize in you; they sense your role, and these titles will remain.

"In other words, without seeking it, you have earned a moral position that no one can take from you, and considering any endeavors that could be undertaken after yours or simultaneous with yours, you will always be known as the founder of the Doctrine. So, ever since that moment, you have possessed a *spiritual tiara*, that is, moral supremacy. Thus, you can see that I told you the truth.

"Do you now believe just a bit more in palm reading?"

"Less than ever, and I am convinced that if you did see something, it was not on my palm but in your own spirit, and I will prove it to you.

"I admit that there are certain physiognomic signs on the hands, as well as the feet, arms and other parts of the body, but each organ displays particular signs according to its use and its connection to the mind. The signs on the hand cannot be the same as those on the feet, arms, mouth, eyes, etc.

"As for the palm lines on the hands, the greater or lesser accentuation they display results from the nature of the skin and the greater or lesser quantity of cellular tissue. Since these parts have no physiological correlation with the organs of the intellectual and mental faculties, they cannot be their expression. Even admitting such a correlation, they might furnish indications about the current state of the individual but they cannot be precursory signs of future or past events independent of his or her will. In the first hypothesis, I would understand that, possibly with the help of such lines, one might be able to tell if a person possesses this or that aptitude, this or that inclination. But plain common sense would reject the notion that one could tell if a person has been married or not, how many times, the number of children, or if widowed or not, and other such things as most fortunetellers allege.

"Among the lines of the palms, there is one well known by all, and which looks like the letter 'M' well enough. They say that if it is quite accentuated, it foretells a *malheureuse* [unhappy] life, but the word *malheur* [unhappiness] is French and one mustn't forget that the equivalent word does not begin with the same letter in all languages, from which one must conclude that the line in question should present a different form according to the particular language.

"As for the *spiritual tiara,* it is evidently something special and exceptional, and to a certain point, individual. I am convinced that you did not come up with that expression in the vocabulary of any treatise on fortunetelling. So, how did it come into your mind? Through intuition, through inspiration, by that sort of prescience peculiar to the double sight that many persons possess without suspecting it. Your attention was focused on the lines of my palm and you fixated your thought on a sign which some other person could have seen as something completely different, or to which you yourself would have attributed a different meaning in another individual."

## FIRST NOTICE OF A NEW INCARNATION

(In Mr. Baudin's home; medium: Miss Baudin)
*January 17, 1857*

The Spirit had promised to write me a letter as the new year arrived. He said that he had something in particular to tell me. Having asked him about it at one of our regular meetings, he said he would give it to the medium in private, who would then transmit it to me. This is the letter:

"Dear friend, I didn't want to write to you last Tuesday in front of everybody, because there are certain things that can be said only between you and me.

"First of all, I want to talk to you about your book, the one about to be published. (*The Spirits' Book* had just gone to press.) Don't wear yourself out from morning to night; you will feel better, and the book will lose nothing by having to wait.

"According to what I have seen, you are quite capable of bringing your undertaking to a successful conclusion and are called to do great things. But don't overdo it. Observe and appraise everything thoroughly and calmly. Don't let yourself be swayed by enthusiasts or by the impatient. Measure all your steps and all your approaches in order to securely reach your goal. Believe only what you can see; don't shun what seems incomprehensible to you. You will know more about it than anyone else because the topics for study will be laid out before your eyes.

"Alas! The truth will neither be known nor believed by everyone except after a very long time! During this lifetime, you will see but the dawning of the success of your work. You will have to come back, *reincarnating in another body,* to complete what you have begun, and then you will be given the satisfaction of seeing the full fructification of the seed that you will have sown in the earth.

"There will be envious and jealous persons that will try to denigrate you and thwart you. Don't get discouraged. Don't concern yourself with what they say or do against you. Pursue your endeavor. Continue working for the progress of humankind and you will be helped by the good Spirits as long as you persevere on the path of the good.

"Do you remember that a year ago I promised my friendship to those who throughout the year had lived rightly? Well then! I can tell you that you are one of those I have chosen from among all the others.

"Your friend who loves and watches over you, Z."

*Remark:* *As I stated earlier, Z was not a high order spirit, although he was very good and benevolent. Perhaps he was more highly evolved than the name he took would imply. One could suppose so, judging from the serious nature and the wisdom of his communications, according to the circumstances. By using such a name he could allow himself a familiar language suitable to the milieu where he manifested, and say – which happened often – hard truths under the light form of witticism. Be that as it may, I have always kept a fond memory of him and have been grateful for the timely warnings he gave me and for the devotion he showed me. He disappeared with the dispersion of the Baudin family, and said that he had to reincarnate soon.*

# REVUE SPIRITE

(In Mr. Dufaux's home; medium: Mrs. E. Dufaux)
*November 15, 1857*

*Question:* *I plan to publish a Spiritist periodical. Do you think I will succeed and would you advise me to do it? I spoke to Mr. Tiedman about it and he doesn't seem to be ready to lend me his financial help.*

*Answer:* *You will succeed if you persevere. The idea is a good one but it needs to be developed a bit more.*

*Q:* I'm afraid someone else might do it ahead of me.

*A:* You need to hurry.

*Q:* There's nothing better that I would like to do, but I lack the time. As you know, I have two jobs, which I really need. I would like to be able to quit them in order to dedicate myself entirely to my endeavor without any other concerns.

*A:* For now, you should not abandon anything. One always finds time for everything; get going and you shall attain.

*Q:* Should I proceed without Mr. Tiedman's help?

*A:* Proceed with or without his help; don't worry about him. You can get by without him.

*Q:* I had the intention of producing a first issue as a trial in order to post the periodical and fix a date, so as to continue later, if possible. What do you think?

*A:* The idea is good, but one issue won't be enough; nonetheless, it is useful and even necessary to pave the way. You will have to proceed very cautiously in order to lay the foundation for a lasting success. If it contains any flaws, better not to have done anything at all, for the first impression could decide its future. Especially at the beginning, it is necessary to satisfy people's curiosity; it must contain the serious and the pleasing at one and the same time: the serious will interest the people of science and the pleasing will delight the common folk. This part is essential, but the other is more important, since without it the periodical will not have a solid foundation. In sum, it is necessary to avoid monotony through variety, to combine solid instruction with interest, and this will be a powerful aid for later works.

*Remark:* *I rushed to write the first issue, and had it published on January 1, 1858, without my having told anyone beforehand. It had no subscribers or investors. I published it assuming all the risks, and I have nothing to regret because its success surpassed all my expectations. Since January 1, the issues have followed one another without interruption, and just as the Spirit had predicted, the periodical became a powerful aid for me. I recognized much later that it was a good thing that I had not had any investors because I had more freedom, whereas another party could have wanted to impose his own ideas and will, and thus hinder my goal. By myself, I did not have to render an accounting to anyone, however hard the burden of my task.*

## FOUNDING OF THE PARISIAN SPIRITIST SOCIETY

*April 1, 1858*

Although there is no instance of foreknowledge regarding it, as a matter of interest I will mention the founding of the Society due to its role in the progress of Spiritism and the subsequent communications it gave rise to.

For nearly six months in my home on Martyrs Street, I held meetings with a few adherents on Tuesdays. The principal medium was Miss E. Dufaux. Although the place was not meant to accommodate more than fifteen to twenty people, there were sometimes up to thirty. These meetings were of great interest due to their serious nature and the far-reaching questions treated at them, and quite often one got to see foreign dignitaries and other distinguished individuals.

The locale was not very comfortable in its layout and, of course, became too cramped. Some of the frequenters proposed contributing to renting a more suitable place, but then it would be necessary to get legal authorization to avoid being bothered by the authorities.[35] Mr. Dufaux, who knew the chief of police personally, took care of the matter. The authorization would also depend on the Secretary of the Interior, General X[36], who was, without our knowledge, sympathetic to our ideas, although he did not understand them entirely. Due to his influence, the authorization, which according to standard procedures would have taken three months, was obtained in fifteen days.

The Society was thus legally constituted and began holding meetings every Tuesday in the room it rented at Palais-Royal, Galerie de Valois. It met there for one year, from April 1, 1858 to April 1, 1859. Unable to continue there, it began meeting on Fridays in one of the rooms of the Donix Restaurant at Palais-Royal, Galerie Montpensier, from April 1, 1859 to April 1, 1860, at which time it moved to its own premises at 59 Sainte-Anne St.

The Society, at first made up of little-homogenous elements and of persons of good will who were accepted a little too easily, went through numerous vicissitudes that were not the smallest troubles of my task.

---

35 At the time, France was under the rule of Napoleon III (1851-1870). Among the restrictions on freedom imposed by the government, meetings with more than 20 persons were prohibited in closed environments without express authorization to the contrary. – Publ.

36 General Charles-Marie-Esprit Espinasse, Secretary of the Interior and General Security for the imperial government of Napoleon III. – Publ.

## THE LENGTH OF MY ENDEAVORS

(In Mr. Forbes' home; medium: Mrs. Forbes)
*January 24, 1860*

In keeping with my way of evaluating things, I calculated that I still had about ten years to finish my endeavors, but I had not told this to anyone. Thus, I was very surprised when I received from one of my Limoges correspondents a communication obtained spontaneously, in which the spirit, speaking of my endeavors, said that it would be ten years before I would finish them.

*Question (asked of Truth):* *How can a spirit, communicating from Limoges – where I have never been – address exactly what I had been thinking about: the length of my endeavors?*

*Answer:* *We know what is yet left for you to do, and consequently, the approximate time you will need to achieve it. Thus, it is quite natural for the Spirits to have mentioned it in Limoges and elsewhere to give an idea of the scope required by the work.*

Nevertheless, ten years is not absolute; it can be prolonged by a few years, depending on unforeseeable circumstances outside your will.

> *Remark (written in December 1866):* I have published four substantial volumes, not to mention supplemental works. The Spirits are urging me to publish *Genesis* in 1867, before the tribulations. During the time of great disturbance, I should work on books supplementary to the Doctrine that cannot appear after the great tempest and for which I need three to four years. At the earliest, that would take me to 1870, that is, about ten years.

## MY MISSION

(In Mr. Dehau's home; medium: Mr. Crozet)

Spontaneous communication received in my absence
*April 12, 1860*

Due to his firmness and perseverance, your President has frustrated the plans of those who had sought to destroy his credibility and to ruin the Society in the hopes of dealing Spiritism a fatal blow. Homage to him! He can be certain that we are at his side and that the Spirits of wisdom will be happy to assist him on his mission. How many there are who would be willing to fulfill this mission because they would receive the benefits derived from it!

But the mission is perilous, and to accomplish it, faith and an unshakable will are necessary, as well as self-denial and courage to brave offenses, sarcasm and disappointments, and not be disturbed by the mud slung by envy and calumny. In such a position, the worst that could happen would be to be labeled a madman and a charlatan. Let them say and think as they wish; everything lasts only a while, except eternal happiness. Everything will be taken into account; and bear in mind that to be happy it is necessary to have contributed to the happiness of the poor beings with whom God has peopled your earth. May your conscience therefore remain in peace and serenity: it is the precursor of heavenly bliss.

## MY RETURN

(In my own home; medium: Mrs. Schmidt)
*June 10, 1860*

*Question (asked of Truth):* *I have just received a letter from Marseille, telling me that they are seriously studying Spiritism and The Spirits' Book in the seminary of that city. What does that mean? Could it be that the clergy are actually taking it to heart?*

*Answer:* *No doubt about it. The clergy are very much taking it to heart because they can foresee the consequences it will have for them; and they are really worried about it. The clergy, especially the enlightened segment, is studying Spiritism more than you might think, but don't think it is out of sympathy; on the contrary, they are looking for ways to combat it, and I assure you that the war they will wage will be fierce. Don't be concerned; continue to act with prudence and circumspection; be on your guard against the traps they set for you. In your speech and writings, cautiously avoid anything that may be used as a weapon against you. Fearlessly continue on your pathway, and if it is sown with thorns, I assure you that you will be greatly pleased before coming back to join us "for a little while."*

*Q:* What do you mean by the words "a little while"?

*A:* I mean that you will not be with us for long. You must return to the earth to conclude the mission that could not be finished in this lifetime. If it were possible, you would not leave at all; however, we are subject to the law of nature. You will be absent for a few years, and when you return, it will be under conditions that will permit you to start working early on. Meanwhile, there is work for you to do before you leave; that is why we will give you enough time to finish it.

*Remark:* *Calculating the approximate amount of time that the remaining work would take, and taking into account the time of my absence and the years of childhood and youth until the age at which a person can play a role in the world, that will necessarily carry us toward the end of this century or the beginning of the next.*

## AUTO DE FE[37] IN BARCELONA.

37 A public ceremony during which the sentences against those brought before the Spanish Inquisition were read, and after which such sentences were carried out by the secular authorities. www.britannica.com. Kardec used the expression for the burning of the books in Barcelona. – Tr.

## CONFISCATION OF THE BOOKS

(In my own home; medium: Mr. d'A…)
*September 21, 1861*

At the request of Mr. Lachatre, then residing in Barcelona, I sent him a certain number of *The Spirits' Book, the Mediums' Book,* issues of *Revue Spirite,* and various other Spiritist works and brochures – a total of nearly three hundred copies. The expediting of the shipment was done in a normal manner through his contact in Paris, in a package containing other merchandise and without the least legal infraction. When the books arrived, the addressee had to pay the import tariffs, but before delivering them the matter had to be referred to the bishop, the ecclesiastical authority that kept an eye on the books being sold in that country. The bishop was in Madrid at the time. Upon his return, based on the report he received, he ordered that the works be confiscated and burned in the public square at the hand of the public executioner. The sentence was set to be carried out on October 9, 1861.

If it had been a case of shipping the works as contraband, the Spanish authorities would have been within their rights to dispose of them as they pleased; however, from the moment that there was neither fraud nor surprise – proven by the tariffs being willingly paid – it would have been the utmost fairness to order the copies to be sent back if they could not be allowed into the country. The complaints made to the French Consul in Barcelona brought no results. Mr. Lachatre asked me if it should be referred to the higher authorities. My advice was to allow the arbitrary act to be carried out; nevertheless, I believed I should hear the opinion of my spirit guide.

*Question (asked of Truth):* *Of course you know what has occurred in Barcelona regarding the Spiritist works. Would you be so kind as to tell me if it would be appropriate to pursue having them returned?*

*Answer:* *By law, you can demand them and you would certainly obtain their restitution if you went to the French Minister of Foreign Relations. But my advice is that this auto de fe will result in a greater amount of good than would have resulted from the reading of a few books. The material loss is nothing compared to the repercussions that such an incident will bring to the Doctrine. You know how much such a ridiculous and antiquated act will aid the progress of Spiritism in Spain. Its ideas will spread so much faster there, and the works will be sought after much more eagerly because they were burned. All will go well.*

*Q:* Would it be appropriate to write an article about this in the next issue of *Revue Spirite?*

*A:* Wait until after the *auto de fe*.

## AUTO DE FE IN BARCELONA

*October 9, 1861*

This date will go down in the annals of Spiritism as that of the *auto de fe* of the Spiritist books in Barcelona. Following is an extract of the execution:

"On this 9th day of October in the year 1861, at 10:30 in the morning in the square of the city of Barcelona, at the place where condemned criminals are executed, and by order of the Bishop of this city, three hundred volumes and brochures on Spiritism were burned, to wit: *The Spirits' Book* by Allan Kardec, etc."

The main newspapers in Spain rendered a detailed account of the incident, which the organs of the liberal press of the country justly denounced. It should be noted that in France the liberal periodicals limited themselves to mentioning it without comment. The *Siècle* itself, so fervent in stigmatizing the abuses of power and the smallest acts of intolerance, did not have one word of reproof for such an act worthy of the Middle Ages. A few minor newspapers even found in it a reason for mockery. Regardless of any beliefs, it was a matter of principle, of international rights of interest to the whole world, which would not have been taken so lightly if it had concerned other works. They spare no blame when it comes to the simple refusal of a stamp for the peddling of a materialistic book. Well! The Inquisition raising its bonfires with all the ancient solemnities at the gates of France: now that surely had quite another magnitude. So why the indifference? Because it involved a doctrine whose progress is regarded with dread by disbelievers. To demand justice on its behalf would be to consecrate its right to the protection of the authorities and would increase its credibility. Be that as it may, the Barcelona *auto de fe* produced the effect hoped for by its repercussions in Spain, where it contributed greatly to spreading Spiritist ideas. (See *Revue Spirite,* November 1861)

That event resulted in numerous communications on the part of the Spirits. The following was obtained spontaneously at the Parisian Society on October 19, upon my return from Bordeaux:

"Something was needed that would jolt certain incarnate spirits so that they would decide to concern themselves with the grand doctrine that shall regenerate the world. Nothing is done pointlessly on the earth in that regard, and we who inspired the *auto de fe* in Barcelona knew very well that by proceeding in such a manner we would enable a large step to be taken forward. That brutal event, unheard of in this day and age, took place in order to grab the attention of journalists who had remained indifferent to the profound agitation stirring the cities and Spiritist centers. They did not interfere, but remained obstinate in turning a deaf ear and responding with silence to the desire of divulgation from the adherents of Spiritism. Like it or not, they are speaking of it now. Some, by admitting the historical fact of what happened in Barcelona and others by denying it, have given rise to a polemic that will travel the world and from which Spiritism will only benefit. That is why today the rearguard of the Inquisition has performed its last *auto de fe* – because we willed it."

A Spirit

*Remark:* *An aquarelle sketch of the auto de fe scene, drawn at the locale by a distinguished artist, was sent to me from Barcelona. I had a photographic reduction made of it. I also possess some ashes taken from the bonfire, containing still-legible fragments of the burnt pages. I put them in a crystal urn.* [38][39]

## MY SUCCESSOR

(In my own home; private communication; medium: Mr. d'A...)

*December 22, 1861*

Since a conversation with the Spirits led to talks of my successor regarding the direction of Spiritism, I posed the following question:

*Question:* *Many of our adherents are worried about what will become of Spiritism after I'm gone, and they are asking about who will replace me since no one has publicly appeared to take over the reins.*

I responded that I did not have the pretense of being indispensable; that God is much too wise to base the future of a doctrine destined to regenerate the world on the life of just one man; moreover, I was always told that my job was to structure the Doctrine and that I would be given the time I needed to do so. The job of my successor will thus be much easier because the trail will have been fully blazed – all he will have to do is to follow it. Nevertheless, if the Spirits deemed it proper to tell me something more positive about the matter, I would be very grateful.

38 The Spiritist Bookstore still has them. – Note in the French edition.

39 The crystal urn was destroyed by the Nazis during WWII. – Publ.

*Answer:* *All of that is completely true; here is what else we can tell you about it. You are right in stating that you are not indispensable; you are only indispensable in human eyes because it was necessary that the work of organization be concentrated in the hands of only one person in order to give it unity; but you are not indispensable in God's eyes. You were chosen; that is why you are alone. But you are not, as you well know, the only one capable of fulfilling this mission. If for some reason it were interrupted, God would have no lack of individuals to replace you. So, come what may, Spiritism cannot be at risk.*

Until the work of development is complete, it has been necessary that you be the only one in evidence because a banner was needed to rally around. It was necessary to consider you indispensable so that the work that leaves your hands would have more authority in the present and the future; it was even necessary to envision fear due to the consequences of your departure.

If the one who is to replace you were designated in advance, the yet unfinished work could be hindered; oppositions aroused by jealousy would form against him; he would be argued over before he could prove himself; the enemies of the Doctrine would try to bar his way, resulting in schisms and divisions. Therefore, he will be revealed when the time comes.

His job will be much easier because, like you said, the trail will have been fully blazed; if he wanders off it, he will get lost, just as those who wanted to get in the way have already gotten lost. His job, however, will be more painful in another sense because he will have to endure harsher struggles. Yours is the responsibility of conception; his is the execution. That's why he will have to be a man of energy and action. Marvel here at God's wisdom regarding the choice of his representatives: you possess the qualities needed for the work you must accomplish, but you do not possess those needed by your successor. For you, the calm and tranquility of the writer who develops ideas in the silence of meditation; for him, the strength of a captain who commands a ship according to the rules traced by science. Free of the work of creating the endeavor under whose weight your body will succumb, he will be freer to apply his faculties to the development and consolidation of the edifice.

*Q:* Could you tell me if the choice of my successor has been set as of this moment?

*A:* It has and it hasn't, since the individual, having free will, can at the last minute withdraw before the task that he himself has chosen. Furthermore, he must prove his capabilities, devotion, disinterestedness and self-denial. If he is led by ambition only and the desire to be recognized, he will certainly be set aside.

*Q:* It has been said several times that many high order spirits will incarnate to help with the movement.

*A:* Undoubtedly, many spirits will have that mission, but each will have their specialty and will act through their position in this or that segment of society. They will all reveal themselves by their deeds, and none by any pretense of supremacy.

## THE IMITATION OF THE GOSPEL

(Segur; August 9, 1863; medium: Mr. d'A…)

*Remark:* *I had not told anyone about the subject of the book I was working on. I kept its title so secret that the publisher, Mr. Didier, only found out what it was at printing time. The title for the first edition was The Imitation of the Gospel. Later, due to reiterated observations by Mr. Didier himself and other persons, it was changed to The Gospel according to Spiritism. Thus, the thoughts contained in the following communications could not be the result of the medium's preconceived ideas.*

*Question:* *What do you think about the new book I'm working on?*

*Answer:* *This doctrinal book will have a considerable influence; in it you touch on crucial issues, and not only will the religious world find in it the maxims that are necessary for the world, but people's practical lives will also glean excellent teachings from it. You have done well to address issues of high practical morality from the point of view of general, social and religious interests. Doubt will be eliminated; the earth and its civilized populations are ready; your friends from the Other Side have been preparing for it for quite some time now. Therefore, sow the seed that we have entrusted to you because it is time for the earth to gravitate in the radiant order of the spheres, and for it to finally exit from the penumbra and the intellectual mists. Finish the book and count on the protection of your guide – the guide of all of us – and on the devoted help of your most devoted Spirits, amongst whose number you may always include me.*

*Q:* What will the clergy say?

*A:* The clergy will cry heresy because it will see that you bluntly attack eternal punishment and other points upon which they base their influence and credibility. They will holler all the more because they will feel much more wounded than by the publication of *The Spirits' Book*, where they could supposedly accept the main principles it contains. Presently, however, you are entering upon a new pathway, on which they will not be able to follow. The secret anathema will become official, and Spiritists, following the Jews and pagans, will be rejected by the Roman Church. On the other hand, Spiritists will see their numbers increase due to this type of persecution, especially when they see priests labeling as absolutely demonic a doctrine whose morality will shine like a ray of sunlight due to the publication of your new book and those that follow.

The time is approaching when it will be necessary for you to announce Spiritism for what it is, and show to all where the true doctrine taught by Christ is to be found. The time is coming when, before heaven and earth, you shall proclaim Spiritism as the only truly Christian tradition, the only truly human and divine institution. In choosing you, the Spirits recognized the solidity of your convictions, and that your faith, like a wall of bronze, would resist all attacks.

Nevertheless, my friend, if your courage has not yet failed under the heavy task that you accepted, be aware that the easiest period is over, and that the time of difficulties has arrived. Yes, dear master, the great battle is made ready; fanaticism and intolerance, stirred up by the success of your writings, will attack you and your loved ones with poisonous weapons. Prepare yourself for the struggle. But I have faith in you, as you have faith in us, because your faith is the kind that moves mountains and enables one to walk on water. Have courage, therefore, and may your book be completed. Count on us, and count especially on the great soul of the Master of us all, who is watching over you in a very special way.

*Paris, September 14, 1863*

*Remark:* *I had asked for a personal communication on any subject and that it be sent to me at my Sainte-Adresse retreat.*

"I would like to speak to you from Paris, although I don't see how it would be useful, since my inner voices may be heard all around you and your brain perceives our inspirations with an ease that not even you suspect. Our activity, especially of the Spirit *Truth,* is constantly around you and in such a way that you cannot dispute it. That is why I won't go into pointless details about the work plan, which, following my secret counsels, you so fully and completely modified. You can now understand why we needed to have you on hand, free from any other concern than the Doctrine. An endeavor like the one we developed together requires reflection and sacred isolation. I have a living interest in your work, which is a considerable step forward and will at last open to Spiritism the broad road of useful applications for the good of society. With this endeavor, the edifice has begun to be freed from its scaffolding and to see its capstone designed on the horizon. So, carry on without impatience or lassitude; the monument will be ready at the appointed hour.

"We have already addressed the incidental issues of the moment with you, that is, the religious issues. *Truth* told you about the uproar already taking place. Such foreseen hostilities are necessary to keep people's attention awake, because they so easily let it wander away from a serious subject. The soldiers who are fighting for the cause will continue to be joined by new combatants whose words and writings will cause a sensation and will bring trouble and confusion to the adversaries' ranks.

"Goodbye, dear companion of yesteryear, faithful disciple of the truth, who has continued throughout his life the work that in times past, before the great Spirit, who loves you and whom I worship, we swore to dedicate our strength and lives to until it is concluded. I salute you."

*Remark:* *In fact, the work plan had been completely modified, which the medium could not possibly have known, since he was in Paris and I was in Sainte-Adresse. He could not have known that Truth had told me about the uproar of the Bishop of Algiers and others. All these circumstances confirmed the part the Spirits were playing in my endeavors.*

## "LIFE OF JESUS" BY RENAN

(Regarding the future of various publications; medium: Mr. d'A…)

*Paris, October 14, 1863*

*Question (asked of Erastus):* *What effect will Renan's Life of Jesus have?*

*Answer:* *The effect will be enormous. The impact will be huge among the clergy because it will hurl to earth the very foundations of the edifice, in which the clergy has sheltered itself for the last eighteen centuries. It is not a faultless book – far from it – because it is the reflection of an exclusive opinion that limits its view to the narrow circle of material life. Although Renan is not a materialist, he belongs to that school which, while not rejecting the spiritual principle, neither attributes to it any effective and direct role in the progress of the things of the world. He is one of those blind intelligences who explain in their own way what they cannot see; who, not understanding the mechanism of remote viewing, imagines that one cannot know a thing but by touching it. Thus, he has reduced Christ to the size of the most ordinary individuals, denying him all the faculties that are the attributes of the spirit free and independent of matter.*

Yet, besides crucial errors – especially in regards to spirituality – the book contains highly correct observations, which until now have escaped commentators, and which, from a certain point of view, give it a far-reaching scope. Its author belongs to that legion of incarnate spirits that may be classified as demolishers of the old world; their mission is to level the terrain upon which a new, more-rational world will be built. God wanted a writer – credited from the talent point of view – to come and shed light on a number of obscure questions tainted by secular prejudices in order to predispose minds to new beliefs. Without suspecting it, Renan has smoothed the way for Spiritism.

## THE NEW GENERATION

(Villon group; medium: Mr. G...)
*Lyon, January 30, 1866*

The earth quivers with joy; the day of the Lord draws nigh; all those among us at the forefront encourage the desire to join in the fray. Already the spirits of more than a few valiant incarnates are gearing up for it. The material flesh does not know what to think; an unknown fire consumes it. These spirits are about to be delivered, for the time has come. An eternity is at the point of expiring; a glorious eternity is about to break forth and God is counting his children.

The kingdom of gold shall give way to a purer kingdom; the mind shall soon be sovereign, and high order spirits, who from the remotest times have illumined the centuries in which they lived and served as beacons for the centuries to come, shall incarnate amongst you. But what am I saying? Many already are incarnate. Their wise word will be a lethal flame that will irreparably ravage the old abuses. How many former prejudices shall come crashing down as the spirit, like a double-edged ax, hacks them at their very foundations!

Yes, the parents of the progress of the human spirit have departed: some, for their radiant dwelling places; others, for the grand endeavors in which happiness is added to the pleasure of learning in order to retake the pilgrim's staff they had laid down at the threshold of the temple of science. Soon, from the four corners of the globe, official scholars will listen in terror to beardless youths, who will use profound language to refute the arguments that they had deemed irrefutable. The mocking smile will no longer be a protective shield, and under the pain of decline, they will be forced to respond. Then, the vicious circle in which the masters of vain philosophy have enclosed themselves will be fully exposed because these new champions will not only bring a torch – the intelligence unburdened of its coarse veils – but many of them will also enjoy that particular state – that privilege of great souls such as Jesus – that gives the power to heal and to perform wonders called miracles. Before the material phenomena, by which the spirit shows itself so very superior to matter, how can the existence of spirits be denied? Materialists will be refuted in their discourses by a word that is more eloquent than their own, and by patent, positive facts that can be proved by all, for, great and small, new St. Thomases will be able to touch them with their finger.

Yes, the old, worn-out world is crumbling; the old world has come to an end and along with it, all those old dogmas that still glitter only because of the gilding that covers them. Valorous spirits, it is up to you to scrape away that false gold. To the rear, all you who wish in vain to shore up the old idol; struck on all sides, it will crumble and drag you down with it in its fall.

To the rear, all you deniers of progress; to the rear, with your beliefs of a bygone era. Why do you deny progress and wish to deter it? It is because wanting to prevail, now and forever, you have focused your thoughts on articles of faith, clamoring to humankind: "You shall always be children, and we, who have illumination from On High, we are destined to lead you."

But you have seen the child's leading-strings resting in your hands as the child leaps ahead of you, and yet you still deny that it can walk on its own! Is it by lashing it with the leading-strings meant to uphold it that you will prove the authority of your arguments? No, and you know it well. But to you, who say you are infallible, it is so pleasing to believe that others have faith in that infallibility, which not even you yourselves believe in any longer!

Ah! What laments are heard in the sanctuary! If one listens closely, it is there that the grieving whispers may be heard. What are you saying, you poor obstinate ones? That the hand of God has fallen on his Church? That everywhere, the free press attacks you and demolishes your arguments? Where is the new St. Chrysostom[40], whose powerful word could reduce to nothing this flood of thinkers? In vain do you wait; the most vigorous and esteemed pens among you can no longer prevail. They insist on clinging to a past that

---

40 Chrysostom (the golden-mouthed), on account of his eloquence, came into the world of Christian parents about the year 344, in the city of Antioch. www.ccel.org. – Tr.

is disappearing while, in an irresistible impulse that impels it forward, a new generation calls out: No; no more of the past; ours is the future; a new dawn is breaking, and that is to where our aspirations are inclined!

Forward! it says. Widen the road; our brothers and sisters will follow us. Follow the tide that is leading us; we need movement, which is life, whereas you offer us immobility, which is death.

Open your tombs, your catacombs; satiate your eyes with the old ruins of a past that no longer exists. Your holy martyrs are not at all dead, so that you can keep them frozen in the present. They foresaw our era, and death for them was the pathway that would take them there. To each era, its own character. We want to seize life because death will be loathed in the centuries that lie ahead of us.

That, my friends, is what the valiant spirits who are incarnating right now will render comprehensible. This century will not end without many remains covering the ground. Deadly, fratricidal war will soon vanish in light of dialogue; reason will replace brute force. And after all those benevolent souls have done battle, they will return to our spirit world to receive the crown of victory.

That is the goal, my friends. The champions are too valiant for success to be in doubt. God has chosen the elite of his combatants and victory is within humankind's reach.

So rejoice, all you who long for happiness, and who want your brothers and sisters to share in it with you. The day has come! The earth leaps with joy because it shall behold the beginning of the kingdom of peace promised by Christ, the divine messenger, a kingdom whose foundations He came to establish.

A Spirit

## AN INSTRUCTION REGARDING ALLAN

## KARDEC'S HEALTH

(Private communication; medium: Mr. D…)
*Paris, April 23, 1866*

In light of Allan Kardec's health continuing to worsen due to excessive work undermining his strength, I feel I must once again repeat to him what I have already told him so many times: You need to rest; human strength has its limits, and your desire to see the teaching progress often leads you to exceed them. You are in the wrong, because by acting like this you will not hasten the progress of Spiritism; on the other hand, acting like this will ruin your health and make it materially impossible to finish the task you have come to accomplish on the earth. Your present infirmity is nothing more than the result of a constant expenditure of vital forces without taking time for the necessary reparation, as well as an *overheating of the body*[41] caused by the complete lack of rest. Rest assured that we are sustaining you, but on the condition that you not undo what we do. What good does it do to rush? Haven't we told you many times that each thing will come in its own time and that the spirits in charge of the movement of ideas will know how to bring about favorable circumstances when the time comes to act?

While all Spiritists are gathering their strength for the battle, do you think it your duty to exhaust yours? No. You must be an example in everything and your place will be on the frontline when danger strikes. What will you do there if your weakened body doesn't allow your spirit to use the weapons that experience and revelation have put in your

41 *Scientific research has demonstrated that vital exhaustion causes an increase in body temperature and critical changes in blood coagulation, increasing the risk for heart attack and stroke.* Yaqub B & Al Deeb S - Heat strokes: Aetiopathogenesis, neurological characteristics, treatment and outcome. J. Neurol. Sci. 156:144–151, 1998.; Kop W. J. et al.: Relationship of Blood Coagulation and Fibrinolysis to Vital Exhaustion. Psychosom. Med. 60(3):352-358,1998; Schuitemaker G.E. et al.: Vital Exhaustion as a Risk Indicator for First Stroke. Psychosomatics 45:114-118, 2004. (Provided by Dr. Sonia Doi, U.S. Spiritist Medical Association) – Tr.

hands? Believe me: leave for later the great works destined to complete the work outlined in your first publications. Your regular work and some small urgent brochures are enough to absorb your time and should be the only objects of your current preoccupations.

I am not speaking in my name only; I am here as the delegate of all the spirits that have contributed so mightily to spreading the teaching through your judicious instructions. Through my intercession, they are telling you that the delay that you regard as harmful to the future of the doctrine is a necessary measure from more than one point of view, whether because certain issues have not yet been fully elucidated, or because people's minds need to be prepared to assimilate them more easily. Others must clear the land and certain theories must prove their insufficiency and create a larger vacuum. In sum, the moment is not right; so spare yourself. When the time does come, your full strength of body and spirit will be necessary. Has Spiritism been the target of many diatribes and stirred many storms thus far? Do you think that all such activities have quieted down, that all the hatred has been assuaged and become powerless? Don't kid yourself. The purifying furnace has not yet purged all the impurities. The future has more trials in store for you and the final crises will not be the least painful ones to bear.

I know that your particular situation imposes on you an enormous amount of secondary tasks that take up most of your time. All sorts of requests overwhelm you and you make it a duty to answer them as much as you can. I will do here what you undoubtedly would not dare do yourself, and addressing Spiritists in general, I ask them, in the interest of Spiritism itself, to spare you any work overload that may take up the time you need to dedicate yourself almost exclusively to finishing the work. Even though your correspondence may suffer a bit because of this, the teaching will profit from it.

Sometimes personal satisfaction has to be sacrificed for the general interest. It is an urgent measure that all sincere adherents will understand and approve of.

The voluminous correspondence you receive is for you a valuable source of documents and pieces of information. It keeps you informed about the true progress of the Doctrine. It is an impartial barometer. Furthermore, it provides you with moral satisfaction, which has upheld your courage more than once, showing you the adhesion that your ideas have encountered all over the world. From that point of view, overabundance is a good thing and not a drawback, but only on the condition of backing your endeavors and not hindering them by creating additional tasks for you.

Dr. Demeure

*Question:* *My good Dr. Demeure, thank you for your wise advice. Thanks to my decision to have someone fill in for me except in exceptional cases, the current correspondence is suffering little now and will not suffer at all in the future. But what am I to do with the more than five hundred letters that have piled up, which, in spite of my good will, I haven't been able to catch up on?*

*Answer:* *As they say in business terms, you need to shift them to the profits and losses account. By announcing this procedure in the* Revue*, your correspondents will know what to do. They will understand the necessity and will consider it justified by the preceding advice. I repeat: it will be impossible for things to go on as they have for much longer. Everything will suffer: your health as well as the Doctrine. You have to know how to make indispensable sacrifices when necessary. With peace-of-mind from now on regarding this point, you will be able to pursue your regular tasks more freely. This is the advice of someone who will always be your devoted friend.*

Demeure

> In taking such wise advice, we have asked those of our correspondents whom we have taken so long to answer to accept our apologies and our regret for not having been able to respond in as much detail as we would have liked to their kind letters, and to collectively accept the expression of our fraternal sentiments.

## THE REGENERATION OF HUMANKIND

(Summary of the communications given through Mrs. M… and T… while in a somnambulistic state)
*Paris, April 25, 1866*

Events are happening quickly, which is why we no longer say to you as before: "The time is drawing nigh." We now say, "The time has come."

By these words you shouldn't imagine a new flood, a cataclysm or a widespread upheaval. Partial convulsions of the globe have taken place in every era and continue to happen because they derive from its constitution – but they do not represent the signs of the times.

Nevertheless, everything that is predicted in the Gospel shall be fulfilled and is being fulfilled right now, as you will realize later on. However, you must take the announced signs only as allegories that are to be understood according to the spirit and not the letter. All *Scriptures* contain great truths under the veil of allegory, and it is because commentators are attached to the letter that they have gone astray. They have lacked the key to understanding their true meaning. This key lies in the discoveries of science and in the laws of the invisible world, which Spiritism has come to reveal to us. From here on out, with the aid of this new knowledge, what used to be obscure will become clear and intelligible.

Everything follows the natural order of things, and God's immutable laws cannot be subverted. Thus, you will see no miracles, no wonders, or anything supernatural in the common meaning attached to these words.

Do not look to the heavens in search of precursory signs, because you will not see them, and those who proclaim them are misleading you. Instead, look around you, in the midst of humankind, for that is where you will find them.

Do you not sense a sort of a wind blowing over the earth and stirring all spirits? The world is taken by expectation and seems to be seized by a vague presentiment that the storm is approaching.

Do not believe in the end of the physical world, however. The earth has been progressing ever since its transformation; it shall progress still and not be destroyed. Humankind, on the other hand, has reached one of the periods of its transformation and the earth will be elevated within the hierarchy of worlds.

Therefore, it is not the end of the physical world that is being prepared, but the end of the moral world. It is the old world – the world of prejudices, of selfishness, of pride, of fanaticism – that is caving in. Each new day brings a little ruin with it. Everything will end with the generation to come, and a new generation will build a new edifice that subsequent generations will consolidate and complete.

From a world of expiation, the earth is destined to become a happy world some day, and to live on it will be a reward instead of a punishment. The kingdom of the good will succeed the kingdom of evil.

So that human beings may be happy, the earth must be populated only by good spirits, both incarnate and discarnate. Since that time has arrived, a great emigration is underway at this moment among the spirits that inhabit it. Because those who practice evil for evil's sake and who are *not touched* by the sentiment of the good are undeserving of a transformed earth, they will be excluded from it because they would once again cause trouble and confusion and would be an obstacle to progress. They will expiate their insensitivity on lower worlds, to which they will take the knowledge they have acquired, with the mission to help such worlds evolve. They will be replaced on the earth by more-evolved spirits, who will see to it that justice, peace and fraternity reign.

We said earlier that the earth will not be transformed by a cataclysm that suddenly wipes out a whole generation. The current generation will disappear gradually and the new one will succeed it in the same way, without any change in the natural order of things. Thus, everything will take place on the outside as usual, with this one sole difference, but one that is crucial: a part of the spirits that used to incarnate on the earth will no longer do so. In every child that is born, instead of a low order spirit inclined toward evil, a more-advanced spirit *inclined toward the good* will reincarnate. So, it will be less of a new generation of physical bodies and more of a new generation of spirits. Hence, those who are expecting to see the transformation result from supernatural and extraordinary effects will be disappointed.

Today's era is one of transition; the members of the two generations are mixed together. Placed at the midway point, you will witness the departure of one and the arrival of the other, and each one can already be identified in the world by its particular characteristics.

These two generations will have completely opposite ideas and points of view. By the nature of their moral dispositions and especially by their *intuitive and inborn* dispositions, it will be easy to tell to which of the two each individual belongs.

Since the new generation will found an era of moral progress, it may be identified by an overall precocious intelligence and reason combined with the *inborn* sentiment of the good and spiritualist beliefs, which is the unmistakable sign of a certain degree of previous advancement. It will not be composed solely of eminently high order spirits, but spirits who, having already progressed, are predisposed to assimilating all sorts of progressive ideas and are capable of aiding the regenerative movement.

On the other hand, what identifies less-evolved spirits is, first of all, rebelliousness against God by denying Providence and any power above humanity; after that, the *instinctive* propensity for degrading passions, the anti-fraternal sentiments of pride, hatred, jealousy and avarice; in sum, the predominance of an attachment to everything material.

These are the vices that the earth will be purged of by the departure of those who refuse to amend themselves because they are incompatible with the kingdom of fraternity; men and women of the good would continue to suffer with their contact. The earth will be delivered from these people and humankind will march forward without obstacles toward the better future that is in store for it as a reward for its efforts and perseverance as it awaits a more complete purification to open the doors to higher worlds.

This emigration of spirits should not be understood as all spirits that are lagging behind being banished from the earth and relegated to lower worlds. Many have yielded to circumstances and example; in them, the rind is worse than the inside. Once removed from the influence of matter and prejudices of the corporeal world, most of them see things in a completely different way than when they were incarnate – according to the numerous examples you have. In this, they are aided by good spirits who are concerned with them, and who make an effort to enlighten them and show them the erroneous path they have followed. Through your prayers and exhortations, you can contribute to their betterment, because there is a perpetual solidarity between the living and the dead.

Consequently, they will be able to return and be happy because it will be their reward. What does it matter what they have been and done if now they are animated by better sentiments? Rather than being hostile toward society and progress, they will be useful helpers because they will belong to the new generation.

Thus, there will not be a definitive banishment except for fundamentally rebellious spirits, those whom pride and selfishness, more than ignorance, has rendered them deaf to the voice of the good and of reason. However, they will not be doomed to everlasting inferiority, for the day will come when they will repudiate their past and open their eyes to the light.

Therefore, pray for hardened hearts so that they may mend their ways while there is still time, for the day of expiation draws nigh.

Unfortunately, disregarding God's voice, the majority will persist in their blindness, and through dreadful struggles, their resistance will mark the end of their reign. In their distraction, they will rush to their own doom; they will cause devastation that will engender countless flagellations and calamities, such that, without meaning to, they will hasten the advent of the era of renewal.

And, as if the destruction were not occurring fast enough, suicides will increase in incredible proportions, even among children. Insanity will have never affected such a huge number of men and women who, even before they die, will be scratched from the number of the living. Such are the real signs of the times, and all will be fulfilled by the chain of events – as we have stated – without the least derogation from the laws of nature.

Nevertheless, through the dark cloud that envelops you, and in whose bosom the storm is rumbling, you can already see the first rays of the new age appear. Fraternity is laying its foundations all over the globe and the nations are joining hands; barbarity becomes familiar with civilization as it comes in contact with it; race and sect prejudices, which have caused tides of blood, are disappearing; fanaticism and intolerance are losing ground, whereas freedom of conscience is being introduced into customs, becoming a right. Ideas are brewing everywhere; evil is being recognized and remedies are being explored, but many proceed without a compass and get lost in utopias. The world is in the middle of an enormous endeavor of a gestation that will have lasted a whole century; in this still-confused endeavor, however, one can see a predominant tendency toward a goal: that of unity and uniformity, which predispose to brotherhood.

Such are also the signs of the times. But while other signs are those of the dying past, the aforementioned are the first cries of the newborn child, the precursors of the dawn that will see the rising of the next century, when the new generation will be in full force. Inasmuch as the 19th century differs from the 18th in certain points of view, the 20th century will differ from the 19th in other points of view.

One of the distinctive characteristics of the new generation will be *inborn* faith; not the exclusive and blind faith that divides people, but rational faith, which enlightens and strengthens, which unites and combines them in a common sentiment of love for God and neighbor. With the generation that is fading away, the last vestiges of disbelief and fanaticism will disappear, both being equally contrary to moral and social progress.

Spiritism is the road leading to renewal because it destroys the two biggest obstacles that oppose it: disbelief and fanaticism. It provides a solid, enlightened faith; it develops all the sentiments and ideas that correspond to the way the new generation sees things. That is why Spiritism is inborn and in a state of intuition in the minds of its representatives. Thus, the new age will see Spiritism expand and prosper because of the force of things. It will become the foundation for all beliefs, the point of support for all institutions.

But from now till then, how many battles must still be waged against those two great enemies: disbelief and fanaticism, which – an odd thing! – have joined hands to strike Spiritism down! They foresee its future and their downfall. That is why they dread Spiritism; they see it already sending down its roots into the ruins of the old selfish world; they see it as the banner that shall bring the peoples together. In the divine maxim *Without charity there is no salvation,* they read their own condemnation, for that phrase is the symbol of the new fraternal alliance proclaimed by Christ, shown to them like the fatal words at the banquet of Belshazzar.[42] Actually, they should bless this maxim because it would defend them against all reprisals from those who persecute them. But no! A blind force drives them to reject the only thing that could save them.

What can they do against the rise of the opinion that opposes them? Spiritism will emerge triumphant from the battle – have no doubt about it – because it lies within the laws of nature and thus cannot perish. Just look at all the ways by which the idea is spreading far and wide: believe that such ways are not fortuitous, but providential. What at first sight would seem to be harmful to Spiritism is precisely what aids in its dissemination.

Soon, Spiritism will see highly devoted champions appear amongst the most respected and qualified, who will support it with the authority of their name and their example, and they will impose silence on its detractors, because no one will dare treat them as crazy. These persons are studying it in silence and will appear when the appropriate time arrives. Until then, it is good that they remain aside.

Soon enough, you will also see the arts drawing from it as a gold mine, and translating the thoughts and horizons that it unveils through painting, music, poetry and literature. You have already been told that someday there will be Spiritist art, like there used to be pagan art and Christian art. This is a great truth, because great masters will be inspired by it. You will see the first sketches soon, and later it will occupy its proper place.

Spiritists! The future belongs to you and to all individuals of heart and devotion. Do not worry about the obstacles, for there is nothing that can hinder the designs

---

42 A reference to the "writing on the wall" in Daniel 5:25 foretelling the Babylonian king's approaching defeat by the Medes and Persians – Tr.

of Providence. Work tirelessly and give thanks to God for having placed you at the forefront of the new phalanx. It is a post of honor, which you yourselves have asked for and for which you must show yourselves worthy with your courage, perseverance and dedication. Happy are they who will die in that struggle, for in the spirit world, shame awaits those who succumbed out of weakness or pusillanimity. Moreover, struggles are necessary to strengthen the soul; contact with evil enables one to better appreciate the advantages of the good. Without the struggles that stimulate the faculties, the spirit would let itself indulge in a disastrous disregard for its advancement. Struggles against the elements develop physical strength and intelligence; struggles against evil develop moral strength.

## THE GRADUAL PROGRESS OF SPIRITISM. DISSENT AND OBSTACLES

(In Mr. Leymarie's home; medium: Mr. L...)
*Paris, April 27, 1866*

Dear fellow disciples: what is true must be; nothing can oppose the emanation of a truth; sometimes people will try to cover it up, persecute it and do to it what shipworms[43] do to Dutch dikes; but a truth is not built on stilts; it travels through space; it is in the ambient air. And if an entire generation could be blinded, there will always be new incarnations, new recruits from the world of spirits, who will bring fertile seeds and other elements, and all sorts of grand undiscovered things.

Do not rush, my friends. Many of you would like to go full steam ahead, and in these times of electricity, as fast as it does. Forgetting the laws of nature, you would like to go faster than the times. However, reflect on how wise God is

43 The naval shipworm, *Teredo navalis,* is not a worm at all. It is a highly specialized bivalve mollusk adapted for boring into and living in submerged wood. www.sms.si.edu. – Tr.

in everything. The elements that constitute your planet have gone through a long and laborious process of creation; before you could exist, everything had to be constituted according to the aptitude of your organs. Matter, minerals, cast and recast, gases, vegetation were harmonized and condensed little by little in order to enable you to appear on the earth. It is the eternal law of labor, which has never stopped governing inorganic as well as intelligent beings.

Spiritism cannot escape that law, the law of labor. Planted in ungrateful soil, it will have its harmful weeds and bad fruits. But also, every day, the bad branches are being cleared, removed or pruned; the soil is being loosened imperceptibly, and when travelers, weary of the struggles of life, see abundance and peace in the shade of a fresh oasis, they will quench their thirst and towel off their sweat in that slowly and wisely prepared kingdom. There, the king is God, the generous dispenser, the judicious egalitarian, who knows well that the pathway to be followed is dolorous but fruitful, pain-filled but necessary. The spirit formed in the school of labor will emerge from it stronger and more capable of great things. To those who become disheartened, the school says, "Have courage," and as supreme hope, it enables even the most ungrateful to foresee the finish line, the salutary point, the pathway marked by reincarnations.

Laugh at the vain declamations; let the dissidents talk; let those, who cannot console themselves for not being first, whine; all this patter will not keep Spiritism from consistently proceeding on its pathway. It is a truth, and just like a river, all truth must follow its course.

## SPIRITIST PUBLICATIONS

(Parisian Society – Medium: Mr. M.... in the somnambulistic state)
*August 16, 1867*

*Remark:* *Mr. L… had announced his proposal to produce Spiritist books that he would sell at greatly reduced prices. Mr. Morin refers to this subject in the following message obtained while in a somnambulistic state:*

"Spiritists are numerous today, but many still do not comprehend the eminently moralizing and emancipating scope of Spiritism. The core that has always followed the good road continues its slow but sure progress. It distances itself from all prejudices and works on those it leaves behind along the way.

"Unfortunately, even among those who form the faithful core there are those who find everything magnificent both on the part of others as well as on their own, and easily and benevolently, they let themselves be led by appearances and foolishly get caught in the web of their enemies, of people who claim to deprive themselves, give their blood, their assets, and their intelligence for the triumph of an idea. Very well! Read again the communication (which he had just written) and you will see that, on the part of certain individuals, such sacrifices cannot be made without ulterior motives.

"One must challenge ostentatious devotion and generosity just like the truthfulness of persons who say they never lie.

"To intend to provide something at an impossible price, without losing anything, is to hide speculation. There's even more: to give away, supposedly out of an excess of zeal, as a bonus, all the elements of a sublime doctrine, is the height of hypocrisy. Spiritists, watch out!"

## MY NEW BOOK ON GENESIS

(Private Séance; medium: Mr. D…)

(Spontaneous communication)
*Ségur, September 9, 1867*

First of all, a few words about the book you are preparing. As we have said many times already, it is urgent to get it underway without delay and to hasten its publication. The first edition has to be ready when the European conflict erupts.[44] If the book is late, the brutal events could divert attention away from purely philosophical works; and since this book is called to play a role in the way things are developing, it has to be introduced when the time is just right. Meanwhile, continue to develop its contents; give it all the breadth you desire; each small part weighs heavily in the balance of action, and at a time as decisive as this one, nothing must be disregarded, whether of a material or moral order.

Personally, I am happy with the work, but my opinion is of little worth next to the happiness of those it is called to transform. What makes me happy the most are the consequences it will have for the masses, both in the spirit world and on the earth.

*Question:* *If there are no mishaps, the book could come out in December. Do you foresee any obstacles?*

*Answer:* *I don't anticipate any insurmountable difficulties. Your health is the main concern, and that is why we are constantly advising you not to neglect it. As for external obstacles, I don't foresee any of a serious nature.*

Dr. D…

## GENESIS

(Private communication; medium: Mr. D…)
*February 22, 1868*

---

44 In 1870, the France of Napoleon III and the Prussia of Bismarck went to war, which ended with the latter annexing Alsace and part of Lorrain to its territory, thereby unleashing a series of conflicts that would culminate with the First World War (1914-1918). In that same year, also by means of a revolution, the Italian states were unified and became one sole nation, drastically reducing the territories and temporal power of the Church, then headed by Pope Pius IX. – Publ.

Following a communication in which Dr. Demeure gave me some very wise advice on changes to be made in the book *Genesis* during its reprinting, which he encouraged me to take care of without delay, I said to him:

"The brisk sales up to this point will cool down, without a doubt. It was an effect of the first moment. Thus, I think that the fourth and fifth editions will take longer to sell out. However, since some time is needed for revision and reprinting, it is important not to be caught off guard. Could you tell me approximately how much time I still have, so that I may act accordingly?[45]

*Answer:* *This revision is a serious endeavor and I would advise you not to take too long to get started. It would be better if you had it ready ahead of time than for them to have to wait for you. However, don't feel too rushed. In spite of the apparent contradiction in my words, you understand me, of course. Get to work on it right away, but don't concentrate on it indefatigably for too long. Take your time; the ideas will be much clearer, and your body will profit from less fatigue.*

Nevertheless, you should anticipate the book going out of stock quickly. When we told you that it would be a big success among all your other successes, we meant both a philosophical success and a material success. As you can see, our predictions were correct. Be ready at all times; things will happen more quickly than you might suppose.

*Remark:* *In a communication on December 18 [1867], he had told me: This will certainly be a big success amongst all your other successes. It is remarkable that in the space of two months another spirit repeated precisely these same words, saying: When WE told you, etc. That word WE*

45 The first three editions of *Genesis* were all exactly the same, with the 2nd and 3rd being simple reprints of the 1st, all three published in 1868. The 4th edition, revised and amplified by the Codifier, and which became the definitive edition, only came out in 1869 and was still at press when he discarnated. – Publ.

*proves that spirits act in accord and that often one speaks on behalf of many.*

## MY PERSONAL WORKS. VARIOUS COUNSELS

(Medium: Mr. D…)
*Paris, July 4, 1868*

Your personal endeavors are going well; pursue the reprinting of your last book; plan things out to the end of the year; that would be something useful; moreover, you can rely on us.

The impact caused by *Genesis* is only just beginning and many of the elements shaken by its appearance will soon line up under your banner; other serious works will appear to complete the elucidation of human thought about the new doctrine.

I also applaud the publication of Lavater's letters: it is a small thing destined to produce big effects. In sum, the year will be fruitful for all the friends of rational and liberal progress.

I am also completely in agreement with publishing the summary you propose to write in the form of a catechism or manual, but I think you should clean it up carefully. When you are ready to make it public, don't forget to consult me about the title. Perhaps I will have some good advice for you at the time, but it will depend on events.

When we recently advised you not to wait too long to revise *Genesis*, we said that you would have to add to it in various spots, fill in a few gaps and condense the material here and there in order to keep it from getting too large.

Our remarks have not been wasted, and we will be as happy to collaborate with its revision as we were to contribute to its writing.

I will engage you today to carefully revise the first chapters especially, where all the ideas are excellent and contain nothing that is not true; still, certain expressions could be interpreted wrongly. Except for these corrections, which I would advise you not to neglect because antagonists reject words when they cannot attack ideas, I have nothing else to advise you in this regard. Thus, I would advise you not to waste any time; it would be better for copies to have to wait for the public than for them to run short. Nothing harms a work more than a gap in its sales. Impatient at not being able to fill orders and thus losing an opportunity to sell books, a publisher will not be interested in the books of an improvident author. The public gets tired of waiting and the bad impression will be hard to erase.

On the other hand, it's good that you have a certain liberty of spirit to avoid the eventualities that may arise around you, and that you can give your attention to your private studies, which, according to events, may be raised currently or put away for a more propitious time.

So, be ready for anything; rid yourself of all impediments, whether to dedicate yourself to a special work, if the overall tranquility allows it, or whether to be prepared for any event if unforeseeable complications require a sudden decision. The coming year will soon be upon us; thus, at the end of this one, put the final finishing touches on the first part of the Spiritist work in order to have the time to finish the task that concerns the future.

## WITHOUT CHARITY THERE IS NO SALVATION

For me, such principles as this do not exist only in theory; I practice them. I practice the good as much as my situation allows. I render service whenever I can. Have the poor ever been turned away at my door or treated harshly? At all hours of the day have they not always been received with the same benevolence? Have I ever complained about my steps or my diligence in rendering service? Have not fathers gotten out of prison thanks to my efforts? Of course, it does not behoove me to make an inventory of the good I might have done; however, at a moment when everything I have done seems to have been forgotten, I think I can remind myself that my conscience tells me that I have done no harm to anyone, and that I have practiced all the good I could without – I repeat – worrying about anyone's opinion. In this regard, my conscience is clear, and the ingratitude I have been shown more than once will never be a reason for me to stop. Any ingratitude I might have received on more than one occasion will not be for me a reason to stop doing it; ingratitude is one of the imperfections of humanity, and since none of us is exempt from reproach, we must excuse others so that they may excuse us, and in this way be able to say like Jesus Christ: *Let him who is without sin cast the first stone.* Thus, I will continue to do all the good within my reach, even to my enemies, because hate has not blinded me. I will always lend them a hand to pull them out of a pit if the occasion presents itself.

That is how I understand Christian charity; I can understand a religion that tells us to repay evil with good, and even more, that we repay good with good. However, I will never understand a religion that prescribes repaying evil with evil. (*Private thoughts of Allan Kardec in a document found among his papers.*)

# 1868 Project

- Central Establishment
- Spiritist Instruction
- Publicity
- Trips

One of the biggest obstacles to the spread of Spiritism would be a lack of unity. The only way to avoid it, if not in the present at least in the future, is to formulate the doctrine in all its parts and up to the smallest detail with so much precision and clarity that any divergent interpretation would be impossible.

If the doctrine of Christ gave way to so many controversies, and if it is still so badly understood nowadays and so diversely practiced, it is because Jesus limited himself to teaching orally and because his apostles transmitted only general principles that each of them interpreted according to his own ideas or interests. If he had formulated the organization of the Christian Church with the precision of a law or a regulation, it is incontestable that such a measure would have prevented most schisms and religious quarrels, as well as the exploitation of religion to feed personal ambitions. Consequently, if Christianity did constitute a cause of serious moral reform for a few enlightened individuals, it was not and still is not for most but an object of blind and fanatical faith, a result which for a great many has engendered doubt and complete disbelief.

Only Spiritism, well understood and well comprehended, can remedy such a state of things and become, as the Spirits have said, the great lever for the transformation of humankind. Experience shall enlighten us as to the path to follow. By showing us the problems of the past, experience clearly tells us that the only way to avoid problems in the future is to set Spiritism on the solid bases of a positive doctrine that leaves nothing to the will of interpretations. The dissents that might arise will melt away by themselves in the fundamental unity that will be established on most-rational bases, if such bases are clearly defined and do not remain vague. Another result of such considerations is that this mode of action, when prudently followed, is the most powerful means of fighting against the Spiritist Doctrine's antagonists. All sophisms would come crashing down upon contact with the principles that no sane reasoning would ever oppose.

Two elements must concur for the progress of Spiritism: the theoretical establishing of the Doctrine and the means of popularizing it. Its daily growth multiplies our relations, which tend only to increase due to the momentum the new edition of *The Spirits' Book* will create and the publicity it will generate.

In order to utilize such relations in a beneficial way, if after having composed the theory I were to concur in its implementation, it would be necessary that, besides the publication of my works, I would have the means of acting more directly. Thus, I believe that it would be useful that the one who has founded the theory could at the same time give it its impulsion, because then there would be more unity. From this point of view, the Society must necessarily exert a great influence – as the Spirits themselves have stated – but its activities would not really be effective unless it served as the center and the rallying point from where a preponderant teaching originates for the public. For that, a stronger organization would be necessary along with elements that it does not yet possess. During our present century, and due to the state of our customs, financial resources are the great engine of all things if used with discernment. In the event that such resources were to come into my hands in one way or another, following is the plan I would propose to pursue, the execution of which would be proportional to the importance of the means and subject to the advice of the Spirits.

## CENTRAL ESTABLISHMENT

The most urgent phase would be to provide a conveniently situated location for meetings and receptions. Without giving it unnecessary luxury, which would be out-of-place, it would have to be furnished in such a way that nothing would denote penury, and it would have to be sufficiently presentable so that distinguished persons could go there and feel comfortable. Besides my private accommodations, it should have:

1. A large room for the Society's séances and large meetings;
2. A reception room;
3. A room dedicated to private evocations, a sort of a sanctuary that would not be tainted by any extraneous use;
4. An office for *Revue Spirite,* archives and the Society's related business.

All this prepared and arranged in a comfortable and appropriate way conducive to its purpose.

A library would be created composed of all French and foreign works, and periodical writings, both old and modern, related to Spiritism.

The reception room would be open every day at certain hours for the Society's members, who could go there and freely confer, read newspapers and consult the archives and library. Foreign adherents passing through Paris would be admitted there upon introduction by a member.

Regular correspondence would be established with the various centers in France and abroad.

The place would have a secretary and an office clerk.

## SPIRITIST INSTRUCTION

A regular course on Spiritism would be taught for the purpose of developing the scientific principles of the Science and spreading a liking for serious study. This course would have the advantage of instituting the unity of principles, of producing educated adherents capable of articulating Spiritist ideas, and of developing a large number of mediums. I consider such a course as being capable of exerting a major influence on the future of Spiritism and its consequences.

## PUBLICITY

The *Revue* would be developed further, either by expanding it or by having a shorter periodicity. A salaried editor would be hired.

A large-scale publicity effort in the more prevalent newspapers would take the knowledge of Spiritist ideas to the entire world – even to the most distant localities – and would awaken the desire to delve into them. Increasing the number of adherents would impose silence on its detractors, who would soon yield to the force of general opinion.

## TRIPS

Two or three months per year would be dedicated to trips to visit the various centers and give them good direction.

If resources allow, an account would be set up to fund a certain number of educated and talented missionaries, who would be responsible for disseminating Spiritism.

A complete organization and assistance of paid aids whom I could count on would free me from a multitude of tasks and material concerns. It would allow me the free time I need to expedite the works I still have to do, and which the current state of affairs prevents me from dedicating myself to as assiduously as needed, since I lack the material time and the physical strength.

If it were given to me to accomplish this project, the execution of which would need the same prudence that I used in the past, it is indubitable that a few years would be sufficient to make Spiritism advance a few centuries.

*****

The Constitution of Spiritism was inserted into the *Revue* by Kardec in December of 1868, but without the comments he added before dying and which we reproduce below textually. Corporeal death deterred him when he was preparing to formulate the *Fundamental Principles of the Spiritist Doctrine Recognized as Incontestable Truths,* a fact that our readers will surely lament as we do, because those principles would have completed this Constitution by means of logical and judicious evaluations. It is the last manuscript by the Master and we read it with deep respect.

# CONSTITUTION OF SPIRITISM

## Exposition of Motives

• Preliminary Considerations
• Schisms
• The Head of Spiritism
• The Central Commission
• The Central Commission's Accessory and Complementary Institutions
• Scope of Action of the Central Commission
• Constitutive Statutes
• List of Beliefs
• Ways and Means
• Allan Kardec and the New Constitution of Spiritism

## I – PRELIMINARY CONSIDERATIONS

Spiritism, like all things, has had its period of gestation, and until all the issues related to it, whether principal or accessory, have been resolved, it could offer only incomplete results. One could glimpse the objective and foresee the consequences, but only in a vague way. From the uncertainty on points not yet settled, differences in the way to consider them would inevitably arise. Unification had to be the work of time, and it had to be effected gradually, as the principles were elucidated. Spiritism will only form a harmonious whole when all the parts it entails have been addressed, and only then will one be able to tell what Spiritism really is.

On the part of adherents, as long as Spiritism was only a philosophical opinion, it could count on the natural sympathy produced by a communion of ideas; however, no serious connection could exist if there were no clearly defined plan. This is, without a doubt, the main cause of the weak cohesion and the instability of groups and societies that have been formed. That is why we incessantly and strongly sought to keep Spiritists from prematurely founding any special institution based on Spiritism before Spiritism itself rested on a solid base. That would have exposed them to unavoidable failures, whose effect would have been disastrous due to the impact such failures would have on the public and the discouragement they would cause adherents. Such failures would perhaps delay by a century the definitive progress of Spiritism, whose powerlessness would have been imputed to a failure that, in reality, was but the result of improvidence. Because they do not know how to wait for the appropriate time to arrive, highly rushed and impatient individuals have compromised the best causes throughout time.[46]

One should ask of things only what they can give according to their readiness to produce; one would not demand from a child what one would expect from an adult, or from a recently planted tree what it will yield only when it is fully grown. Spiritism, while developing, could only give individual results; collective and general results will be the fruit of complete Spiritism, which will develop successively.

Although Spiritism has not yet given its final word on all points, its completion is at hand. The moment has come to give it a strong and durable base, capable, however, of receiving all the developments entailed by ulterior circumstances, as well as giving full security to those who wonder who will take its reins after the one who has guided its first steps.

Undoubtedly, Spiritism is imperishable because it rests upon the Laws of Nature, and because, better than any other, it answers the true aspirations of humankind. Its diffusion and

---

46 For a broader treatment of the issue regarding Spiritist institutions, see the July 1866 edition of *Revue Spirite*. – Note from the French.

final implementation, however, can be advanced or held back by various circumstances, some of which are subordinate to the general progress of things, while others are inherent to Spiritism itself, its constitution and organization.

While the fundamental question is preponderant in everything and ends up always prevailing, the question of form has crucial importance here; it can even temporarily prevail and cause obstacles and delays, depending on how it is resolved.

Thus, we would have done an incomplete thing and left big obstacles for the future if we had not foreseen the difficulties that might arise. It is with the intention of attending to them that we have prepared an organization plan, drawing on the experience of the past in order to avoid the pitfalls that most of the doctrines that have appeared in the world have come up against.

The plan described herein was conceived some time ago because we have always been concerned with the future of Spiritism. We have let it be sensed on many occasions – vaguely it is true – but enough to show that it is not a new concept at this point, and that by working on the theoretical part of the endeavor, we have not neglected the practical side.

## II – SCHISMS

One matter that presents itself first of all to our minds is that of the schisms that could arise in the midst of Spiritism. Will Spiritism be spared them?

Certainly not, because, especially at the start, it will have to struggle against personal ideas, which are always absolute, tenacious and slow to rally to the ideas of others. It will also have to struggle against the ambition of those who want to link their names to any innovation; who create novelties only to be able to say they do not think or act like the others, or who do so because their pride suffers for occupying only a secondary position.

If Spiritism cannot escape human weaknesses, which one can always count on, it can at least neutralize their consequences – and this is crucial.

It is worth noting that the many divergent systems that arose at the origin of Spiritism regarding the way in which the phenomena should be explained all disappeared as Spiritism became complete by means of observation and a rational theory. Today, those early systems have few followers. This is a well-known fact, from which one may conclude that the final disagreements will be dissipated with the full elucidation of all the parts of Spiritism. But there will always be prejudiced dissidents, always interested for one reason or another in doing things their own way. It is against their intentions that one must be attentive.

To ensure future unity, one condition is indispensable: all the parts of the entire Doctrine must be established with precision and clarity, without leaving anything vague. To accomplish that, we have proceeded in such a way that our writings do not lend themselves to any contradictory interpretation and we have made efforts for it to always be that way. When it is clearly and unambiguously stated that two plus two is four, no one can say that we meant to say that two plus two is five. Therefore, *alongside* Spiritism, sects may form that do not adopt its principles, or at least all of them, but not *within* Spiritism due to the interpretation of the texts, like the many interpretations that have been formed regarding the meaning of the words of the Gospel. This is a primary point of crucial importance.

The second point is not to leave the ambit of practical ideas. If it is true that the utopia of yesterday often becomes the truth of tomorrow, let us leave to tomorrow the care to realize the utopia of yesterday, but let us not hinder Spiritism with principles that will be considered chimerical and be rejected by scientifically-minded individuals.

The third point is inherent to the essentially progressive character of Spiritism. From the fact that it does not delude itself with unrealizable dreams in the present, it does not follow that it is stuck in the present. Based exclusively on the Laws of Nature, it cannot go beyond those laws; but if a new law were discovered, it would have to harmonize with it. It cannot in any way close the door to progress – that would be suicide. Assimilating all the ideas recognized to be just, of whatever order they may be, physical or metaphysical, it will never be surpassed, and this is one of the principal guarantees of its perpetuity.

Therefore, if a sect is formed alongside Spiritism, founded or not on its principles, one of two things would apply: either that sect would possess the truth or it would not. If not, it would fall by itself under the influence of reason and common sense, as many others have already fallen throughout the centuries. If its ideas are correct, even concerning one single point, Spiritism, which seeks the good and the true wherever they are, would assimilate them so that, instead of being absorbed, it would be Spiritism that does the absorbing.

If a number of its adherents eventually leave it, it will be because they think they can do something that is better; if they really do something better, Spiritism will imitate it; if they were to do much good, Spiritism would endeavor to do as much, and more if possible. If they were to do much evil, on the other hand, it would let them do so, certain that, sooner or later, the good will prevail over evil, and the true over the false. This is the only struggle it would take on.

We would add that tolerance, the consequence of charity, which is the basis of Spiritist morality, makes it a duty to respect all beliefs. Wanting to be freely accepted by conviction and not by force, proclaiming freedom of conscience to be a natural, indefeasible right, it says: *If I am right, everyone will end up thinking as I do; if I am wrong, I will end up thinking like the others.* In virtue of such a principle – not casting stones at anyone – it will give no reason for reprisals and will leave dissenters the full responsibility for their words and actions.

Thus, the plan for Spiritism will only be invariable with respect to the principles that have passed to the condition of proven truths. With respect to the others, it will not accept them, as it has always not done, except as hypotheses until they are confirmed. If it is shown that it is mistaken on any one point, it will modify itself regarding that point.

Absolute truth is eternal, and for that very reason, invariable. But who could pride themselves on possessing it in its entirety? In the state of imperfection of our knowledge, what seems erroneous today may be recognized as true tomorrow due to the discovery of new laws. This applies to the moral as well as to the physical order. Against that eventuality, Spiritism should never be unprepared. The progressive principle, which it has inscribed into its code, will guarantee its perpetuity, and its unity will be maintained precisely because it is not based on the principle of immobility.

Instead of being a force, immobility becomes a cause of failure and ruin for those who do not follow the overall movement. It breaks up unity because those who want to progress are separated from those who insist on remaining behind. However, following the progressive movement requires prudence and being on guard against the reveries of utopias and theories. It must be done at the right time – neither too early nor too late – and with full knowledge of the facts.

Undoubtedly, a doctrine set on such bases will be really strong, capable of defying any competition and neutralizing the intentions of its competitors.

Furthermore, experience has already justified such foresight. Having progressed along such a pathway from its beginning, Spiritism has continuously advanced, but unhurriedly, always checking to see if the ground is solid, and measuring its steps by the state of opinion. It has proceeded like the navigator who does not set sail without a sounding line in hand and without testing the winds.

## III – THE HEAD OF SPIRITISM

But who should be in charge of keeping Spiritism on this path? Who has the spare time and the perseverance to devote to the incessant work such a job demands? If Spiritism were left to its own devices without a guide, should we not fear that it might wander off course? And that malevolence, to which it will still be exposed to for a long time, will it not make an effort to denature its character? This, in fact, is a vital question, whose solution is of major interest for the future of Spiritism.

The need for a higher central supervision, a watchful guardian of the progressive unity and the overall interests of Spiritism, is so obvious that there is already concern for not yet seeing a leader appearing on the horizon. It is understood that without a moral authority capable of centralizing endeavors, studies and observations, of giving impulse, encouraging diligence, defending the weak, upholding the irresolute, helping with the advice of experience, and settling uncertain points, Spiritism would run the risk of going adrift. Not only is this guidance necessary, but it needs to be strong and stable enough to weather every storm.

Those who do not want for there to be such authority do not understand the true interests of Spiritism. If some think they can dispense with any supervision, the majority, who do not believe in their infallibility and who do not have full confidence in their own knowledge, feel the need for a point of support, a guide, if only to help them advance further with more assurance and security. (See article: "Independent Spiritism" in the April 1866 issue of *Revue Spirite*.")

The need for direction established, from whom would the head get his powers? Would he be acclaimed by the universality of Spiritism's adherents? That would be an impracticable matter. If he imposed himself on his own authority, he would be accepted by some and rejected by others, and twenty contenders could surface, hoisting banner against banner. It would be despotism and anarchy at the same time. Such an act would be characteristic of someone who was ambitious, and no one would be less suitable than an ambitious – and therefore prideful – person to head a doctrine based on selflessness, dedication, disinterestedness and humility. Placed outside the fundamental principle of Spiritism, he would do nothing but falsify its spirit. This is what will unavoidably happen if effective measures are not adopted beforehand to prevent it.

Let us say, for instance, that someone has all the qualities required to accomplish his mandate, and that he somehow becomes the supreme head: individuals succeed one another and they are not similar to one another; after a good one, a bad one could follow; with the individual, the character of leadership could change; lacking any bad intent, he could, nevertheless, have views that are more just or less just; but if he wanted his personal ideas to prevail, he could lead Spiritism astray, incite divisions, and the same difficulties would be renewed with each change. One must not lose sight of the fact that Spiritism has not yet reached its full strength. From the organizational point of view, it is a child that has barely begun to walk. Thus, especially at the start, it is important to guard it against the difficulties of the path.

But – it might be asked – could not one of the spirits announced to take part in the regeneration become the head of Spiritism? Possibly; however, since such spirits do not have a sign on their forehead to make themselves recognizable, they will affirm themselves by their *actions,* and will, in their majority, be acknowledged as such only after having died, according to what they have produced while alive; moreover, since they would not be perpetual, all eventualities must be foreseen.

We know that the mission of such spirits will be multiple; that they will belong to all levels of the scale and the various branches of the social economy, where each one will exert its influence on behalf of new ideas, according to the specialty of its position; that all will thus labor for the establishment of Spiritism, in one field or another – some as heads of State, others as legislators, magistrates, scientists, writers, orators, industrialists, etc.; that each one will prove itself in its field, from the proletarian to the sovereign, *without anything to distinguish it from the ordinary person except its deeds.* If one of them should be responsible for taking part in guiding Spiritism, it is probable that it will be put providentially in the appropriate position to get there through legal means; apparently fortuitous circumstances would lead it there without any premeditated plan on its part and without it having any awareness of its mission. (See "The Messiahs of Spiritism" in the Feb. and March 1868 *Revue Spirite* issues.)

In such a case, the worst of all heads would be the one who considered himself to be God's elect. Since it is irrational to believe that God entrusts such missions to the ambitious or prideful, the characteristic virtues of a true messiah must be, above all else, simplicity, humility and modesty; in other words, the most complete material and moral disinterestedness.

Hence, the mere pretension of being a messiah would constitute a negation of such essential qualities; it would prove in those that availed themselves of such a title either a presumptuous foolishness if taken in good faith, or a remarkable imposture. There will be no lack of schemers or so-called Spiritists who would like to assume the position out of pride, ambition or cupidity, and others who would boast of pretentious revelations with the help of those who will seek to stand out and to fascinate overly credulous minds. We must also foresee that, under false appearances, there would be individuals who would try to take over the helm with the preconceived idea of wrecking the ship by steering it off course. It would not sink, but it would suffer harmful delays that must be avoided. These are, without contest, the major stumbling blocks that Spiritism must guard itself against. The more consistency it acquires, the more traps its adversaries will lay.

Therefore, it is the duty of all sincere Spiritists to frustrate the wiles of intrigue that could undermine the smallest as well as the largest centers. First of all, they must completely repudiate all those who present themselves as messiahs, whether as the head of Spiritism, or as a mere apostle of Spiritism. The tree is known by its fruit, so wait for the tree to bear its fruit before deciding if it is good, and see whether or not the fruit is worm-eaten. (See *The Gospel according to Spiritism,* chap. XXI, no. 9: "Characteristics of the True Prophet")

Someone has proposed that candidates be appointed by the Spirits themselves in each Spiritist group or society. While this measure would not prevent every inconvenience, it would present others, peculiar to such a way of proceeding, which experience has already revealed and which would be superfluous to recall here. We must not lose sight of the fact that the mission of the Spirits consists in instructing us so that we may make ourselves better individuals – not replacing the initiative of our free will. They suggest ideas; they assist us with their counsels – especially in regards to moral issues – but they leave to our own judgment the job of dealing with material matters, which is not their mission to spare us from resolving. Human beings should be content with being assisted and watched over by good spirits, but they should not charge them with the role incumbent on incarnates.

Furthermore, such a measure would cause more problems than might be supposed due to the difficulty of making all groups participate in such an election. It would be a complicated process, and the simpler the process, the less susceptible it would be of breaking down. Hence, the problem is one of constructing a strong and stable central direction that could protect Spiritism from all fluctuations, one that would respond to all the needs of the cause, one that would set up an insurmountable barrier to the wiles of intrigue and ambition. Such is the objective of the plan of which we will give a brief outline.

## IV – THE CENTRAL COMMISSION

During its developmental period, the guidance of Spiritism had to be individual; it was necessary that all the constitutive elements of Spiritism, coming in its embryonic stage from a multitude of focal points, focus on a common center in order to be examined and collated there, and that a single thought preside over their coordination to establish unity for the whole and harmony among all the parts. If it had been otherwise, Spiritism would have been like a mechanism whose parts did not fit together precisely.

Because it is an uncontested, clearly demonstrated truth, we have stated that the Spiritist Doctrine could not have come from a single center any more than all astronomy could have come from a single observatory. Any center that tried to construct it exclusively upon its own observations would have done something incomplete; upon an infinite number of points, it would have found itself in contradiction with the others. If a thousand centers would have wanted to come up with their own doctrine, there would not have been two that were the same on all points. If they would have been in agreement on the fundamentals, they would inevitably have differed on the form. Hence, since there are a lot of people who concern themselves with the form rather than the fundamentals, there would be as many sects as different forms. Unity could only come from the whole and from the comparison of all the partial results. That is why the concentration of all the endeavors was necessary. (See *Genesis,* chap. 1: "Character of the Spiritist Revelation," no. 51ff.)

But whatever was advantageous for a certain time would later become an inconvenience. Today, now that the preparatory work on the fundamental issues is finished, and the general principles of the science have been established, the guidance, which had to be individual in the beginning, must become collective: first, because a time will come when its weight will exceed the strength of one person, and second, because there is a greater guarantee of stability in an ensemble of individuals, each having but his or her own voice and not being able to do anything without the concourse of the others, than one sole individual capable of abusing his or her authority and wanting his or her personal ideas to predominate.

Instead of a single person in command, the leadership will be entrusted to a permanent *central commission,* whose organization and attributions will be defined in a way not to leave anything to anyone's whims. This commission will be composed of twelve charter members at most, who will fulfill certain desirable conditions to this effect, and an equal number of counselors. It will complete itself according to equally determined regulations as their positions become vacant due to death or other causes. A special guideline will establish the manner in which the first twelve are appointed.

The commission will appoint its president for one year.

The authority of the president will be merely administrative. He or she will chair the commission's deliberations and supervise the execution of its work and the handling of its day-to-day matters; but beyond the attributions conferred on him or her by the bylaws, he or she cannot make any decisions without the agreement of the commission. Consequently, there will be no possibility for abuse, no fuel for ambition, no pretexts for intrigue or jealousy, no harmful supremacy.

Therefore, the central commission will be the true head of Spiritism, a collective head that can do nothing without the consent of the majority. Large enough to clarify matters by discussing them, it will not be so large as to foster confusion.

The central commission's authority will be monitored and its actions overseen by congresses or general assemblies, which we will address later.

For the community of adherents, the approval or disapproval, sanction or refusal of decisions of a constitutive body representing the collective opinion will inevitably have an authority it would never have if it emanated from a sole individual representing only a personal opinion. Often one rejects the opinion of one individual because it is humiliating to submit to it, but one has no problem with deferring to the opinion of many.

It is well understood that we are talking here about a moral authority in what concerns the interpretation and application of the Doctrine's principles, and not about any sort of disciplinary power. In matters of Spiritism, this authority will be like an academy in matters of Science.

For the larger public, a constituted body has greater authority and preponderance against adversaries; it presents, especially, a force of resistance and provides a means of action that one sole individual would not have; it can fight with infinitely greater advantages. One individual may be attacked and harmed, but not a collective entity.

A collective entity also offers guarantees of stability that do not exist when everything rests on one head. If an individual is impeded by some cause, everything might be hindered. A collective entity, on the other hand, continues unceasingly. Although it may lose one or more of its members, nothing is endangered.

The essential thing is for all the members to be in accord on the fundamental principles; that will be the absolute condition for their admission, just as it will be for all those who participate in the endeavor. Concerning details on pending questions, it does not matter if there are disagreements, since it is the opinion of the majority that will prevail. Those whose way of seeing things is correct will not lack good reasons to justify it. If someone quits, upset that his or her ideas were not accepted, matters will continue to follow their course; there will be no reason to regret his or her departure, since he or she will have displayed a prideful, non-Spiritist susceptibility that would be capable of causing trouble.

The most common cause of division among parties is a conflict of interests and the possibility of some supplanting others to their own advantage. This cause has no reason to exist, since the harm of one cannot benefit the others, because they stand together and thus they can only lose instead of winning from the disunion. This is a matter of detail foreseen in the organization.

Let us say, for instance, that among the members of the commission, there is a false brother, a traitor, won over by the enemies of the cause: what harm could he do since he is not the only voice in the decision-making process? Let us suppose, as far-fetched as it might seem, that the entire commission heads down the wrong pathway: congresses will be there to set things straight.

Overseeing the actions of the administration will be the job of such congresses, which will be able to decree a censure or an accusation against the central commission for breaking its mandate, for violating established principles, or for establishing measures harmful to Spiritism. Therefore, it will refer to the congresses in circumstances where it deems its responsibility could be seriously affected.

Therefore, if congresses act as a brake for the commission, the commission in turn will draw new strength from their approval. This way, the collective head will depend on the general opinion in the end, and will not be able to wander off the correct path without risk to itself.

The main responsibilities of the central commission will be the following:

1. Watch over the interests of Spiritism and its propagation; maintain its usefulness by preserving the integrity of the recognized principles; watch over the development of its results.
2. Study new principles susceptible of being included in the body of Spiritism.
3. Collect all documents and information that might be of interest to Spiritism.
4. Be in charge of correspondence.
5. Maintain, consolidate and extend the bonds of fraternity among the adherents and particular societies of the different countries.
6. Direct *Revue Spirite,* which will be the official journal of Spiritism, and to which another periodic publication may be added.
7. Examine and evaluate books, newspaper articles, and any writings of interest to Spiritism; refute any attacks when they occur.
8. Publish the fundamental works of Spiritism in the way most favorable for their dissemination; write and publish the works which we will outline and which we will not have time to do while alive; encourage publications that may be profitable to the cause.
9. Create and maintain the library, the archives and the museum.
10. Administer the relief fund, the dispensary and the rest home.
11. Administer material undertakings.
12. Direct the Society's séances.
13. Conduct oral teaching.
14. Visit and instruct at meetings and the particular societies that will place themselves under its care.
15. Convene congresses and general assemblies.

These responsibilities will be distributed among the commission's members according to each one's specialty. If need be, they will be assisted by a sufficient number of auxiliary members or simple employees.

## V – THE CENTRAL COMMISSION'S ACCESSORY AND COMPLEMENTARY INSTITUTIONS

Several complementary institutions will be annexed to the central commission as local auxiliaries as circumstances allow, to wit:

1. A *Library,* which will contain all the works of interest to Spiritism. These works may be consulted on site or loaned to readers.
2. A *Museum*, which will contain the first works of Spiritist art, the more noteworthy mediumistic works, portraits of adherents to whom the Cause owes much because of their dedication, of individuals to whom Spiritism renders homage, though they are outside the Doctrine, as benefactors of humanity, great missionaries of progress, etc.
3. A *dispensary,* which will be used for *free* medical consultations and the treatment of certain ailments under the direction of a licensed physician.
4. A relief and contingency fund, when it becomes practical.
5. A rest home.
6. A society of adherents, which holds regular séances.

Without going into a premature examination in this regard, it would be useful here to say a few words about two of the articles that might give rise to misunderstandings.

Setting up a general relief fund is an impractical thing, which would present serious problems, as shown in a special article (See *Revue* of July 1866). Thus, the commission should not set a course it would soon be forced to abandon, nor should it undertake anything that it is not certain it could accomplish. It needs to be positive and not nourish chimerical illusions, because that is the route to follow securely for the long haul. Therefore, in everything it must work within the limits of the possible.

A relief fund cannot and must not be more than a local measure, with a restricted action, whose prudent organization may serve as a model for others of the same type, which individual societies could create. It is due to their multiplicity that they would be able to render effective service, and not by centralizing the means of action.

The fund will be fed by: 1) amounts designated for it, taken from the income of the general Spiritism fund; 2) special donations. It will invest the amounts received in order to bring in revenue. It is from this revenue that it will render temporary or lifelong relief and will fulfill the obligations of its mandate, which will be stipulated in the rules for its constitution.

The plan for a rest home, in the full definition of the term, cannot be implemented at the beginning due to the monies such an institution would require, and also because the administration would need time to settle in and begin functioning regularly before complicating its responsibilities with undertakings that might run it aground. It would be imprudent to attempt too many things before being certain about the means to execute them. This is easily understood if one ponders all the details inherent to establishments of this sort. Good intentions are fine, but before anything else, it must be possible to accomplish them.

## SCOPE OF ACTION OF THE CENTRAL

## COMMISSION

At the beginning a center for the development of ideas was formed without any premeditated plan, by necessity, but without any official character. Such center was necessary because if it had not existed, what would be the connecting point for Spiritists scattered throughout different countries? If it could not communicate its ideas, impressions and observations to all the other individual centers also scattered and often inconsistent, it would have remained isolated and the spreading of Spiritism would have suffered. Thus, a point where everything was concentrated was crucial, a point from where everything could radiate. Far from rendering this center useless, the development of Spiritist ideas will make the necessity for it to be felt even more deeply, because the need to come together and work in unison will be even more considerable as the number of adherents increases. By regularizing the state of things, the Constitution of Spiritism will result in a greater advantage for Spiritism and will close the gaps it presents. The center it creates is not an individuality, but a focus of collective activity, acting in the general interest, and where all personal authority disappears.

But what will be the scope of the center's circle of activity? Is it destined to govern the world and become the universal arbiter of truth? If it harbored such a pretense, it would misunderstand the spirit of Spiritism, which, for the same reason that it proclaims the principles of free examination and freedom of conscience, it repudiates the idea of setting itself up as an autocracy; from the very start, it would enter upon a fatal pathway.

Because they are founded on the laws of nature and not on metaphysical abstractions, Spiritism's principles tend to become – and one day will certainly be – those of all human beings. All will accept them because they will be palpable and demonstrated truths, just as the theory of the earth's movement around the sun was accepted. However, to claim that Spiritism will be organized everywhere in the same manner, that Spiritists all over the world will be subject to a uniform regime and one way to proceed, that they should wait for the light to come to them from one set point upon which they should set their eyes, would be as absurd of a utopia as planning for all the peoples of the earth to someday form one sole nation governed by one sole head, ruled by one code of laws and subjected to the same customs. Although there are general laws that may be common to all peoples, these laws, as far as the details of application and form are concerned, will always be appropriate for the customs, characteristics and environs of each one.

The same will happen with organized Spiritism. Spiritists all over the world will have common principles that will connect them to the larger family through the sacred bond of fraternity. Applying these principles, however, might vary according to country, without breaking Spiritism's fundamental unity, and without forming dissident sects that would cast stones and anathemas at one another – which would really be highly anti-Spiritist. Thus, general centers in different countries can and will inevitably form, without any other bond than the communion of faith and moral solidarity, without subordination to one another, and without the one in France, for example, having the intention of imposing itself on American Spiritists and vice-versa.

The comparison of the observatories we cited earlier is perfectly correct. There are observatories at different points of the globe; all of them, whatever nation they belong to, are founded on general principles recognized by Astronomy. But that fact does not make them branches of one another. Each tailors its work as it sees fit; they all exchange observations and make the most of their peers' scientific discoveries. The same will happen with the general centers of Spiritism; they will be the observatories of the invisible world, and will borrow reciprocally what they have that is good and applicable to the customs of the countries where they are established, their objective being the good of humankind and not the satisfaction of personal ambitions. Spiritism is a matter of depth; to attach it to the form would be a puerility unworthy of the grandeur of the subject. That is why the diverse centers penetrated by the true spirit of Spiritism will fraternally join hands and unite to fight their two common enemies: disbelief and fanaticism.

# VII – CONSTITUTIVE STATUTES

Drawing up the constitutive statutes had to precede all execution. If drawing them up had been entrusted to an assembly, it would not have been necessary to set the conditions to be fulfilled in advance for those in charge of the work. The lack of a prior basis, a divergence of opinions, personal intentions, as well as plots by adversaries, could lead to divisions. An undertaking of such a large scope could not be improvised; it demanded lengthy preparation and knowledge of Spiritism's true needs acquired through experience and serious thought for the unity of viewpoints, harmony and coordination of all the parts of the whole; it could only emanate from individual initiative to later receive the sanction of interested parties. From the start, however, it needed to have a regulation, a course laid out, a determined objective. Once the rules are established, one proceeds with security, without trying and failing, without hesitation.

Nonetheless, since it is not conferred on anyone to possess universal knowledge, nor to do things to absolute perfection; since a person may be mistaken about his or her own ideas and since others may see what that person does not; and since the intention of imposing oneself would be abusive, the constitutive statutes will be submitted for revision to the upcoming congress, which can make the corrections deemed useful.

But no constitution, no matter how good, can last forever. What is good in one era might become insufficient later on. Needs change with the times and with the development of ideas. If we want it for the long run, without falling into disuse or one day being violently repealed by progressive ideas, it must march in step with such ideas. This fact applies to all philosophical doctrines and particular societies, as well as politics and religion: following or not following progress is a matter of life and death. In the matter at hand, it would thus be a grave mistake to bind the future by a regulation declared inflexible.

It would be no less of a serious mistake to frequently introduce into the organic constitution changes that would jeopardize its stability. It is necessary to act with maturity and circumspection. One can evaluate the real usefulness of changes only after a while. Thus, who can be the judge in such a case? Not one person only, who usually sees things from his or her own perspective. Not even the author of the original draft, who might evaluate the work with too much complacency. It is the interested parties themselves, because they experience in a direct and permanent manner the effects of the institution and can tell where it comes up short.

The revision of the constitutive statutes will be done by *ordinary congresses,* transformed for the purpose into *organic congresses* at certain times; thus it will proceed indefinitely in order to maintain them without interruption at the level of the needs and progress of ideas – even a thousand years from now.

The time for revision being periodic and known ahead of time, there will be no reason for any special convocations. Revision will be not only a right but a duty of the congress at the indicated time; it will be put beforehand on the agenda in order not to subordinate it to the good will of anyone in particular, and to prevent anyone from arrogating to him or herself the right of deciding by his or her own authority, whether or not opportune. If after reading the statutes the congress deems any change unnecessary, it will declare them unchanged in their entirety.

With the number of congress members being inevitably limited, taking into account the material impossibility of bringing together all those interested, and in order not to be deprived of the input of those who are absent, members can send their observations to the central commission from whatever part of the world they may find themselves, during the break between two regular congresses, and such items will be put on the agenda of the following congress.

No appreciable movement of ideas occurs in less than a quarter of a century; every twenty-five years, therefore, the original constitution of Spiritism will be subject to revision. Without being too long, this span of time is sufficient to allow for the appraisal of new necessities and to prevent the instability of too frequent modifications.

However, since it is in the first years that most of the preparatory work occurs, that the social movement that is presently ongoing may give rise to unforeseen necessities until the society has firmed up its steps, and that it is important to take advantage without delay of the lessons of experience, the times for revision will be closer to one another, but always determined beforehand, until the end of the current century [$19^{th}$]. Over the course of the first thirty years, the constitution will have been sufficiently completed and rectified to enjoy a relative stability. At this point, the 25-year periods can begin without any inconvenience.

This way, the early individual work that cleared the way becomes in reality the collective work of all those interested, with the advantage inherent to those two modes, without the inconveniences; it will modify itself under the influence of progressive ideas and experience, but without jolts and haste, because the principle rests on the constitution itself.

## VIII – LIST OF BELIEFS

The absolute requirement of vitality for every meeting or association, whatever its objective, is homogeneity, that is, unity of viewpoints, principles and sentiments, the tendency toward the same determined goal; in short, the communion of thoughts. Every time people gather on behalf of a vague idea, they never reach an agreement, because each one understands the idea in his or her own way. Every meeting formed of heterogeneous members contains its own seeds of dissolution since it is composed of divergent material or self-centered interests, tending toward different goals, which conflict and which are very rarely disposed to making concessions to the common interest, or even to reason; they support the opinion of the majority if they cannot do otherwise, but they never really come together.

That is how it always was until Spiritism came along. Formed gradually, through successive observations – like all sciences – its acceptance has expanded bit by bit. The designation "Spiritist," applied successively to all degrees of belief, comprises an infinity of nuances, from the simple belief in the manifestations to the loftiest moral and philosophical deductions; from those who, remaining on the surface, see in the phenomena nothing but a pastime, to those who search for the concordance of its principles with the universal laws and their application to the common interests of humankind; and finally, from those who see in it nothing but a means of exploitation for their own profit, to those who draw from it the elements for their own moral growth.

Thus, to call oneself a convicted Spiritist does not in any way indicate the measure of one's belief, because the term means much to some but very little to others. A gathering to which all those who call themselves Spiritists are summoned would present an amalgam of divergent opinions that could not be mutually assimilated, and it would not lead to anything productive; not to mention the doors being thrown wide open to those interested in fomenting discord.

Such lack of preciseness, unavoidable in the beginning and during the time of development, frequently caused regrettable mistakes, in which Spiritism was attributed with what had been nothing more than an abuse or an aberration. It is due to the wrongful application commonly made to the Spiritist label that critics, inquiring very little about the depths of matters and even less about the serious side of Spiritism, find in it material for mockery. Although they are actually nothing more than mountebanks, if certain people call themselves Spiritists, or try to make of Spiritism what illusionists try to make of physics, in the eyes of critics, they are a representative of Spiritism.

It is true that a distinction has been made between good and bad, true and false Spiritists, more-enlightened and less-enlightened Spiritists, more-convinced and less-convinced Spiritists, hardcore Spiritists, etc. Always vague, such designations possess nothing authentic, nothing that would characterize Spiritists if one did not know the individuals, and if there has been no opportunity to appraise them by their works.

Thus, one may be deceived by appearances. The result is that the Spiritist label, not allowing but an incomplete application, is not an absolute definition. Such uncertainty instills minds with a sort of mistrust that prevents the establishment of a serious bond of fraternity among adherents.

Now that all the fundamental points of Spiritism have been set, as well as the duties that are incumbent upon all serious adherents, the Spiritist label may have a defined character that it did not have previously. A form of profession of faith could be established, and adhesion to it in writing would be an authentic testimony of the manner in which to regard Spiritism. Moreover, this adhesion, ascertaining the uniformity of principles, would be a bond that would unite adherents into one large family, without distinction of nationalities, within the empire of the same faith, communion of thoughts, opinions and aspirations.

Belief in Spiritism will not be a simple, often partial, acquiescence to a vague idea, but a motivated adhesion, made knowingly, and ascertained by an official title issued to the adherent. To avoid the inconveniences of a lack of precision as to what Spiritists actually are, signers of the profession of faith would take the title of *professing Spiritists.*

Resting on a precise and definite basis, this designation would leave no room for any mistake, and would enable adherents who profess the same principle and follow the same pathway to recognize one another with no other formality than the declaration of their designation, and if need be, the presentation of their title. A meeting composed of professing Spiritists will necessarily be as homogenous as being human allows.

A detailed and clearly defined profession of faith will be the road to follow; the title of *professing Spiritist* will be the rallying word.

But, one will ask, is such a title enough guarantee against individuals of questionable sincerity?

A full guarantee against bad faith is impossible, for there are those who make a game of the most solemn acts; however, we hold that such guarantee is better than no guarantee at all. Furthermore, those who without scruples pretend to be what they are not when the matter concerns only words, often retreat before a written affirmation which leaves marks behind and which could be used against them in case they wander off the right pathway. Even if there are a few who are not hindered by this consideration, their number will be negligible and without influence. Moreover, this possibility is foreseen in the statutes, and provided for therein by a special clause.

Such a measure will inevitably keep away from serious meetings persons who do not belong there. If it keeps a few Spiritists of good faith away, it would always be those who are not secure enough to assert themselves, the timorous ones who dread being put on the spot, and those who in any circumstance are never the first to give their opinion, wanting to see in advance how things will turn out. With time, some will see things more clearly, whereas others will not be counted among the solid defenders of the cause. As for those one might truly regret, their number will be small and will decrease each day.

Since nothing in this world is perfect, the best things have their drawbacks. If we wanted to reject everything that is not exempt of problems, nothing would be acceptable. In everything, it is necessary to weigh the advantages and the disadvantages. In this case, it is more than obvious that the former outweigh the latter.

Thus, not all those who call themselves Spiritists will rally around the constitution – that is certain; consequently, it is only for those who freely and willingly accept it, since it does not have the purpose of being imposed on anyone.

Since Spiritism is not understood in the same way by everyone, the constitution will appeal to those who envisage its point of view, with the objective of supporting it when they find themselves isolated and of strengthening the bonds of the large Spiritist family through the unity of belief. But faithful to the principle of freedom of conscience, which Spiritism acknowledges as a natural right, it will respect all sincere convictions and will not anathematize those who hold different ideas; it will not profit any less from the knowledge they might put forward outside its circle.

What is essential, therefore, is to know those who are on the same pathway. But how to know for certain? It is materially impossible to do so by means of individual interrogatories, and what is more, no one can be invested with the right to scrutinize consciences. The only means, the simplest and most permissible means, would be to establish a schedule of principles that sum up the state of the current knowledge arising from observation and which are sanctioned by the overall teaching of the Spirits, to which each person is free to adhere. Written adhesion is a profession of faith that dispenses with any further inquiry, thus giving full liberty to everyone.

Consequently, the constitution of Spiritism would therefore have as a necessary complement a list of defined principles as far as faith is concerned, without which it would be an endeavor with neither scope nor future. This list, the result of acquired experience, will be the indicator of the pathway. In addition to an organic constitution, a constitution of faith would be necessary to progress securely, that is, a *creed* – if one would prefer – which would be the reference point for all adherents.

This plan, however, which is no more than an organic constitution, should not and ought not hamper the future, under the risk of succumbing sooner or later to the grip of progress. Founded on the present state of knowledge, it will be changed and completed as new observations expose deficiencies or defects. Such changes, however, must not be made lightly or hastily. They will be the endeavor of organic congresses, which, with the periodic revision of the constitutive statutes, will add that of the formulary of principles.

Constantly walking hand in hand in harmony with progress, both constitution and creed will survive the test of time.

## IX – WAYS AND MEANS

Without a doubt, it is regrettable to have to embark upon considerations of a material order to reach a wholly spiritual objective. However, we must note that the very spirituality of the endeavor has to do with the question of earthly humankind and its well-being; it does not only concern the spreading of a few philosophical ideas, but the founding of something positive and long-lasting on behalf of the expansion and consideration of Spiritism so that it can produce the fruit it is capable of producing. To think that we are still in a time in which a few apostles could set out on the road with a walking stick, without worrying about shelter and their daily bread, would be an illusion quickly destroyed by bitter disappointment. To accomplish anything serious, one must submit to the necessities imposed by the customs of the times in which one lives, and such necessities are much different than those of patriarchal life. The very interest of Spiritism thus demands that we assess the means of action so as not to be stopped halfway down the road; therefore, let us assess them, because we live in a century where everything must be counted.

As one can plainly see, the attributions of the central commission are large enough to require a true administration. Since each one of its members has an active and assiduous role, if it were composed solely of persons of good will, the endeavors might be harmed, as no one would feel he or she had the right to criticize the negligent. For the regularity of endeavors and normality of day-to-day matters, it is necessary to have individuals whose assiduity can be counted on, and whose functions would not be simple acts of kindness. The more independent they are regarding their personal resources, the less they will have to worry about other occupations; if they lack resources, they will not be able to dedicate their time. Hence, it is important that they be rewarded just like the administrative personnel. As a result, Spiritism will gain in strength, stability and punctuality while being at the same time a means of rendering services to persons who might be in need of them.

An essential point in the economy of any foresightful administration is that its existence should not rest on occasional income that may run short, but on sure, regular resources, so that its progress, whatever happens, is not hindered. Thus, it is essential that the persons called on to lend their support do not have any worries regarding their future. Experience has shown that resources based only on revenue from contributions, always facultative, are highly unpredictable, whatever commitments have been entered into, and are often difficult to collect. To establish permanent and regular expenses on occasional resources would be a lack of foresight that might be regretted some day. The consequences are certainly less serious when it is a matter of temporary foundations that last as long as possible. Here, however, it is a matter of the future. The fate of an administration such as this one cannot be subject to the hazards of a commercial business. From the beginning it must be, if not as thriving, at least as stable as possible one century from now. The more solid its base, the less exposed it will be to the blows of intrigue.

In such case, minimum prudence requires that monies be inalienably invested as they are received in order to provide ongoing revenue that is protected against all eventualities. By regulating its expenses based on its income, the administration will not see its existence compromised in any case, since it will always have the means to function. At first, it can be organized on a smaller scale; the members of the commission can be provisionally limited to five or six, with the personnel and administrative expenses reduced to a minimum, except when the development of resources and the necessities of the cause call for an increase; but still, the necessary is needed.

It is with a view to preparing the way for this installation that we have dedicated the fruits of our endeavors up to now, as we stated previously. If our personal resources do not allow us to do more, we shall at least have the satisfaction of having laid the first stone.

Let us say, for example, that at a given time, the central commission will be able to function on a fixed income of 25,000 to 30,000 francs in one way or another. By restricting its expenses at the beginning, all the resources it will have available in capital and occasional revenue will constitute the *Spiritism Relief Fund,* which will be subject to strict accounting. With obligatory expenses regulated, surplus income will augment the ordinary capital. Proportionally, with the resources of that capital, the commission will provide for the various expenses that are advantageous to the development of Spiritism, without ever making a personal profit from it, or making it a source of speculation for any of its members. Furthermore, the use of the funds and the accounting will be subject to verification by special commissioners appointed for such a task by congresses or general assemblies.

One of the chief concerns of the commission will be the publications, without having to attend to them by means of aid coming from income, if possible. In reality, the funds meant for this endeavor will be no more than an advance because they will be returned to the account via the sale of books, whose revenue will be returned to the common capital. This is an administrative matter.

## X – ALLAN KARDEC AND THE NEW CONSTITUTION OF SPIRITISM

The considerations contained in the excerpt below, after the report on the Spiritism Relief Fund, presented by Allan Kardec to the Parisian Society on May 5, 1865, being the prelude to the new constitution of Spiritism he was putting together, as well as the presentation of his views regarding his personal position, have their rightful place in this preamble.

"A lot has been said about the royalties I have received from my books. Of course, no serious person would ever believe that I have made millions, in spite of the affirmation of those who say they heard from a reliable source that I enjoy a princely life, carriages pulled by four horses, and that in my home we only walk on Aubusson rugs (*Revue Spirite,* June 1862). Furthermore, whatever the author of a brochure you are familiar with might have said, demonstrating through hyperbolic calculations that my receipts surpass the civil list[47] of the most powerful sovereign in Europe, since in France

47 In the United Kingdom, the Civil List is the list of sums appropriated annually by Parliament to pay the expenses of the sovereign and his or her household. www.britannica.com. – Tr.

alone 20 million Spiritists pay fees to me (*Revue,* June 1863), there is one fact that is more authentic than his calculations; that is, that I have never asked anyone for anything, that no one has ever given me anything for my personal use; in other words, *I do not live at anyone's expense,* because of all the funds that have been voluntarily given to me in the interest of Spiritism, not one cent has been diverted for my personal use.[48]

"My 'immense wealth,' therefore, would have to come from my Spiritist works. Although these works have enjoyed an unexpected success, one would need to know only a little about the book business to know that it is not possible to amass millions in five or six years from philosophical books, with authors making no more than what amounts to a few cents per copy in royalties. But large or small, since such income is the fruit of my labor, no one has the right to meddle in what I do with it.

"Commercially speaking, I am in the position of any man who reaps the fruits of his labor; I run the risk of every writer, who may wind up being a success or a failure.

"Even though I do not have to render an account on this issue, I deem it appropriate, on behalf of the cause to which I have dedicated myself, to offer a few explanations.

"Whoever saw our home as it used to be and sees it as it now is can attest to the fact that nothing about our lifestyle has changed since I began to concern myself with Spiritism; it is as plain now as it was then. Hence, there can be no doubt that my profits, whatever they might have been, have not provided us with the delights of luxury. So, where are they going?

"By lifting me from obscurity, Spiritism set me on a new course; I soon found myself pulled into a movement

---

48 At that time, these amounts came to a total of 14,100 francs for the Doctrine exclusively, proven by a rendering of accounts. – Note from the original French (A.K.)

I was far from anticipating. When I conceived the idea of *The Spirits' Book,* it was my intention not to put myself in the spotlight but to remain anonymous; however, quickly surpassing expectations, that became impossible; I had to renounce my love for isolation, under penalty of abdicating the work undertaken and which kept expanding every day; I had to yield to the impetus and take the reins. As it developed further, a broader horizon opened up before me and its limits were pushed wider. I then understood the immensity of my task and the importance of the endeavor that was up to me to complete. Far from intimidating me, the difficulties and obstacles redoubled my energy. I could see the objective and decided to achieve it with the help of the good Spirits. I felt I had no time to waste and I did not waste it, either on useless visits or on futile ceremonies; it was my life's work. I gave it all my time and I sacrificed my rest and health to it, because the future was written before me in indelible letters.

"Without keeping me from my way of life, this exceptional situation did not create any necessities that my very limited personal resources did not enable me to satisfy. It would be hard for anyone to imagine the multiplicity of expenses it entailed, and which, apart from it, I could have avoided.

"Well then, ladies and gentlemen! What provided me with this supplement of resources was the product of my works. I can happily say that it was with my own work, with the fruit of my own efforts that I provided for the material necessities – most of them, at least – for consolidating Spiritism. I have thus made a large contribution to the Spiritism Relief Fund. Those who help with the dissemination of the works cannot say that they are toiling away to make me rich, because the product from the sale of every book and every subscription to the *Revue* is used on behalf of Spiritism and not the individual.

"But providing for the present was not everything; it was also important to think about the future and to prepare a foundation, which, after me, could aid the one who replaces me in the great task to be carried out. That foundation, of which I should not speak yet, is tied to my property, and it is in light of that fact that I am using part of my earnings to improve it. Since I am far from possessing the millions attributed to me, I strongly doubt that, despite my savings, my resources will ever enable me to give this foundation the complement I would like to see it have while I am alive. However, since its realization is in the designs of my spirit guides, if I myself do not accomplish it, it is probable that, one day or another, it will get done. While I am waiting, I am developing plans for it.

"Far from me, ladies and gentlemen, be the thought of the least vanity from what I have just conveyed to you. It took the obstinacy of certain diatribes to engage me – albeit regretfully – to break the silence about a few facts concerning me personally. Later on, everything that malevolence has distorted will be brought to light through authentic documents; the time for these explanations, however, has not yet arrived. The only thing that has mattered to me in the meantime is that you be informed about the use of the funds that Providence has made pass through my hands, whatever their origin. I regard myself as no more than a trustee, even of the funds that I have earned, and even more so of those that have been entrusted to me.

"Someone once asked me – without curiosity, of course, but just a simple question without ulterior motive – what I would do with a million francs if I had it. I responded that the use of that amount would be quite different nowadays than what it would have been at first. Formerly, I would have advertised by using plenty of publicity; now, I can see that that would have been a waste, because our adversaries took care of that at their own expense. Since I did not have large resources at my disposal for that purpose, the Spirits wanted to show that Spiritism owes its success to its own power.

"Now that the horizon has broadened and the future has unfolded, the necessities are proving to be much different. An amount like that would be better employed. Without going into premature details, I will only say that part of it would be used to convert my property into a special Spiritist retreat, whose visitors would reap the benefits of our moral doctrine; another part would be used to build an *inalienable* income to: 1) maintain the establishment; 2) ensure an independent existence for the one who replaces me and those who help him carry out his mission; 3) provide for the current needs of Spiritism, without being dependent on occasional revenue, as is my case, since most of the resources are the result of my work, which will end.

"That is what I would do; but if I am not given such satisfaction, I know that, in one way or another, the Spirits who are guiding the Movement will provide for all necessities at the right time. That is why I am not at all worried and am focusing on what is essential to me: the achievement of the works I still have to complete. That done, I shall depart whenever it pleases God to call me."

To what Kardec said then, he now adds:

"Once the commission is organized, I will be part of it as a mere member and will give it my collaboration, without demanding any personal primacy, titles or privileges.

"Although an active member of the commission, I will in no way be a burden on its budget, either because of a salary, travel expenses, or any other cause. If I have never asked anyone for anything personally, I would do so even less under such circumstances. My time, my life and all my physical and intellectual energies belong to Spiritism. Thus, I formally state that no part of the resources available to the commission will be diverted on my behalf.

"On the contrary, I will give it my share as follows:

1) By handing over the income from my works – finished and to be finished;

2) By transferring securities and real estate.

"Once Spiritism is organized by the central commission's constitution, my works will become the property of Spiritism in the name of that same commission, which will oversee their management and publication by the means most appropriate for popularizing them. It will also oversee their translation into the main foreign languages.

"Till now, the *Revue* has been, and could not have been otherwise, a personal endeavor, since it is part of our doctrinal works, all constituting the annals of Spiritism. It is therein that all the new principles are developed and studied. Hence, it was necessary that it maintain its individual character for the foundation of unity.

"I have been asked several times to issue it more frequently. But despite how flattering that wish may be, I cannot grant it; first, because physical time would not allow me the additional work, and second, because it must not lose its essential character, which is not that of a journal per se.

"Now that my personal work is nearing its end, the necessities are no longer the same; the *Revue*, like my other finished and unfinished works, will become the collective property of the commission, which will guide it in the best direction possible to benefit Spiritism the most; meanwhile, I will continue to lend it my collaboration.

"To complete my doctrinal endeavor, I still need to publish several works, which are neither its least difficult aspect nor its least laborious. Although I already have all the elements, and the plan for each one has already been delineated up to the final chapter, I could give them more assiduous attention and get started on them if, by instituting the central commission, I were free of the details that absorb a great deal of my time.

*****

"The early period of Spiritism was devoted to the study of the principles and laws, which together would comprise Spiritism; in other words, to prepare the materials while concurrently spreading the idea: the sowing of the seed, which like the seed in the Gospel parable, would not bear fruit everywhere equally. The child has grown; it is an adult, and the time has come, when, helped by sincere adherents and devotees, it shall advance toward the objective traced out for it, without being held back by laggards.

"But how to form this team of adherents and devotees? Who would dare assume the responsibility for passing judgment on individual consciences? The best, therefore, would be for the team to be formed by itself, and for that the way would be quite simple. It would suffice to put up a banner and say: Those who adopt this banner, follow it!

"In taking the initiative of Spiritism's constitution, I used a common right given to all humans, to complete as they wish the work they have begun and to be the judges of the opportunity. From the instant in which each person is free to accept or not accept such work, none can complain of suffering any arbitrary pressure. I created the word *Spiritism* to meet the necessities of the cause; thus, I have every right to determine its applications and to define the qualities and beliefs of the true Spiritist. (*Revue Spirite,* April 1866)

"After all of the foregoing, one can easily understand why it was impossible and premature to establish this constitution at the start. If the Spiritist Doctrine had been formed in all parts, like all personal conceptions, it would have been complete from the very first day, and nothing would have been simpler than to constitute it. However, since it developed gradually as a consequence of successive acquisitions, its constitution would have undoubtedly brought together all the lovers of novelties; soon, however, it would have been abandoned by those who did not accept all its consequences.

"Nonetheless, some might say: Aren't you causing a schism amongst the adherents? By setting up two opposing camps, isn't that weakening the phalanx?

"Not all those who call themselves Spiritists think alike on every point; the division does exist in fact, and it is much more harmful because it may be the case that one cannot tell if a particular Spiritist is an ally or an enemy. What lends it its power is its universality. Hence, a sincere union could not exist amongst morally or materially self-interested persons who do not follow the same path or pursue the same objective. Ten persons sincerely united by a common thought are stronger than a hundred who do not understand one another. In such a case, the mélange of divergent viewpoints takes away the power of cohesion from those who would desire to progress together, just like a liquid, which, infiltrating a body, is an obstacle to the aggregation of molecules.

"If the constitution has the effect of temporarily diminishing the apparent number of Spiritists, it will have the inevitable consequence of lending more power to those who will progress in accord toward the realization of the grand humanitarian objective that Spiritism shall reach. They will know each other and will be able to join hands from one end of the world to the other.

Furthermore, the constitution will have the effect of setting up a barrier to ambitions, which, by imposing themselves, would attempt to divert it to their profit and to deviate it from its course. Everything is calculated in light of this outcome, through the suppression of every autocracy or personal supremacy.

# The Spiritist Creed

- Preamble
- Fundamental Principles of Spiritism Recognized as Incontestable Truths

## PREAMBLE

The ills of humankind result from the imperfection of human beings; it is because of their vices that they harm one another. As long as they are vice-ridden they will be unhappy because the clash of interests will engender continual misery.

Of course, good laws contribute to improving societal conditions, but they are powerless to ensure the happiness of humankind because they do nothing more than restrain the worst passions without eliminating them. They are also more repressive than moralizing, and they only repress the most obvious bad actions without, however, eliminating their causes. Moreover, the goodness of laws is in direct relation to the goodness of people; as long as people are dominated by pride and selfishness, they will make laws that benefit their own personal ambitions. Civil law only changes what is on the outside; only moral law can pierce the inner forum of the conscience and reform it.

Thus, realizing that it is the strain caused by the contact with vice that renders human beings unhappy, the sole remedy for their ills lies in their moral improvement. Since the source of ills is found in their imperfections, happiness will increase as such imperfections decrease.

Regardless of how good a social institution may be, if people are bad, they will distort and denature its spirit to exploit it for their own benefit. Once people become good, they will organize good institutions that will last because all will have an interest in preserving them.

Consequently, the social issue does not have its starting point in the form of this or that institution; it lies fully in the moral improvement of individuals and the masses. That is where the principle can be found, the true key to humankind's happiness, because then people will no longer even think about harming one another. It is not enough to varnish over vice; it must be uprooted.

The principle of improvement lies in the nature of beliefs because beliefs are the motive behind actions and they modify sentiments. It also lies in the ideas inculcated since childhood and identified with the spirit, as well as in the ideas that the subsequent development of the intelligence and reason can strengthen and not destroy. It is through education, more than through instruction, that humankind will be transformed.

People who make a serious effort to improve themselves ensure their happiness in this very lifetime. Besides the satisfaction of their conscience, they are spared the material and moral miseries that are the inevitable consequence of their imperfections. They will have peace-of-mind because vicissitudes will touch them only lightly. They will enjoy health because they will not abuse their bodies with excesses. They will be wealthy because one is always wealthy when one knows how to be content with the necessities. They will have peace-of-mind because they will not have fictitious necessities, nor will they be tormented by the desire for honors and superfluities, the fever of ambition, envy or jealousy. Indulgent towards the imperfections of others, they will suffer less because of them; they will regard them with pity instead of anger. Avoiding everything that may harm their neighbor through words and actions, seeking instead everything that may be useful and pleasing to others, no one will suffer in contact with them.

They will guarantee their happiness in the future life because the more they purify themselves, the higher they will rise in the hierarchy of intelligent beings; they will abandon this earth of trials for higher worlds because the evils they have redressed in this life will not have to be redressed in others; because in the errant state they will encounter only friendly and sympathetic spirits, and will not be tormented by the constant sight of those who would have reason to complain against them.

Any group of people animated by such sentiments will be as happy as our earth allows them to be; if step by step an entire nation, an entire race – all humankind – were to acquire such sentiments, our globe would take its place amongst the happy worlds.

Is this a chimera, a utopia? Yes, for those who do not believe in the progress of the soul; no, for those who believe in its unlimited perfectibility.

Overall progress is the result of all individual progress; but individual progress does not consist only in developing the intelligence or acquiring a bit of knowledge. That is only one part of progress, which does not necessarily lead to the good, since we see people making a very bad use of their knowledge. It consists above all in moral improvement, the purification of the spirit, the extirpation of the bad seeds that exist in us. That is true progress, the only kind that can guarantee happiness to humankind, because it is the very negation of evil. Individuals with an advanced intelligence can commit much evil; those who are morally advanced will only do the good. Thus, the moral progress of humankind is in everyone's interest.

However, for those who believe everything ends with death, what does the improvement and happiness of future generations matter? What interest do they have in bettering themselves, in repressing and controlling their lower passions, and in depriving themselves for others? None. Logic itself tells them that their interest lies in immediate pleasure by all means possible, since tomorrow they may be no more.

The doctrine of nihilism is the paralysis of human progress because it circumscribes people's views to the imperceptible point of their present existence; because it narrows their ideas and unavoidably concentrates them on the material life. With this doctrine, since humans were nothing before and will be nothing hereafter, with all their social relationships ending after life, solidarity is a meaningless word; fraternity, a baseless theory; self-denial on behalf of others, a mere deception, and selfishness with its maxim *Every man for himself* a natural right; vengeance, a reasonable act; happiness, the privilege of the strongest and most cunning; and suicide, the logical end for those who, bereft of resources and means, expect nothing from life and cannot pull themselves out of the mire. A society founded on nihilism would contain in itself the seed of its own dissolution.

Quite different are the sentiments of those who have faith in the future; who know that nothing they have acquired in the way of knowledge and morality is lost; that the efforts of today will bear fruit tomorrow; that they themselves will be part of those more advanced and happier future generations. They know that by laboring for others, they labor for themselves. Not limited to the earth, their vision encompasses the infinity of worlds that will be their dwelling places some day; they can foresee the glorious place that will be theirs, as it will be for all who have reached perfection.

With faith in the future life, the circle of their ideas expands; the future belongs to them; personal progress has an aim, an *effective* usefulness. From the continuity of relationships amongst people, solidarity is born; fraternity is founded on a law of nature and in the interest of all.

Belief in the future is thus the element of progress because it is a stimulant for the spirit; only this belief can instill courage in people during their trials because it gives them the reason for such trials, and it gives them perseverance in the struggle against evil because it shows them an objective. It is therefore their job to instill this belief in the minds of the masses.

This belief is inherent to human beings. All religions proclaim it. Why has it not yet yielded the results that one would expect? Because, in general, it is presented in conditions unacceptable to reason. According to the way it has always been shown, it breaks all relationships with the present: once we leave the earth, we become foreigners to humankind. There is no solidarity between the living and the dead; progress is purely individual; in working for the future, one works only for oneself and only considers oneself with a vague objective in mind that has nothing definite, nothing positive upon which thought could rest with assurance; it is more of a hope than a material certainty. Hence, for some it results in indifference; for others, a mystical exaltation, which, by isolating the individual from the earth, is essentially harmful to the true progress of humankind since it neglects concern for material progress, to which nature makes it a duty for us to contribute.

However, as incomplete as the results may be, they are no less real, nonetheless. How many people, in fact, have been encouraged and sustained on the pathway of the good by that vague hope! How many have stopped at the precipice of evil for fear of compromising the future! How many noble virtues this belief has developed! Let us not disdain the beliefs of the past, no matter how imperfect, when they lead to the good: they have corresponded to the degree of humankind's advancement.

But having progressed, humankind wants beliefs that are in harmony with the new ideas. If the elements of faith remain stationary and kept at a distance by the mind, they lose all their influence; the good they have produced over a certain amount of time cannot continue because they are not in tandem with the circumstances.

So that the doctrine of the future life may from now on yield the results that should be expected, it must above all else completely satisfy reason; it must correspond to the idea we have about the wisdom, justice and goodness of God; and it must not receive any denial from science. The future life must not leave any doubt or uncertainty in one's mind; it must be as positive as the present life, of which it is the continuation, just as tomorrow is the continuation of the previous day. It must be seen, grasped and touched with the finger, so to speak. Lastly, the connection between the past, present and future through many different existences must be made obvious.

Such is the idea that Spiritism provides of the future life. What gives it strength is that it is not a human conception whose only merit would be of being more rational, without offering any more certainty than the others. Rather, it is the result of the studies conducted on the examples furnished by different categories of spirits who presented themselves in the manifestations that have enabled us to explore extra-corporeal life in all its phases, from the upper to the lower degree on the scale of beings. Consequently, the facts concerning the future life are not a mere theory, a more or less probable hypothesis, but the result of observation. It is the inhabitants of the invisible world themselves who have come to describe their conditions, and it is this situation that the most fertile imagination could not have conceived if it were not shown to the eyes of the observer.

Giving us material proof of the existence and immortality of the soul, initiating us into the mysteries of birth, death, the future life and the universal life, and making palpable to us the unavoidable consequences of good and evil, Spiritism, better than any other, emphasizes the need for individual improvement. By means of Spiritism, people know where they have come from, where they are going and why they are here; the good has an objective, a practical usefulness. It is not limited to preparing people for the future; it also molds them for the present, for society. By growing morally, people will prepare earth for the kingdom of peace and fraternity.

Spiritism is thus the most powerful element for moralization, because it affects the heart, the mind and well-understood personal interest all at the same time. By its very essence, Spiritism participates in all branches of physical, metaphysical and moral knowledge. The issues it encompasses are innumerable, but they can be summed up in the following points, which, being considered incontestable truths, form the list of Spiritist beliefs.

## FUNDAMENTAL PRINCIPLES OF SPIRITISM RECOGNIZED AS INCONTESTABLE TRUTHS

*********

The bodily death of Allan Kardec interrupted the *Posthumous Works* of that eminent spirit. This volume ends with a question mark, and many readers would like to see it answered logically, as the knowledgeable teacher in matters of Spiritism could do so well. Doubtlessly, it would be that way.

During the International Spiritist and Spiritualist Conference of 1890, its members declared that, starting in 1869, continuous studies have revealed new things, and that according to the teaching foreseen by Allan Kardec, some of the principles of Spiritism, upon which the master based his teaching, had to be revisited and made to agree with the progress of general science over the last twenty years.

That stream of ideas, common to the members of that Conference, who came from all parts of the earth, demonstrated that a new volume was needed to combine Kardec's teachings with what the search for truth constantly provides us.

That will be the work of the *Advertising Commission.* We can truly count on the good counsels of the brothers and sisters, who, during the Conference demonstrated their competence regarding the most important philosophical issues to aid the Commission in the development of a collective and unceasingly progressive endeavor. In turn, that volume will have to be revised when a new Conference decides to do so.

Allan Kardec stated:

"Science is called to construct the true genesis according to the Laws of Nature.

"The discoveries of science glorify God rather than demean God. They destroy only what humans have built upon their erroneous ideas about God.

"Pressing forward with progress, Spiritism will never be surpassed, because if new discoveries were to show it to be in error on one point, it would modify itself on that point; if a new truth is revealed, it will accept it."[49]

P.G. Leymarie

---

49 *Genesis,* chap. I – Character of the Spiritist Revelation; International Spiritist Counsel, 1st ed. 2009 – Tr.

www.ingramcontent.com/pod-product-compliance
Lightning Source LLC
LaVergne TN
LVHW010051110826
845155LV00028B/292

* 9 7 8 1 9 4 8 1 0 9 5 1 2 *